Thomas Benedikte

Language Policy and Linguistic Minorities in India

LIT Studies on Asia

Volume 3

This study was written for the European Academy of Bolzano/Bozen (EURAC), Institute for Minority Rights, in the frame of an exchange-program on supranational (regional) policies and instruments for the promotion of human rights and the management of minority issues. The publication is based on extensive research in eight Indian States, carried out in 2008 and 2009, with the support of the European Academy of Bozen/Bolzano and the Mahanirban Calcutta Research Group, Kolkata.

EURAC research

Partners of the exchange-program:
Accademia Europea Bolzano/Europäische Akademie Bozen (EURAC) – Bolzano/Bozen (Italy)
Brunel University – West London (UK)
Johann Wolfgang Goethe-Universität – Frankfurt am Main (Germany)
Mahanirban Calcutta Research Group (India)
South Asian Forum for Human Rights (Nepal)
Democratic Commission of Human Development (Pakistan),
and University of Dhaka (Bangladesh)

LIT

Thomas Benedikter

Language Policy and Linguistic Minorities in India

An appraisal of the linguistic rights of minorities in India

LIT

Author: Thomas Benedikter (EURAC)
Proofreading: Catherine Gordley
Lay-out: Hanna Battisti
All photographs: Thomas Benedikter

Cover photo: Karbi in Diphu, Autonomous District of Karbi Anglong (Assam), photo by Thomas Benedikter

Bibliographic information published by the Deutsche Nationalbibliothek
The Deutsche Nationalbibliothek lists this publication in the Deutsche Nationalbibliografie; detailed bibliographic data are available in the Internet at http://dnb.d-nb.de.

ISBN 978-3-643-10231-7

A catalogue record for this book is available from the British Library

Fresnostr. 2 D-48159 Münster
Tel. +49 (0) 2 51-620 32 22 Fax +49 (0) 2 51-922 60 99
e-Mail: lit@lit-verlag.de http://www.lit-verlag.de

Distribution:

In Germany: LIT Verlag Fresnostr. 2, D-48159 Münster
Tel. +49 (0) 2 51-620 32 22, Fax +49 (0) 2 51-922 60 99, e-Mail: vertrieb@lit-verlag.de

In Austria: Medienlogistik Pichler-ÖBZ GmbH & Co KG
IZ-NÖ, Süd, Straße 1, Objekt 34, A-2355 Wiener Neudorf
Tel. +43 (0) 22 36-63 53 52 90, Fax +43 (0) 22 36-63 53 52 43, e-Mail: mlo@medien-logistik.at

In Switzerland: B + M Buch- und Medienvertriebs AG
Hochstr. 357, CH-8200 Schaffhausen
Tel. +41 (0) 52-643 54 85, Fax +41 (0) 52-643 54 35, e-Mail: order@buch-medien.ch

Distributed in the UK by: Global Book Marketing, 99B Wallis Rd, London, E9 5LN
Phone: +44 (0) 20 8533 5800 – Fax: +44 (0) 1600 775 663
http://www.centralbooks.co.uk/html

Distributed in North America by:

Transaction Publishers
New Brunswick (U.S.A.) and London (U.K.)

Transaction Publishers
Rutgers University
35 Berrue Circle
Piscataway, NJ 08854

Phone: +1 (732) 445 - 2280
Fax: + 1 (732) 445 - 3138
for orders (U. S. only):
toll free (888) 999 - 6778
e-mail: orders@transactionpub.com

Content

Page

List of tables

Maps

Abbreviations

SRC – State Reorganization Commission
TLF – Three Languages Formula
NCLM – National Commissioner for Linguistic Minorities
CIIL - Central Institute of Indian Languages
ST – Scheduled Tribes
SC – Scheduled Castes
UT – Union Territory

Acknowledgements

My heartfelt thanks for support, suggestions, comments and assistance of any kind go to:
Dr. Günther Rautz, co-ordinating director of the Institute of Minority Rights, EURAC Bozen
Prof. Ranabir Samaddar, director of the Mahanirban Calcutta Research Group, Kolkata
Ms Chatterji, secretary general, MCRG, Kolkata
Dr. Jennifer Bayer, Central Institute of Indian Languages CIIL, Mysore
Prof. Shailendra Kumar Singh, Head of the Department of Linguistics, NEHU Shillong
Dr. Curiously Bareh, Researcher, Department of Linguistics, NEHU Shillong
Dr. Sylvanus Lamaré, St. Edmund's College, Shillong
S. K. Upadhyaya, National Commission for Linguistic Minorities, Kolkata
Prof. Dyutish Chakraborty, Department of Political Science, University of Northern Bengal, Siliguri
Prof. Omkar N. Koul, chairman, Indian Institute of Language Study, New Delhi
M.K. Khanna, National Commission for Minorities, New Delhi
Ms Kamala Devi Tokchom, Imphal (Manipur)
Subodh Hansda, ASECA (All Santal Educational Conference), Kolkata
Dr. Klaus Voll, New Delhi
Prof. Dipankar Basu, Darjeeling
Dr. T. Kumzang, Secretary General of the Ladakh Buddhist Association, Leh (Ladakh)
Prof. Anjani Kumar Sinha, University of Delhi, New Delhi
Südasien-Institut (SAI) of the University of Heidelberg (Germany)
Dr. Farah Fahim, EURAC Bozen/Bolzano
Ms. Catherine Gordley, Bolzano/Bozen
Dr. Hanna Battisti, Kaltern

Introduction

Linguistic human rights in the Indian context

The present analysis deals with language rights as a subset of human rights in an area of the world exhibiting particular linguistic diversity. It is an effort to map India's linguistic minorities and to assess their major grievances and the provisions for their protection. Linguistic human rights have been coherently defined on a theoretical level[1] and through some early legal approaches.[2] The right to speak, to learn, to educate and unfold all cultural activities in one's own mother tongue, in addition to other official languages, is also enshrined in many Constitutions of the world. "Linguistic rights should be considered basic human rights. Linguistic majorities, speakers of a dominant language, usually enjoy all those linguistic human rights which can be seen as fundamental, regardless how they are defined. Most linguistic minorities in the world do not enjoy these rights. It is only a few hundreds of the world's 6.000 odd languages that have any kind of official status, and it is only speakers of official languages who enjoy all linguistic human rights."[3] Thus, in a world organised in states with one single, or some few official majority languages, linguistic minorities are compelled to defend their linguistic rights.

The latest edition of UNESCO's Atlas of World's Languages in Danger of Disappearing[4] classifies around 2,500 of the 6,000 languages of the world as to some extent endangered: 538 critically endangered, 502 severely endangered, 632 definitely endangered and 607 unsafe. Within India's linguis-

1 See Robert Phillipson – Mart Rannut – Tove Skutnabb-Kangas, *Linguistic Human Rights – Overcoming Linguistic Discrimination,* Mouton De Gruyter, Berlin-New York 1994; a good introduction ti linguistic rights is provided by Peter L. Patrick, *Linguistic Human Rights: A Sociolinguistic Introduction*, at: http://privatewww.essex.ac.uk/patrickp/lhr/lhrintro.htm; Jacques Maurais/Michael Morris, *Languages in a Globalising World*, Cambridge University Press, 2003; Will Kymlicka/Wayne Norman, *Citizenship in Diverse Societies*, Oxford University Press, 2000.

2 *The Universal Declaration of Linguistic Rights*, Institut d'Edicions de la Diputació de Barcelona, 1998; *The European Charter for Regional and Minority Languages*, at: http://conventions.coe.int/Treaty/EN/Treaties/Html/148.htm; *The UN-Declaration on the Rights of Persons belonging National or Ethnic, Linguistic and Religious Minorities*: http://www.unhchr.ch/html/menu3/b/d_minori.htm ; *UN-Declaration on the Rights of Indigenous Peoples:* http://www.iwgia.org/graphics/Synkron-library/Documents/InternationalProcesses/DraftDeclaration/07-09-13ResolutiontextDeclaration.pdf

3 Phillipson – Mart Rannut – Tove Skutnabb-Kangas, *Linguistic Human Rights*, Introduction

4 Available at: http://www.unesco.org:80/culture/ich/index.php?pg=00206

tic landscape on a total of 196 languages included in the UNESCO-Atlas 84 are considered unsafe, 62 definitely endangered, 6 severely endangered, 35 critically endangered and 9 extinct (since the 1950s). "Unsafe" under UNESCO's definition means that a language is still spoken also by younger generations, but limited to very few domains. Although some of these results may require more require more precise and comprehensive data,[5] the overall diagnosis does appear rather critical.

India, however, is a language policy-making laboratory, seeking to cope with a multilingual reality and accommodate almost a hundred minority languages. The world's major democratic and federal state, while economically opening up to global markets, and culturally keen on pushing national integration and international exchange, has to come to terms with its complex internal multilingualism. While the Indian way to internal multilingualism privileges the major languages with official recognition, many millions of minority language speakers are deprived of important linguistic rights and are discriminated against by the current language policy of the Union and the States. They are facing the decision whether to retain or to renounce on their traditional language in the education of their children, and are living with the daily experience that their mother tongues are deemed worthless dialects without utility in modern life.

In India's minority rights discourse the issue of linguistic rights has not been of much concern. This is unjust, as the denial of linguistic rights not only hampers the cultural development of a community, but is also detrimental for the social and economic development of a minority and for the society as such. While the culture industry and the big media privilege a few dominant languages, minority languages and tribal cultures alike are dying a silent and slow death. In India many such languages have definitely disappeared and several more are on the edge of extinction. This fact is not unknown to politicians, rather it is taken as the inevitable price to be paid for economic modernization and cultural homogenization.

The principle underlying the concept of universal human rights is that individuals and groups, irrespective of where they live, are entitled to norms that no state can be justified in restricting or violating. But not all human rights are a question of death penalty, torture or arbitrary imprisonment.

5 Looking on the results of the Indian population census of 1961, 1971, 1981 and 1991 other authors conclude „..that none of these languages is going to die out, because in all cases the percentage has shown an increase between 1981 and 1991." See: Bharati Wangkheimayum/ Anjani Kumar Sinha, *Survival of Minority Languages in a Multilingual Set-up*, in: South Asian Language Review, Vol IX, No 1-2, Delhi 2000, p. 153

Often individuals and groups are treated unjustly and suppressed by means of language and the denial of cultural rights. People who are deprived of linguistic human rights may thereby be prevented from enjoying other human rights, including fair political representation and participation, fair trials and access to education, access to information and freedom of speech, and maintenance of their cultural heritage, right to social security and equality in the labour market. Therefore it is important to formulate, codify and implement minimum standards for the enjoyment of linguistic human rights, which should be made an integral part of international and national law.[6]

Why are linguistic rights important? Observing linguistic human rights implies at an individual level that everyone can identify positively with this mother tongue, and have that identification respected by others, irrespective of whether their mother tongue is a minority language or a majority language. It means the right to learn the mother tongue, including at least basic education through the medium of the mother tongue, and the right to use it in the most important contexts of public and community life. But it means also the right to learn at least one of the official languages in one's country of residence. If a growing share of people, living in their traditional home areas, involuntarily shift to dominant languages something in language policy went wrong.

Respecting linguistic human rights implies at a collective level respecting the right of a minority to exist. It implies respecting its right to enjoy and develop its language, and to establish and maintain schools and other training and educational institutions, with control of the curricula and instruction in its own language. It also involves guarantees of representation in the political affairs of the state or region, and being granted forms of autonomy to administer matters internal to the group, at least in the fields of culture, education, religion, information and social affairs; it also means being endowed with the minimum financial means to fulfil these functions.

Representatives of the linguistic majorities often are view such rights as a means to prevent the minorities from being absorbed into "mainstream" society. The widely branded ideal is still linguistic homogeneity and efficiency in communication, particularly in decisive domains in politics, administration and business. Whereas in Europe, the nation-state-ideology is softened by the requirements of multilingualism in a Union of independent states that each keep their national languages, in India fostering linguistic diversity is no longer seen as a threat to political unity, as multilingualism has been

---

6 Phillipson/Mart Rannut/Tove Skutnabb-Kangas, *Linguistic Human Rights*, Introduction, p.2

accepted as a basic fact and value of the "Indian civilisation". In India it is politically correct to look at it as a resource, not as a problem. But what's about internal multilingualism embracing the smaller languages spoken on a territory? Is multilingualism also appreciated on the larger level, when it comes to protect smaller linguistic communities and tribal languages without lakhs of daily newspaper readers? Some States of India are reluctant to grant a sufficient range of rights to such linguistic minorities. They still fear that granting linguistic and cultural rights to minorities will induce them to strive for autonomy and a state of their own (linguistic state), and that this could end in the disintegration of their States or even of the federal state. But linguistic rights do not pose any threat to the integrity of a state, rather they respond to basic human needs and rights. They give no legitimacy to self-determination claims. The opposite may be true: the denial of linguistic and cultural rights can provoke popular resistance and political opposition or even violent rebellion. The question is rather whether such rights can be ensured and unfold only if they are linked to specific territory or whether protection and some cultural autonomy can be granted even for speech communities that have dispersed settlements.

In India, the federation has been vested with the responsibility of safeguarding the minimum standards protecting the rights of linguistic minorities. Having given way 40-50 years ago to the reorganization of the States along linguistic lines, the multilingual political elite of India felt the moral obligation to grant linguistic rights as well. This was done to prevent both conflicts among States with regard to "kin-minorities," and conflicts with minority groups and peoples who risk discrimination by the dominant linguistic majority. As the example of Assam confirms, this risk was and still is quite serious. But despite many political proclamations to multilingualism, the overall impression is still that many Indian States want to be seen as doing something rather than in fact committing themselves fully to maintaining minority languages. This impression echoes in the annual reports the National Commissioner for Linguistic Minorities must submit to the President and Parliament. "Except in some states which are committed to the cause, the very term 'linguistic minorities' raises eyebrows. The issue is not a burning issue. It does not result in violent protests and since we are living in the days of immediate reaction and expedient policies, the long term implications of neglect of the linguistic minorities or the minority languages does not appear to be a problem worth spending a few minutes of concentrated thinking. In my visits to various places, I have met many officers who were in a hurry to get away from the meeting as they had to attend to much more pressing issues...."[7]

7 National Comm. for Linguistic Minorities, 42 report, 2004, p. 4, at: http://nclm.nic.in

Linguistic rights are in the hands of State policy makers. "Minorities, on the other hand, can not 'take rights' themselves just by proclaiming and exercising them. Linguistic rights need official recognition, need instruments, infrastructures and funds of application, need a secure and clear legal framework, need validation and support from the State, which exercises sovereignty and public power. Spontaneous activity in language and culture might be important as it is the speakers' community to maintain and develop a minority language."[8] But historical experience has shown that there is no chance of long-term survival if a language is not allowed to cover some of the decisive public domains of its speakers. A linguistic community must have linguistic rights in the public sphere, in public education, and in media, if its language is to be taken seriously. What might have been true for tribal languages in the past centuries – survival due to isolation – does not apply to most of India's linguistic minorities today. Rather, they are integrated in the general society and economy, and the protection of their language does not depend not on them alone.

After acknowledging this responsibility, the first step is the recognition of minority languages. The second must be language status planning and language acquisition planning. Society must pay a price to achieve this, investing in education and culture, adopting appropriate rules in public administration and services, strengthening the role of minority languages in the media, and recognising the protection of languages as a fundamental human right. In this regard, India has been a shining example for other countries. Hence we return to the starting point: if considered only as efficient procedures of public administration, or in terms of economic productivity or of multilingualism projected to international competition, minority languages are in dire straits. But if the States and political actors become aware of the significance of language rights as basic human rights and of their potential as resources to develop the human and cultural potential of all members of the society, including the linguistic minorities, they must develop corresponding legal regulation and political implementation.

The present study is, first of all, an appraisal of the rights of linguistic minorities in India. The first chapters include stocktaking of existing linguistic diversity and its most salient features, as well as the legal safeguards provided on various government levels. India's tribal peoples are a matter of particular concern, as they are culturally vulnerable minorities everywhere. The following chapters deal with the major public domains of languages, education, public administration and media, and culminate in an assessment of the appropriateness of the Three-Language-Formula for

8 *ibidem*, p.3

accommodating the interests of linguistic minorities. Finally, I conclude this analysis by measuring the present situation of linguistic minorities with the European standards of language rights of ethno-linguistic minorities. May this study prove helpful for further exchanges between Europe and India critically assessing linguistic human rights in both areas.

Thomas Benedikter

Bozen/Bolzano (South Tyrol, Italy), May 2009

Chapter 1

An overview on India's linguistic landscape

1.1 India's languages in history

The Indian state was created in 1947, and was built upon a conglomerate of territories and peoples, which before that time were either directly or indirectly dominated by a colonial power – the British Empire. The language of the ruling power and of its civil and military administration was English. Thus the language offering social status, success, and career prospects was the language forced upon the subcontinent by the foreign rulers. A "nation" in the European sense, based on a common culture, history and language, did not exist in India until the 20th century. India's religious, cultural and linguistic diversity and spiritual profusion impressed the world, but politically it composed a great patchwork. A sense of group solidarity based on a culturally defined "nation", and state power organized along ethnic or linguistic lines were rather uncommon. "Nation-building" happened only later, when the new state allowed for new communication possibilities, mobility, education facilities and government structures, which propelled a process of national identity building. As this state was a legacy of colonial rule over an entire subcontinent, India's population is very heterogeneous, or "by history" multicultural and multilingual.

Initially India's national movement did not seek independence, but only equal rights in the framework of the existing power structures. The refusal of colonial rule and the claim for full independence came later, when all attempts to gain equal rights had failed. While India's anti-colonial movements strengthened pre-existing awareness of indigenous ancient cultures and traditions, these did not constitute a unitary or overarching "national self-consciousness" for the whole geographical area of the subcontinent. Certainly, classical education up to a certain level and in those domains not directly concerned by the colonial domination was possible (in Sanskrit, Urdu, Persian, Tamil), but during the colonial rule English had been firmly established in the most important domains of life (public administration, business, higher education and science, armed forces, international communication). The discovery that Sanskrit was a language even older than the most revered European languages Latin and Greek, and even that many Indo-European languages were derived from Sanskrit, added to the national self-consciousness of the Indian elite. Tamil also has a literary tradition more than 2,000 years old. More generally, the recognition of the Dravidian language family and of other linguistic groups raised awareness among

Map 1 - Language families in South Asia

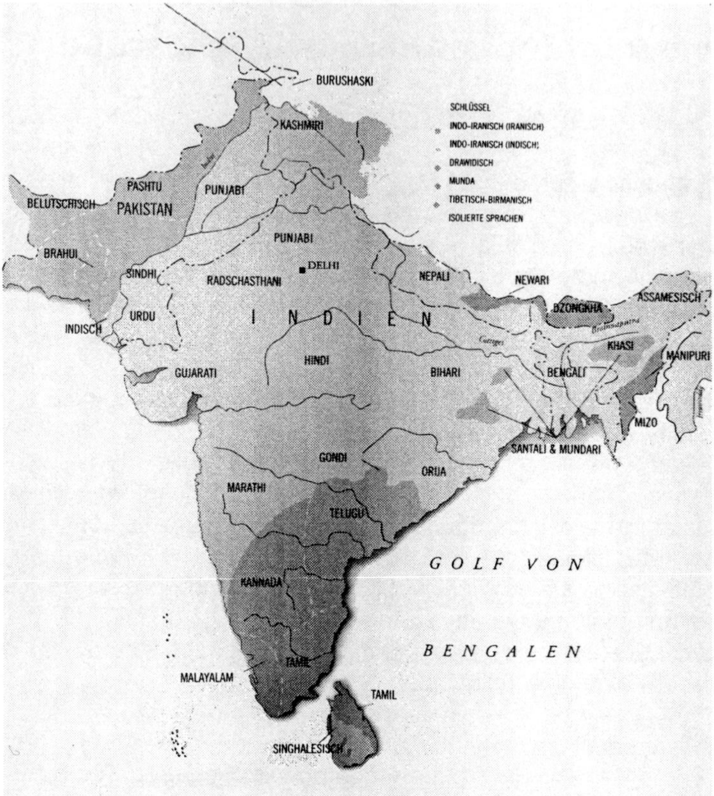

Source: Bildatlas der Sprachen, Bechtermünz Verlag, 1998

Indians of the coexistence and intermingling of several language families and their value in cultural history. Not only could the "big" 12 languages refer to an age-old tradition, but so too could many smaller linguistic communities.

Unlike religion and religiously based nationalism (Ali Jinnah and his Muslim League in the 1940 'Pakistan Resolution') language has held a less important role in India's nation building process. At that time a considerable part of British India's population, being not Hindu, but Muslim, developed another linguistic tradition (Urdu) or cultivated their "regional" traditional languages and dialects. Hence, in the run-up to independence neither Sanskrit nor Hinduism could offer the substratum for creating a culturally defined nationalism in India; rather, linguistically based sub-nationalism gained ground. Neither the truth languages[9] (Sanskrit, Persian or Arabic), nor the colonial language (English) could be used for mobilising the masses. Thus, the nation was conceived as a primordial community bound together by the Vedanta philosophy and other religious classics. Despite the adoption of an "official language" (Hindi) and the standardisation of the major languages such as Urdu, Bengali, Tamil, Telugu, Marathi, and Malayalam, India remained a basically multicultural and multi-religious area.[10]

Although a dream of some Moghul emperors and perhaps of king Ashoka many centuries earlier, the idea of an independent unitary state on the territory of the whole subcontinent could only stir and grow on the basis of a corresponding colonial territory, the largest colony that ever existed. Apart from a very few territories, India for over 200 years has been ruled by just one colonial power imposing just one language – English – for just some political purposes. India's linguistic diversity did not bother the colonial rulers; on the contrary, it supported their project of maintaining power over a politically divided country. The British tolerated regional traditions, smaller languages, sub-nationalism of all kinds, while the idea of an Indian nation seeking an independent state truly terrified them. In the administrative and territorial framework of the British colony a national movement would develop that was united against the colonial power neither by a common religion nor by a common superposed language. A modern and secular state along the British model was propagated, in which regional peculiarities and linguistic diversities were expected, but were not to play a major role.[11] Only the conflict between Hindi and Urdu, tightly linked to the religious division of India's population, raised a linguistic cleavage alongside the religious and political conflict. Consequently, partition was not proclaimed on linguistic grounds, but based on opposed and conflicting concepts of nation and state in an imagined united India. According to Gandhi's vision, both Hindi and Urdu would have been declared the state languages of a politically united sub-continent, and only later, after independence, the internal linguistic division of the new Indian Federation would gain momentum. But conflicts

9 Benedict Anderson, *Imagined Communities, Reflections on the origin and spread of Nationalism*, London/New York, 1983, p. 21 and p. 41-49

10 In this regard the development of „national state languages“ has been much more smooth in Indonesia and Malaysia. Both languages, Bahasa Indonesia and Bahasa Malaysia, could be formed in short time from the preexisting Basar Malay, which neither was the language of politically or economically dominant groups nor was it connected to e religion or a particular race.;

11 An exception from the overwhelming disdain of the vernacular languages among the British rulers was William Campbell, who supported the recognition of Indian languages. See William Campbell, *In Defence of Vernaculars*, edited by M. S. Thirumalai/B. Mallikarjun, Critical Quest, New Delhi 2006

also arose about which language, Hindi or English, should be adopted as "national language". As no "vernacular language" could convincingly assume this role, the former colonial language was adopted as happened in so many former colonies in Africa and Asia.

Is India's federalism a tribute to its heterogeneity? India inherited both its constitution and federal structure from the British. By transferring some powers to the provinces the British rulers made some concessions to the Indian independence movement, without questioning their overall rule. Federalism in India did not grow up from the bottom, but was declared from above. In addition, the British also invented the institution of "President's rule", which could be proclaimed in case of instability in one federated unit, and which allows the recall of a chief minister and his replacement by a governor nominated from the centre. President's rule is limited to 6 months, but after this period new elections may be held. This kind of central interference in States' affairs was exercised hundreds of times, particularly in the 1970s and 1990s.

In India, compared with some Western federal states, the powers of the states are rather limited. The federated states also dispose of fewer budgetary means than under the standard models of federal constitution around the world. Indian federalism can therefore be defined as "federalism from above" or "federalism until revoked". This particular form of federalism, based on strong central power, allowed for the "co-operative" re-organisation of India's subdivision in States along linguistic criteria beginning in 1956, which aimed to create more linguistic and cultural homogeneity. Later, responding to huge political and sometimes military pressure, new states were created, in some cases for ethno-linguistic reasons. This political factor is of utmost importance to India's present linguistic landscape: the major "regional" languages had a towering importance in building up functioning sub-federal unities, and this kind of reform, in turn, could restrain secessionism and foster a "national" civic polity feeling part of India.

Indian society presents not only a cultural-geographical segmentation, but also a complex social stratification, again linked to religion and ethnicity. Some social groups considered discriminated or disadvantaged were recognised in special sections (Schedules) of the Constitution. These groups, as the scheduled castes, scheduled tribes and other backward classes, enjoy special rights, such as quotas to access universities and public employment. The Indian legislator never built a quota system on the basis of language. Hence, neither is the population of a State or region classified according to such a scheme, nor is the whole concept of the federated states imbued by it. India remains basically a secular and multinational state rather than homeland of a particular group co-existing with some minorities. This was also due the need to distinguish the very character of the state from Pakistan. But it did not prevent the rise of widespread communalism, which is causing the major cleavages and group conflicts in modern India – mostly between Hindi and Muslims. No wonder then, that the conflicts among religious communities today dominate India's minority rights discourse, pushing the linguistic issues into shadows.

Compared with the social and communal conflicts, and compared with some self-determination struggles in the Northwest and Northeast of the country, the linguistic issue in independent India retained a much lower profile.[12] Following the linguistic re-organization of the States in the 1950s and 1960s, the overwhelming majority of the big linguistic groups[13] lived in States with the corresponding official language. However, at present at least 120 million Indian citizens belong to a linguistic minority with a mother tongue different from the official language of the State in which they reside, but mostly one of the "scheduled" languages.

According to the Indian census of 2001, and after the inclusion of four more languages in the 8th Schedule of the Indian Constitution, 97% of the people in India speak one of the 22 "scheduled languages" as a first language, whereas 3% speak one of the remaining 92 languages not included in the Constitutional list so far, out of a total of 114 languages recognised as such in the census. The Third All India Education Survey reports the use of 58 languages in school curricula and of 47 languages in public administration. Radio programs are broadcast in 91 languages, print-media products are available in 87 languages,[14] and the Federal and State governments are propagating mass multilingualism under the banner of the Three-Language-Formula (TLF). A multilingual idyll, then?

1.2 India's languages in figures

India's linguistic landscape is shaped by four language families. These are, from north to south: the Tibeto-Burmese, Indo-European (Indo-Aryan), Austro-Asiatic (Munda, Khasi) and Dravidian family. There are also some

12 In fact, no linguistic criterion is applied for scheduling tribal peoples. Almost half of their members do not any more retain their traditional language.

13 In India's scholar and political discourse the term people or nation for a ethnolinguistic community is strictly avoided.

14 See J.C. Sharma, *Multilingualism in India*, in Language in India, CIIL 8-12-2001

isolated languages, such as Arbi (Arabic, thus Hamito-semitic family), while Kusunda and Andamese are probably linked to the Indo-Pacific family. In the past, many more languages must have been spoken, as the little-studied linguistic substrates indicate. Just one example: some 30% of the agricultural vocabulary of modern Hindi are from an unknown source. The same is reported for many other Northern Indian languages, whereas there has been less research conducted on the Southern languages.[15]

Table 1 - The Indian language families

	Number of languages	Percentage on total population
Austro-Asian	14	1.13%
Dravidian	17	22.53%
Indo-European	20	75.30%
Tibeto-Burmese	62	0.97%
Semito-Hamitic	1	0.1 %

Note: English is included in the Indo-European family.

Most probably the Dravidian languages covered most of the entire subcontinent some 3,000 years ago, before being slowly replaced in Northern India by the Indo-Aryan languages brought with the immigrating peoples from Central Asia. The modern Indo-Aryan languages evolved from ancient Sanskrit, the language of the holy texts, which today is used only for religious rituals and ceremonies. Hindi has a huge range of regional varieties and dialects, which are being spoken by about 420 million people today. Standardised Hindi (khari boli) was originally spoken only in Delhi. In 1991, Hindi had 48 variants. Urdu, the major minority language in the so-called "Hindi-belt", generally can be understood by Hindi speakers, but as it was developed as the language of the Islamic conquerors, using an Arabic-Persian script and adding a great deal of vocabulary from that cultural area, it is not spoken as a mother tongue by a majority of any Indian State, not even in Jammu and Kashmir.

The Austro-Asiatic language family comprises the speakers of Munda, probably one of the oldest group of languages of the subcontinent. The Khasi (Meghalaya) and the Mon-Khmer (Andaman and Nicobar Islands) are also part of this family. In India's Northeast and in some Himalayan regions various Tibeto-Burmese languages are spoken by less than 1% of India's total population, constituting the numerically most diverse language family of the country. Without the 62 languages of this tiny part of the Indian Union

15 See Michael Witzel, *Languages and Scripts*, in: Encyclopedia of India New Delhi 2002, p. 50-55

Assamese women at a Hindu-festival in Guwahati

(4% of the population and 8% of its territory) India's linguistic diversity would be cut in half.

There is no official inventory of languages spoken in India that reports all languages recognised by linguists. The only source listing the languages is the official Indian census, which reported 114 languages and 216 "mother tongues" spoken by more than 10,000 people in 1991. Since 1991 the census has neglected the smaller language groups, which in sum comprise about 566,000 speakers. In other words: the official language policy has simply given up such small languages. All States have linguistic minorities; no State is monolingual with reference to its autochthonous population. In India the question of mother tongue is often conflated with region, religion, profession, ethnicity, caste names and similar characteristics. A clear classification of languages, as distinct from dialects, from a linguistic point of view is still lacking.[16]

16 Bhattacharya, *ibidem*, p. 59. Information regarding mother tongue and bilingualism remain fairly stable and widespread. Both these concepts play significant roles in planning ethno-linguistic identity, since languages and identity are interrelated. In India, for all communities, other than scheduled tribes, the only identity provided to a group is its mother tongue.

Pnar and Khasi students in Nartiang (Jaintia Hills, Meghalaya)

Statistical information on languages in India was first collected in 1881, but methodological differences that have arisen since do not always allow for an immediate comparison with this data.[17] The final result of the 1881 census yielded 162 languages, 116 of which were Indian. This approximates the census results of 120 years later (114 languages). By 1891, the number of languages was reduced to 150. A landmark census took place in 1901, which provided a great deal of detailed linguistic data. The Census of India of 1931 lists 141 languages; 294 mother tongues were identified in 1971. In 1981, 109 languages were counted, but the census was based on different definitions of which language could be defined as such.[18] In 2001 the census registered 114 languages.

17 See S.S. Bhattacharya, *Languages in India – Status and functions*, p.54

18 The definition used in 2001 was the following: "The language spoken in childhood by the person's mother to the person. If the mother died in infancy, the language spoken in the person's home in childhood." It has to be taken into account, that in intensely charged environment, answers are often influenced by emotional and other considerations. See Khubchandani, p.7

Table 2 - India's 22 major languages (1991) and the 22 scheduled languages (in 2001)

	language	Speakers (1991)	percen-tage	Rank in 2001	language	Speakers (2001)	percen-tage
1	Hindi	337,272,114	40.0%	1	Hindi	422,048,642	41.03%
2	Bengali	69,595,738	8.30%	2	Bengali	83,369,769	8.11%
3	Telugu	66,017,615	7.87%	3	Telugu	74,002,856	7.19%
4	Marathi	62,481,681	7.45%	4	Marathi	71,936,894	6.99%
5	Tamil	53,006,368	7.32%	5	Tamil	60,793,814	5.91%
6	Urdu	43,406,932	5.18%	6	Urdu	51,536,111	5.01%
7	Gujarati	40,673,814	4.85%	7	Gujarati	46,091,617	4.48%
8	Kannada	32,753,676	3.91%	8	Kannada	37,924,011	3.69%
9	Malayalam	30,377,176	3.62%	9	Malayalam	33,066,392	3.21%
10	Oriya	28,061,313	3.35%	10	Oriya	33,017,446	3.21%
11	Punjabi	23,378,744	2.79%	11	Punjabi	29,102,477	2.83%
12	Assamese	13,079,696	1.56%	12	Assamese	13,168,484	1.28%
13	Bhili/ Bhilodi**	5,572,308	0.665%	13	Maithili***	12,179,122	1.18%
14	Santali	5,216,325	0.622%	14	Santali***	6,469,600	0.63%
15	Gondi**	2,124,852	0.253%	15	Kashmiri	5,527,698	0.54%
16	Sindhi	2,122,848	0.253%	16	Nepali	2,871,749	0.28%
17	Nepali	2,076,645	0.248%	17	Sindhi	2,535,485	0.25%
18	Konkani	1,760,607	0.210%	18	Konkani	2,489,015	0.24%
19	Tulu**	1,552,259	0.185%	19	Dogri***	2,282,589	0.22%
20	Kurukh**	1,426,618	0.170%	20	Meitei (Manipuri)*	1,466,705*	0.14%
21	Meitei (Manipuri)	1,270,216	0.151%	21	Bodo***	1,350,478	0.13%
22	Bodo	1,221,881	0.146%	22	Sanskrit	14,135	N

Source: Census of India 1991 and 2001

*The percentage of speakers of each language for 2001 has been worked out on the total population of India excluding the population of Mao-Maram, Paomata and Purul subdivisions of Senapati district of Manipur due to cancellation of census results. In 2001 India's total population was 1,027,015,247 N - Stands for negligible.
** Non scheduled languages *** scheduled only in 2003.
Also note that the names of languages given here are rather cover terms, in some sense. Each language, for which the population figure is given in the table above, also includes some other languages, or dialects that are not explicitly presented in the table. For example, the cover term Kannada also includes the language or dialect Badaga.

India's linguistic landscape has been extensively described also by Roland J.L. Breton, Languages and Ethnic Communities in South Asia (updated edition), Sage publication, London/New Delhi 1997

Despite the existence of many regions and areas of linguistically mixed populations, there is a geographical concentration of speakers of the main languages (except Urdu and Sindhi) in a few major regions, which shows stability over time. But because India did not evolve in terms of "nation states", as had occurred in Europe, the boundaries between such linguistic areas have been blurring and overlapping.[19]

In colonial times, British rulers and Indian elite regarded all minority languages that did not have a written tradition as 'dialects' of the dominant language of the region. This interpretation amounted to an implicit denial of equal rights to linguistic minorities on the grounds of practicability.[20] Moreover, India must come to terms with mass illiteracy, and therefore some bias towards languages with higher prestige and script can be detected in the census. The official census returned an enormous list of mother tongues, many of which were just dialects. Looking at the census language figures, India still has a problem correctly registering the smaller, especially non-written languages, used primarily by tribal peoples. In such cases many speakers do not completely self-identify with their language nor do the authorities classify the language as such. The census results on bi- and multilingualism are also questionable.

Table 3 - India's non-scheduled languages in 1991[21]

No.	Language	speakers	No.	Language	speakers
1.	Adi	158,409	49.	Kuki	58,263
2.	Anal	12,156	50.	Kurukh/Oraon	1,426,618
3.	Angami	97,631	51.	Lahauli	22,027
4.	Ao	172,449	52.	Lahnda	27,386
5.	Arabic/Arbi	21,975	53.	Lakher	22,947
6.	Bhili/Bhilodi	5,572,308	54.	Lalung	33,746
7.	Bhotia	55,483	55.	Lepcha	39,342
8.	Bhumij	45,302	56.	Liangmei	27,478
9.	Bishnupuriya	59,233	57.	Limbu	28,174
10.	*Bodo/Boro*	1,221,881	58.	Lotha	85,802
11.	Chakesang	30,985	59.	Lushai/Mizo	538,842
12.	Chakru/Chokri	48,207	60.	Malto	108,148
13.	Chang	32,478	61.	Mao	77,810
14.	Coorgi/Kodagu	97,011	62.	Maram	10,144

19 A large number of ethnic communities have switched over to other languages of the region. Many ethnic communities, which include all tribal peoples, may also speak the same language prevalent in the region. See Bhattacharya, p. 60

20 Lachman Khubchandani, Language Demography and Language in Education, in UNESCO, 2001, New Delhi

21 Population figures and other statistical information is available at: http://www.censusindia.net/t_00_005.html

15.	Deori	17,901	63.	Maring	15,268
16.	Dimasa	88,543	64.	Miri/Mishing	390,583
17.	*Dogri*	89,681	65.	Mishmi	29,000
18.	English	178,598	66.	Mogh	28,135
19.	Gadaba	28,158	67.	Monpa	43,226
20.	Gangte	13,695	68.	Munda	413,894
21.	Garo	675,642	69.	Mundari	816,378
22.	Gondi	2,124,852	70.	Nicobarese	26,261
23.	Halabi	534,313	71.	Nissi/Dafla	173,791
24.	Halam	29,322	72.	Nocte	30,441
25.	Hmar	65,204	73.	Paite	49,237
26.	Ho	949,216	74.	Parji	44,001
27.	Jatapu	25,730	75.	Pawi	15,346
28.	Juang	16,858	76.	Phom	65,350
29.	Kabui	68,925	77.	Pochury	11,231
30.	Karbi/Mikri	366,229	78.	Rabha	139,365
31.	Khandeshi	973,709	79.	Rengma	37,521
32.	Kharia	225,556	80.	Sangtam	47,461
33.	Khasa	912,283	81.	*Santali*	5,216,325
34.	Khezha	13,004	82.	Savara	273,168
35.	Khiemnungan	23,544	83.	Sema	166,157
36.	Khond/Kondh	220,783	84.	Sherpa	16,105
37.	Kinnauri	61,794	85.	Tangkhul	101,841
38.	Kisan	162,088	86.	Tangsa	28,121
39.	Koch	26,179	87.	Thado	107,992
40.	Koda/Kora	28,200	88.	Tibetan	69,416
41.	Kolami	98,281	89.	Tripuri	694,940
42.	Kom	13,548	90.	Tulu	1,552,259
43.	Konda	17,864	91.	Vaiphei	26,185
44.	Konyak	137,722	92.	Wancho	39,600
45.	Korku	466,073	93.	Yimchungre	47,227
46.	Korwa	27,485	94.	Zeliang	35,079
47.	Koya	270,994	95.	Zemi	22,634
48.	Kui	641,662	96.	Zou	15,966
	total	**31,126,32**	**97.**	**Other languages***	**566,000**

Source: Census of India, 1991

Notes: Dogri, Maithili, Bodo and Santali have been scheduled in 2003. The figure of Dogri refers only to Dogri-speakers outside of Jammu and Kashmir, but in reality there are more than 2 million Dogri-speakers in Jammu. No figure for Maithili has been registered in the census of 1991. The Indian Census Organization reports that "the population of Jammu and Kashmir is not included in these figures as the 1991 census was not conducted there due to disturbed conditions."

*The Indian census of 1961 recognised 1,652 different languages in India (including languages not native to the subcontinent). According to the 1971 census 281 languages have been spoken by more than 5.000 speakers and 221 by more than 10.000 speakers. In 2001, after a further regrouping, just 114 languages with more than 10.000 speakers were left. More than 100 languages are likely to be spoken by less than 10.000 speakers, summing up to 566.000 persons.

Apparently in India there still is no popularly accepted codex of what languages and dialects are, although "...it is reported that the correlation between language ability and language identity is an overwhelming 97% and above."[22] Just as Hindi now (since the census of 2001) comprises 48 varieties, almost all languages listed in the 8th Schedule of the Constitution have absorbed other variants and have thus gone through a process of standardisation. Some languages are close relatives, sharing the same grammar and other linguistic features. Punjabi and Konkani could resist assimilation into the neighbouring languages of Hindi and Marathi, as this process supported by political and religious divisions. For a long time Konkani was regarded as just a dialect or variety of Marathi, which has a long and flourishing literary tradition. Nevertheless Konkani could be established as the official language of the State of Goa, whose population indicates that 51.5% have Konkani as their mother tongue (1991 Census).[23]

In 1991 and 2001 the results of the census regarding the mother tongue question were processed and regrouped in order to reach a consistent list of "rationalised mother tongues". The census 1991 listed 1576 "rationalised mother tongues", but these subsequently regrouped into 114 languages. While presenting the abstract of languages and mother tongues, the Census Organization issued a statement saying: "Presented below is an alphabetical abstract of languages and the mother tongues with strength of 10,000 and above at the all India level, included under each language. In 1991 there have been a total of 114 languages and 216 mother tongues, 18 scheduled languages and 96 not specified in the Schedule." In 2008, 22 languages are scheduled, 92 not. The total remains 114 languages. An official recognition, based on scientific criteria, of what exactly a language is, would avoid both political arbitrariness regarding the attribution of official recognition and rights, and biased subjective self-classification.

1.3 Scheduled and non-scheduled languages

In India, language status planning occurred through "officialization"

22 Bhattacharya, p.55. Linguists generally distinguish the terms "language" and "dialects" on the basis of 'mutual comprehension'. The Indian census uses two specific classifications in its own unique way: "language" and "mother tongue". The 'mother tongues' are grouped within each 'language'. Many 'mother tongues' so defined would be considered a language rather than a dialect by linguistic standards. This is specially so for many 'mother tongues' with tens of millions of speakers that is officially grouped under the 'language' Hindi. In Europe, on contrary, only few such cases of disputed classification as a distinct language exist even in popular understanding (e.g. Scots, Letzeburgisch).

23 Population figures and other statistical information is available at: http://www.censusindia.net/t_00_005.html

Bhotia-girl in Dhankar, Spiti Valley (Himachal Pradesh)

(recognition as a scheduled language) in a special section of the Constitution, the 8th Schedule of the Constitution. This Schedule's original purpose was stated in Article 351 of the Constitution in relation to the corpus planning of Hindi: "It shall be the duty of the Union to promote the spread of the Hindi language, to develop it so that it may serve as a medium of expression for all the elements of the composite culture of India and to secure its enrichment by assimilating without interfering with its genius, the forms, style and expressions used in Hindustani and in the other languages of India specified in the 8th Schedule and secondarily on other languages."

At the time the Constitution was enacted, inclusion in this list meant that the language was entitled to representation on the Official Language Commission, and that the language would be one of the bases that would be drawn upon to enrich Hindi, the official language of the Union. The list has since acquired further significance. The Government of India is now under an obligation to take measures for the development of these languages, such that "they grow rapidly in richness and become effective means of communicating modern knowledge."

In addition, a candidate taking an examination for public service at a higher level is entitled to use any of these scheduled languages in his answer. The following table lists the languages set out in the 8th Schedule as of May 2007, together with the regions in which they are used:

No.	Language	State(s)/Union Territories
1.	Assamese/ Asomiya	Assam
2.	Bengali/Bangla	Andaman & Nicobar Islands, Tripura, West Bengal
3.	Bodo	Assam
4.	Dogri	Jammu and Kashmir
5.	Gujarati	Dadra and Nagar Haveli, Daman and Diu, Gujarat
6.	Hindi	Andaman and Nicobar Islands, Arunachal Pradesh, Bihar, Chandigarh, Chhattisgarh, Delhi, Haryana, Himachal Pradesh, Jharkhand, Madhy Pradesh, Rajasthan, Uttar Pradesh and Uttarakhand
7.	Kannada	Karnataka,Andhra Pradesh
8.	Kashmiri	Jammu and Kashmir
9.	Konkani	Goa, Karnataka, Maharashtra, Kerala
10.	Maithili	Bihar
11.	Malayalam	Kerala, Andaman and Nicobar Islands, Lakshadweep, Puducherry
12.	Manipuri (also Meitei)	Manipur
13.	Marathi	Maharashtra, Goa Dadra & Nagar Haveli, Daman and Diu, Madhya Pradesh, Karnataka
14.	Nepali	Sikkim, West Bengal, Assam
15.	Oriya	Orissa
16.	Punjabi	Chandigarh, Delhi, Haryana, Punjab
17.	Sanskrit	Primary liturgical language of Hinduism. Also declared a „Classical Language of India"
18.	Santhali	Santhal tribals of the Chota Nagpur Plateau (comprising the states of Bihar, Chattisgarh, Jharkhand, Orissa and West Bengal)
19.	Sindhi	Sindhi community spread over various States
20.	Tamil	Tamil Nadu, Andaman & Nicobar Islands, Puducherry (also designated a classical language)
21.	Telugu	Andaman & Nicobar Islands Andhra Pradesh, Karnataka, Orissa, Tamil Nadu, Puducherry
22.	Urdu	Jammu and Kashmir, Uttar Pradesh, Bihar, Andhra Pradesh, Maharashtra, Karnataka, Uttarakhand and Delhi

The 8th Schedule is "the most important language policy statement" in India. Out of a total of 114 languages in 28 states and 7 UTs, 22 languages have now been scheduled, and 92 are still not scheduled. The list of tribes – most of which speak their own language – in the Indian Constitution is kept separate from the list of scheduled languages.

The 14 languages originally listed in the 8th Schedule in 1950 were: Assamese, Bengali, Gujarati, Hindi, Kannada, Kashmiri, Malayalam, Marathi, Oriya, Punjabi, Sanskrit, Tamil, Telugu and Urdu. Sindhi was added through the 21st amendment in 1967, and in 1992 the 71st amendment brought the total number to 18 with the addition of Nepali, Manipuri and Konkani. In 2003, the 100th amendment, supported by all 338 members present in Parliament,[24] added Maithili, Dogri, Santhali and Bodo. 33 languages are still on the "waiting list" to be included in the list of scheduled languages. The languages of the Schedule are given some preferential treatment; for instance they are considered first for any and almost every language planning and development activity, and are granted all facilities including those needed to absorb government language technology initiatives.

As for the numbers of speakers, in this analysis the more detailed census figures refer mostly to the 1991census, as the detailed language data of 2001 are not yet available. According to the 1991 census, 22 'languages' had more than a million native speakers, 50 had more than 100,000 and 114 had more than 10,000 native speakers. The remaining accounted for a total of 566,000 native speakers (out of a total of 838 million Indian citizens in 1991).

There is no "right to be scheduled" on the grounds of sheer numbers of speakers. According to the most recent census of 2001, 29 'languages' have more than one million native speakers, 60 have more than 100,000 and 122 have more than 10,000 native speakers. Languages with less than 10,000 speakers are not registered by the Indian census. Some of the non-scheduled languages have 3, 4 or 5 million speakers – more than some medium-size European national languages. In 2001 the group speaking non-scheduled languages made up 3% of the total population (around 30 million speakers). In 2004, 42% of Indians spoke Hindi as mother tongue or in combination with a dialect considered a variant of Hindi. Totalling more than 430 million people, by numbers this is the second language of the world after Chinese. A slight majority of the Indian population speaks Hindi as first or second language.

Status policy planning of a language begins with its recognition as a language.[25] Often linguistic minorities are denied rights when their language is not recognized. Current politics in many countries try to minimise the size

24 See *Language in India*, Vol.4, 1 January 2004, Language News, at: http://www.languageinindia.com/index.html

25 What is the status of a language: "Status of a language is the total sum of what one can do with a language, legally, culturally, economically, politically and demographically. The status of a language varies in time and space, and the status may be changed by promotion or by pressure", Bhattacharya, p. 62

and importance of minority languages, seeking to avoid any subsequent support. In India, due to the 2003 recognition, the number of speakers of scheduled languages reached 97% of India's total population. But what rights can these speakers derive from recognition under the 8th Schedule? Languages of the 8th Schedule are gaining greater importance due to their dominance in the field of education, mass media, and examinations by the Public Service Commission for recruitment, and generally due to government policy to strictly implement their language policies. But there is no legal provision setting out which rights a scheduled language can legitimately claim.[26]

The denial of recognition within the 8th Schedule to so many languages, and even to quite large ones by number of native speakers, appears rather arbitrary and conditioned largely by politics. There are no precise criteria for scheduling, and scheduling is certainly not based only on the number of speakers. Some languages with a large number of speakers still are not "scheduled", the largest of these being Bhili/Bhilodi with 9.6 million native speakers (ranked 14th), Gondi with 2.7 million speakers (ranked 18th) and Khandesi with 2.1 million speakers (ranked 22nd). Only Santhali, with 6.5 million speakers (ranked 15th) in 2003, succeeded in being admitted to the 8th Schedule as the first Adivasi-language. On the other hand, two languages with fewer than 2 million native speakers have recently been included in the 8th Schedule for largely political reasons: Manipuri/Meitei with 1.5 million speakers (ranked 25th) and Bodo with 1,4 million speakers (ranked 26th). For cultural/historical reasons Sanskrit is on the official Schedule though only 14,000 people claim it as their language, but many more study it in school as the classical language of India.

---

26 Articles 344 and 351 of the Constitution have assigned two specific functions to the 8th Schedule: Article 344 constitutes a "Commission and Committee of Parliament on official language, which will make recommendations on the progressive use of Hindi for the official purposes of the Union, language to be used in the Supreme Court and the High Courts and for Acts, Bills, and for the communication between the Union and a State or between one State and another and restrictions on the use of English for all or any of the official purposes of the Union".

Article 351 relates to the development of Hindi. It assigns the duty to the Union to promote the spread of Hindi, which should develop to serve as a medium of expression for all the elements of the composite culture of India. It has to enrich by assimilating the forms, style and expressions used in Hindustani and in other languages. And it should enrich itself by drawing vocabulary primarily from Sanskrit and secondarily from other languages. Thus the constitutional assignment is for the development of official Hindi. Article 344 (1) is considered as inoperative, and Article 351 as recommendatory. Also the 8th Schedule is considered as anachronistic, but attempts are being made to make it relevant. See Mallikarjun, "*The 8th Schedule Languages – A Critical Appraisal*", in: *Language and the State – The 8th Schedule*, New Delhi 1995, p. 72

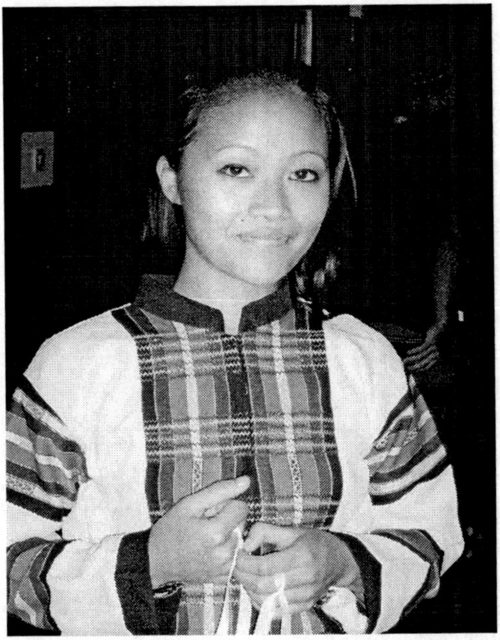

Mizo student, member of a dance group (Aizawl, Mizoram)

Does recognition of just 22 languages out of a total of 114 spoken Indian languages impinge upon equal opportunities for all Indian citizens? Indeed, it is difficult to find sufficient justification for the list of the 8th Schedule as it is in force today.[27] Two entire language families, the Sino-Tibetan and Austro-Asiatic family, were almost disregarded under the 8th Schedule. Vishvanatham identifies one main reason: "That is, that only languages with large numbers of speakers spread over and concentrated in large geographical areas, with cultivated and well developed literatures, having their own scripts, and publishing newspapers and magazines were included in the list. Written literatures with own scripts made them distinctively different and independent. Under this list 12 languages satisfy the conditions of large numbers of speakers, geographical region, written literature with specified scripts. Sanskrit was added due to its vast and rich ancient literature and heritage, Urdu because of its importance as the language of India's Muslim tradition."[28] Sindhi was added to the 8th Schedule in 1966 in recognition the presence in India of the sizeable ethnic linguistic group forced out of its former homeland of Sindh (today Pakistan) at the time of partition of the subcontinent. Nevertheless, a clear set of criteria has never been applied in according this kind of recognition: "Most scholars search

27 Bhattacharya, p. 299

28 *ibidem*, p. 305

out for a set of criteria, or try to construct one that is supposedly implicit, that forms the basis for the inclusion of languages in the 8th Schedule. But this search would lead nowhere."[29]

What are the benefits of official language recognition within the 8th Schedule? "One example of such a useful nature of recognition is the potential for employment of the speakers of that language. The conferment of official status leads to programmes which require speakers of the language to participate as teachers, literacy workers, translators and so on. The resulting jobs are newly created and do not take people away from their communities. This is not always true, particularly when a exogenous language like English in India is gaining in strength as a job-select language and the language of power, business and technology. But, the official recognition might offer a direction for future changes."[30]

Minority language speakers' struggle for the recognition of their languages under the 8th Schedule of the Constitution continues. "Such inclusion, like issues related to land and forest resources, is central to the future of the non-scheduled languages. First, the official recognition in the 8th Schedule will lead to respect for such languages and their speakers. Secondly, such an appeal to the revitalization and empowerment of the formally and consequently socially marginalized languages is urgent, necessary and important".[31] Nevertheless, when languages are recognised, as in the recent cases of Nepali, Konkani and Manipuri, they are not recognized out of Government benevolence, but as the result of appeals from actual and potential troublesome pressure groups. Official recognition also responds to what we might consider to be calls for a voice by the people in the periphery or the people internally colonized. "The assumption is not that these people do not talk, but that the talk of the colonized people is not recognized by the dominant groups and the powers-that-be as being worthy of being heard. Most of these groups have lived through a long period during which not only their languages and cultures have been actively devalued, but their speakers have also been exploited socially and economically."[32]

---

29 Kailash S. Aggarwal, *Epilogue*, in: R.S. Gupta/Anvita Albi/Kailash S. Aggarval (eds.), *Language and the State - The 8th Schedule*, Creative Books, New Delhi 1995

30 *ibidem*, p. 223. K. Aggarwal adds: "The overall implication is that the inclusion of a language in the 8th Schedule needs to be supported because its speakers strongly fell about it and request it and to abrogate the defaults of the past."

31*ibidem*, p. 224

32 Kailash Aggarwal, *Epilogue*, R.S. Gupta/Anvita Albi/Kailash S. Aggarval (eds.), *Language and the State*, Creative Books, New Delhi 1995, p. 224

Monks in the monastery of Dhankar, Spiti Valley (Himachal Pradesh)

As the official policy of language recognition is so inherently biased, the inclusion of a language in the 8th Schedule has depended largely on the ability of its speakers to influence the political process: "Any plea for recognition is met with standard refrain that the administrative costs of implementing any such decision would be prohibitive and would ultimately set a trend wherein all the 1.652 mother tongues would have to be recognized. As a result there is forced bilingualism and there is a continuous threat of a language being wiped out due to sheer lack of usage. It is estimated that in India half of the tribal people have lost or shifted their mother tongues."[33] If not the numerical strength of a language, then does its literary tradition contribute to recognition? There are some languages still excluded from the 8th Schedule that have a literary tradition, as Oraon, Bhili, Gondi. On the other hand, how can they be in the condition to produce more literature if public support in language planning is denied? India's sociolinguists assert that "the actual theme underlying the 8th Schedule is that of cultural superiority. Implicitly the State encourages language competitiveness as the languages in the 8th Schedule are advanced and enjoy public support, while the rest are merely also-rans".[34]

33 *Ibidem*, p. 225

34 Nikhil Nayyar, in: *Language and the State - The 8th Schedule*, New Delhi 1995, p. 151

1.4 The quest of choosing a "national language"

Articles 343 and 344 of the Indian Constitution of 26-1-1950 declared the official language of India to be Hindi, written in the Devanagari script with English as an auxiliary official language to be reconsidered in 15 years. Concerning the States, the Constitution allows for the free choice of official language: "The Legislature of a State may by law adopt any one or more of the languages in use in the State or Hindi as languages to be used for all or any of the official purposes of that State. Provided that, until the Legislature of the State otherwise provides by law, the English language shall continue to be used for those official purposes within the State for which it was being used immediately before the commencement of this Constitution" (Article 345, Const.). Also included in Articles 346-349 Const. are provisions for the language use of the Supreme Court and High Courts and for communication between states and with the central government. The Constitution also established the right of the President to recognise a regional language, given that this was needed and wanted by a significant portion of a State's population.

The choice of one language as the language of the Indian Constitution was intended as an act of definition of national identity. The Constituent Assembly[35] wished to establish a "national language" instead of English, which was considered a symbol of colonial rule. Hindi in the Devanagari script was adopted with 63 to 32 votes to replace English in the administration and educational system. Thus, Article 343 (1) of the Constitution states: "The official language of the Union shall be Hindi in Devanagari script". Moreover it was stated that the Union should be in charge of developing the Hindi language so "...that it may serve as a medium of expression for all elements of the composite culture of India".[36] The Constituent Assembly convened to give the Federal institutions 15 years from the approval of the Constitution to further develop Hindi as the national language in order to definitely replace English. Thirteen other languages were listed in the 8th Schedule of the Constitution as an act of formal recognition of those languages and of India's multilingualism. Almost all States subsequently set up advisory committees for their language policies and special institutions for the development of their regional languages.

Nevertheless the Official Language Act retained the use of English for most official purposes. The underlying conflict between the advocates of Hindi as the only national language on the one hand and of English on the other

35 See A.G. Noorani, *Constitutional Questions in India*, Clarendon Press, Oxford 2000
36 Constitution of India, Article 351, 1; at: http//www.constitution.org/cons/india/

was only postponed. Since the first years of independence Southern India's Dravidian language communities were reluctant to accept Hindi, fearing a lasting cultural dominance of the Hindi speaking North. The Devanagari script is also unfamiliar to the speakers of the Dravidian languages.

In 1958, the Prime Minister of Madras organised an "All India Language Conference", which rejected the establishment of Hindi as India's only official language on the federal level. The formulation in the Official Language Act of 1963 – "English may be used as..." – alarmed South India's States, and the Madras State Anti-Hindi Conference 1965 tried to unite the forces contrary to Hindi as only national language. Fierce demonstrations were held against the language policy of the Union's government. The Southern States succeeded in maintaining the legal status of English as official language. This was confirmed in 1967 through the Official (Amendment) Languages Act.
The central and most sensitive issue is the language to be used in the political institutions and in the federal administration and judiciary. In India, the non-Hindi speakers were afraid of having to compete with Hindi-speakers for employment opportunities in the "All India Service". Hindi, the language of the relative majority (around 40% of Indian citizens) and official state language in 8 federated States, maintains a strong position. Therefore, the major advocates of English as an official federal language came from the South. Hence, English can be chosen as language for the examinations, which give access to public employment in all States and Union Territories, whereas Hindi is accepted as the examination language in only in a part of the federal administration.[37] The other scheduled languages, recognized since the "Official Languages (Amendment) Act" entered into force in 1967, are also accepted as examination languages.

According to the Constitution (Article 346), communication between the Centre and the States can be carried out in Hindi or in English with the possibility of replacing English step by step with Hindi. According to the Official Language Amendment Act of 1967, documents written in Hindi must be accompanied by an English translation, whereas English documents do not require any translation. Haryana, Himachal Pradesh, Uttar Pradesh, Uttaranchal, Bihar, Rajastahan, Madhya Pradesh, Chattisgarh, Jharkhand, Gujarat, Maharashtra and Punjab decided to adopt bilingual communication with the Centre. The latter three States have official languages other than Hindi. In the remaining States, the prevailing language in communication with the Centre is English. There are also differences between English and Hindi with regard to the content of these communications. Bilingual documents

37 See NCLM, Annual Report 2004, S. 47

predominately deal with general issues, but specific and important documents such as treaties and agreements are usually written in English.[38]

As English has been adopted as the language of the higher federal judiciary and of legislation in India (Constitution, Article 348, 1), both languages can be used in Parliament, as can each of the other scheduled languages, subject to Presidential approval (Article 120 of the Constitution). In practice, however, English is also widely used in parliamentary debates. An English version must be provided for draft laws and laws relevant for all States, which also serves as the decisive version. In most of India's states and Union Territories official translation offices – the Central Hindi Directorate until 1970 and since 1971 the "Central Translation Bureau" – have been established to tackle this translation work.[39] Federal provisions are mostly translated into Hindi by the competent Federal ministry.

A State Governor, with the approval of the State President, can allow Hindi or any other scheduled language to be used in the High Courts of the State (Article 348, 2 Constitution). The lower the level of the judiciary, the more frequent use is made of regional languages. The States have significantly less freedom to determine the language in which judicial proceedings in their respective High Courts will be conducted. The Constitution gives the power to authorise the use of Hindi, or the state's official language, in proceedings of the High Court, to the Governor rather than to the State legislature. It also requires the Governor to obtain the consent of the President of India, who in these matters acts on the advice of the Government of India. The Official Languages Act gives the Governor a similar power in relation to the language in which the High Court's judgments will be delivered, subject to similar conditions. Four states - Bihar, Uttar Pradesh, Madhya Pradesh and Rajasthan - have been granted the right to conduct proceedings in their High Courts in their official language, which in each case was Hindi. However, the only non-Hindi State to seek a similar power - Tamil Nadu, which sought the right to conduct its High Court proceedings in Tamil - had its application rejected by the central government earlier, upon the advice of the Supreme Court. Now, in a new move the federal ministry of justice stated that it will not object to Tamil Nadu's claim to have Tamil as an official language to conduct proceedings in its High Court.

Today, the definitive adoption of Hindi as the only official language of the

38 Das Gupta Jyotirindra, *Language Conflict and National Development, Group Politics and National Language Policy in India*, Berkeley/Los Angeles/London 1970, p.17
39 See the 29th report of the National Commissioner for Linguistic Minorities 1988/89, at: http://nclm.nic.in

Naga students at the Northeastern Hill University NEHU, Shillong (Meghalaya)

Union shall depend on the unanimous will of all Indian States, which appears unlikely. The political project to establish a national (historically Indian) link language for all India turned out to be impracticable, and English continued to be tolerated on all levels. In the end, Indian democracy was flexible enough to accept a compromise.

Chapter 2

2. The linguistic reorganisation of the Indian Union

2.1 Redrawing the States' boundaries

While the history of the reorganisation of Indian provinces on a linguistic basis can be traced back to 1858, drawing boundaries along linguistic lines was not a political reality until the 1950s. In the British Parliament at that time, John Bright said that the provinces of India should be grouped into 5 administrative groups on the basis of geography and language. In 1896, Mahesh Narayan of Bihar began a movement for the removal of Hindi speaking parts from Bengal to keep Hindi speaking regions under one sole administration. With the vivisection of Bengal by Lord Curzon in 1905, the leaders of the nationalist movement began to grant importance to the organization of States on a language basis for the first time. In 1908, Lokamanya Tilak said before the Royal Commission that the States of India should be organized on a language basis, and from then on he became the forefront leader advocating this principle.

The idea of redrawing India's internal boundaries has been raised since 1920. In order to be effective and to reach the people in their own language and to achieve its goals, in December 1920 the All India Congress Committee at Nagpur organized its administrative divisions based on language. The All Parties Conference set up the Motilal Nehru Committee (1928) to look into the aspects of reorganisation and supported the organisation of regions along linguistic principles. The Indian National Congress reaffirmed the principle of linguistic reorganisation on three occasions between 1928 and 1947. In a meeting from August 28th to 31st, 1928, the All Party Conference resolved to accept the reorganisation of States on linguistic principles. Finally, in its 1945 election manifesto, the All India Congress declared that it was its aim to provide opportunities to the people to develop according to their intentions, and every group of people and every region of the country should have the opportunity to develop culturally. In order to achieve this, the Congress decided to organize the States on the basis of language and culture. The first linguistic states to be formed were Orissa and Sindh in 1936.

In 1948, after independence, when the demand for a separate Telugu State was voiced, the Linguistic Provinces Commission was appointed under the Chairmanship of S.K. Dar (1948). Its report recommended that "the emphasis should be primarily on administrative convenience, whereas homogeneity of language will enter into consideration only as a matter of administrative convenience and not by its own independent force".[40] In paragraph 125 of the report the Commission said: "Linguistic homogeneity in the formation of new provinces is certainly attainable within certain limits, but only at the cost of creating a fresh minority problem. And nowhere will it be possible to form a linguistic province of more than 70 to 80 percent of the people speaking the same language, thus leaving in each province a minority of at least 20% of people speaking other languages".[41] Probably this aspect of the Commission's views was not sufficiently deliberated. Linguistic re-organization alone, however, was not the only or major factor triggering new language movements in later periods.

Upon the recommendation of the Dar Committee, the Government intended to postpone the reorganisation. However, due to pressure from the public to revive the reorganisation of the States, in 1948 the All India Congress Committee at Jaipur created the JVP Committee (Jawaharlal Nehru, Vallabhbhai Patel and Pattabhi Sitaramaiah), which worked out the foundation for the second significant event of the century after the independence: on December 22nd, 1953, Jawaharlal Nehru announced the Resolution of the Government of India relating to the reorganisation in the Parliament. He stated: "...the language and culture of an area have an undoubted importance as they represent a pattern of living which is common in that area. In considering a reorganisation of States, however, there are other important factors which have also to be borne in mind. The first essential consideration is the preservation and strengthening of the unity and security of India. Financial, economic and administrative considerations are almost equally important, not only from the point of view of each State, but for the whole nation".[42]

Reviewing the then existing linguistic scenario in the States, the States Reorganization Commission (SRC), in a report dated 30-9-1955, noted:

1. Not all the language groups are so placed that they can be grouped into separate States;
2. There are large numbers of bilingual belts between different linguistic areas;

40 See Jennifer Bayer, *Language and Law*, CIIL Mysore, at: http://www.ciil-ebooks.net/html/disorder/index.htm

41 For this chapter see especially Jennifer Bayer, *Law and Language*, CIIL-e-books at: http://www.ciil-ebooks.net/html/disorder/index.htm

42 Jennifer Bayer, *ibidem*

3. There exist areas with a mixed population even within monolingual areas.[43]

The four principles that the SRC followed in the reorganization of the States are:

1. Preservation and strengthening of the unity and security of India
2. Linguistic and cultural homogeneity
3. Financial, economic and administrative considerations
4. Successful function of the national plan

Guided by these principles, the Commission put major emphasis on the criterion of a minimum standard of internal cohesion within the population of a State. The new States should not only have a common language to promote the growth of such regional consciousness, but also to foster administrative convenience. In the democratic life of such States, the government should ensure that the administration is conducted in a language the people can understand.

The Commission also had to face the issue of newly-formed linguistic minorities. To safeguard the peculiar interests of minority groups, the SRC suggested, with reference to the use of languages in administration, that:

a) A State should be considered monolingual when about 70% or more of the entire population of the State speaks the same language;
b) A State should be considered as bilingual when about 30% or more of the entire population of the state speaks a language other than the language of the region;
c) The language of the minority should be used for conducting official business in a district and not the official language of the State, if 70% or more of the population of the district speaks it;
d) In bilingual districts, municipal areas or in taluks, where minorities contribute 15% to 20%, documents like Government notices, electoral rolls, ration cards, etc., are to be reprinted in both languages.

Andhra Pradesh was carved out in October 1953, and the subsequent mounting pressure for the creation of other States resulted in the formation of the States Re-organisation Commission in December 1953. In October 1955, it submitted its report, which was neither binding nor ever fully implemented. Its impact was nevertheless felt in the 7th Amendment of the Indian Constitution, in which language was a major consideration if not the sole consideration in re-ordering the political boundaries of states. The establishment of the Naga Hills-Tuensang area in 1957 was a concession

43 The National Commissioner of Linguistic Minorities, Official presentation of the CLM, leaflet 2008; further information on: http://nclm.nic.in;

to the ethnic movement of the Naga people, who struggled and achieved statehood for Nagaland in 1963. The partition of Bombay into Maharashtra and Gujarat was the second landmark. The partition of Punjab in 1966 (Punjabi Suba and Haryana) and the creation of Himachal Pradesh was a natural consequence. Most subsequent political changes after have taken place in the Northeast. Meghalaya was established in 1970 on linguistic grounds and attained full status as a State in 1972. At the same time the Union Territories of Arunachal Pradesh and Mizoram were established. Manipur and Tripura, Union Territories since 1956, became federated States in the 1970s and Sikkim became an Indian State in 1975.

The reorganisation of the Indian Union along linguistic lines, launched in 1954, was certainly the single most important act of language policy of independent India. The process of reorganising the States of Central and Southern India according to linguistic majorities between 1954 and 1960 was complicated and conflicted. The Congress, dominated by North Indian politicians, was reluctant to give in to the claims of the Dravidian South and to capture fully the linguistic complexity of Southern India: the creation of Andhra Pradesh set a case of precedence. Eventually the SRC decided not to apply only linguistic criteria, rejecting the principle of "one state – one language" as being in contradiction with the constitutional principle of equality of all citizens. Religious criteria were also to be excluded, as India was considered a secular state. Until 1960 all Southern India was restructured: after Andhra Pradesh (Telugu majority, State in 1953), Gujarat was carved out of Maharashtra. Kerala was created in 1956, Maharashtra in 1969. In 1966 Punjab was divided into the Punjabi-speaking 'Punjab-Suba' and Hindi-speaking Haryana. Karnataka, with a majority of Kannada speakers, was shaped from the former Mysore state. Assam, starting with the institution of Nagaland in 1963, was divided into 7 states in the 1970s and 1980s. Where several minority languages coexisted within a geographic area, a request for separate statehood was sometimes first denied, and only later conceded (e.g. Jharkhand was carved out of Bihar only in 2000, after a long political struggle). The process of sorting out the States according to majority languages led to more pronounced linguistic homogeneity, as is mirrored in the majority languages of the Indian States today.

The Indian Constitution does not specify the official languages to be used by the States in official functions and leaves each State free to adopt any language used in its territory, Hindi, or English as its own official language. This official language need not be one of those listed in the 8th Schedule, and several States have adopted official languages not listed in the 8th Schedule, such as Kokborok in Tripura, Mizo in Mizoram, Khasi, Garo and Jaintia in

Meghalaya and French in Pondicherry (a Union Territory). Nevertheless, the linguistic reorganisation of States succeeded in bringing together in one or more States the majority of the speakers of the major (and scheduled) languages. Thus, these States may legitimately be called the "home states" of those languages.[44]

Table 5 Majority languages, speakers of minority languages (1991)

Territory	Majority language (and % of its speakers)		% of speakers of minority language
Andhra Pradesh	Telugu	85.13	14.87
Arunachal Pradesh	Nissi/Dafla*	23.40	76.60
Assam	Assamese	60.89	39.11
Bihar	Hindi	80.17	19.83
Goa	Konkani	56.65	43.35
Gujarat	Gujarati	90.73	9.28
Haryana	Hindi	88.77	11.23
Himachal Pradesh	Hindi	88.95	11.05
Jammu&Kashmir	Kashmiri**	52.73	47.27
Karnataka	Kannada	65.69	34.31
Kerala	Malayalam	95.99	4.01
Madhya Pradesh	Hindi	84.73	15.63
Maharashtra	Marathi	73.62	26.38
Manipur	Manipuri/Meitei	62.36	37.64
Meghalaya	Khasi**	47.45	52.55
Mizoram	Mizo/Lushai	77.58	22.42
Nagaland	Ao*	13.93	86.07
Orissa	Oriya	82.23	17.77
Punjab	Punjabi	84.88	15.12
Rajasthan	Hindi	89.89	10.11
Sikkim	Nepali	60.97	39.03
Tamil Nadu	Tamil	85.35	14.65
Tripura	Bengali	69.59	30.41
Uttar Pradesh	Hindi	89.68	10.32
West Bengal	Bengali	86.34	13.66

Source: figures elaborated from the Census of India 2001

Notes: *In these two cases of indigenous languages one can hardly speak of a "majority language", as it is just the language spoken by the relatively major share of population.

**In Jammu&Kashmir Kashmiri is the absolute majority language of the Kashmir

44 Rajendra Pandey, *Minorities in India*, Delhi 1997, p.81. During the linguistic reorganization, several conflicts arose regarding the boundaries of the States. This issue is also discussed by Jennifer Bayer, *Language and Law*, CIIL Mysore, at: http://www.ciil-ebooks.net/html/disorder/index.htm

Valley; in Meghalaya Garo and Khasi share the role of most important languages in the State, but none of them is the official language of the respective State.

There are two pan-Indian languages (English and Hindi), two languages without a specific region (Urdu and Sindhi), and 18 languages concentrated in different regions. The situation of Sindhi and Urdu is different, as they do not have a contiguous territory that might be called "home state" or "home-region" crosscutting several States. Due to the effects of migration fluxes after the partition in 1947, Sindhi is spread over Gujarat, Maharashtra and Madhya Pradesh, where over 90% of the Sindhi speaking population lives.

Table 6 – Official status of languages, State/district level (2001)

Language	State, where it is official	Area where it is regional official
1. Assamese	Assam	
2. Bengali	West Bengal, Tripura	District of Cachar (Assam)
3. Gujarati	Gujarat	
4. Hindi	UP, Bihar, M.P., Rajasthan, Haryana, H.P., Delhi, Chandigarh, Gujarat	Some units of Karnataka
5. Kannada	Karnataka	
6. Kashmiri	-	-
7. Malayalam	Kerala	Mahe in Pondicherry, some units of Karnataka
8. Marathi	Maharashtra	
9. Oriya	Orissa	
10. Punjabi	Punjab	
11. Sanskrit	-	-
12. Sindhi	-	-
13. Tamil	Tamil Nadu, Pondicherry	Some units of Karnataka
14. Telugu	Andhra Pradesh	Some units of Karnataka, Yamen of Pondicherry, Ganjam/Koraput of Orissa
15. Urdu	Jammu&Kashmir, UP, West Bengal	
16. Konkani	Goa	
17. Manipuri	Manipur	
18. Nepali	Sikkim (with Bhotia and Lepcha)	3 subdivisions of district Darjeeling
19. Bhotia*	Sikkim (with Nepali and Lepcha)	
20. Lepcha*	Sikkim (with Bhotia and Nepali)	
21. Mizo*	Mizoram	Lunglei/Simtupui districts of Mizoram
22. Kokborok*	Tripura (Second official language)	
23. Bodo		Bodoland Autonomous Hill District (Assam)
24. Maithili	-	-
25. Dogri	-	-
26. Santhali	-	-

* not recognized with the 8th Schedule of the Constitution.

** Khasi and Garo are recognised as "Associate official languages" of Meghalaya in 2005. *Source: S.S. Bhattacharya, Languages in India – Their Status and Function, in: Itagi/ Singh (eds.) Linguistic Landscape in India, CIIL Mysore, 2002, p. 91*

Urdu is even more widely dispersed and is linked to the historical development of Islam in India during the period of the Moghul empires. Since 1947, English has emerged as an even stronger link-language for all Indian communication. The preference for Hindi as a link-language depends mostly on geographic area of residence and social strata. Upper classes of society prefer English, which has generally become the language of higher, especially academic, education.

In the single States, usually the major regional language spoken in the territory has been declared the official language. An exception was made in Jammu and Kashmir, which adopted Urdu as the official language, as well as some smaller states in the North East like Arunachal Pradesh (English), Meghalaya (English), Nagaland (English), Tripura (English), as there are several major languages, some tribal languages without a script, and no other indigenous "link-language". Tripura, along with Sikkim and some other areas of the Northeast, is an example of the transformation of majority languages into minority languages due to immigration in a relatively short historical period. Whereas the autochthonous tribal population speaking the main language Kokborok accounted for 52.8% in 1901, after a century of Bengali speaking immigration, the proportion shrunk to 31.05% (2001 census). In Sikkim the Nepali speaking population only overturned the indigenous peoples in numerical terms in the 1960s.

Although "linguistic homogenisation" operated through the reorganisation of the States, there are sizeable minority language groups belonging to the 8th Schedule in almost all of the 17 larger States. Most live in the border areas between the States or in the larger cities. These groups, which can be termed "relative minorities" (speaking a language which is official in another state), comprise substantial numbers of Bengali, Kannada, Punjabi and Telugu speakers. Hindi speakers live in sizeable numbers in Jammu and Kashmir and Punjab, to a lesser extent in West Bengal, Assam, Maharashtra and to a still lesser extent in Andhra Pradesh, Orissa, Gujarat and Karnataka. In the other two Southern States they are negligible (Tamil Nadu and Kerala). The Urdu speaking population is to be found in the wider Hindi belt, except Punjab and Himachal Pradesh, as well as in Karnataka, Andhra Pradesh and Maharashtra and to a lesser extent in West Bengal, Orissa, Gujarat and Tamil Nadu. They are negligible in Assam and Kerala.

The changes in linguistic geography occasioned by this reorganization of the Indian States did little to solve the problem of minority languages or to promote their status vis-à-vis the regional languages. According to Srivastava, however, the reorganisation of States along linguistic lines had another long-term impact: it changed the nature of non-conflicting bilingualism into a competing type.[45]

It is true that, in addition to linguistic factors, factors like ethnic and religious composition and geographical factors including distance from the capital and economic and social backwardness of the regions played a major part in carving out States. The creation of two of the three youngest Indian States in 2000 – Uttarakhand, Jharkhand and Chattisgarh – was also motivated by the language factor. Further political reorganisation along linguistic lines is not excluded, as at least 120 million Indian citizens belong to linguistic minorities with regard to their State of residence. It is important to know that many areas inhabited by linguistic minorities are linguistically not homogeneous and require linguistic regulations and safeguards for the minorities rather than the redrawing of State borders. The founding fathers of the Indian Constitution did anticipate some of these problems and tried to incorporate some provisions relating to language use. The stated goal of the language policy was to help all languages develop into fit vehicles of communication in their designated areas of use irrespective of majority or minority status.[46] "When language becomes a barrier between the accused and justice, then justice and equity are not meted out to the accused. when equality of opportunity is not provided to different linguistic groups in education, employment and mass communication, then social justice is denied to them. When the public administration was operating in one official State language only, linguistic minorities would sooner or later feel alienated."[47]

2.2 India's "linguistic federalism"

After the linguistic reorganisation of federal India and the territorial subdivision of the Union into federated States, Union Territories mirrored the linguistic landscape much more precisely. In essence India applied a division principle dictated by the linguistic majority of a territory, which in Europe would be called "state titular majority" or "national or state language". Subsequently, the State adopted the dominant language of the majority of the population as the official language. This State should not be confused with the historical process of "nation building" that moulded European history. Languages in India do not constitute "nations". At the same time, accept-

45 See Rakesh Bhatt/Ahmar Mahboob, *Minority languages and their status*, in: Kachru/Kachru/Sridhar, *Language in South Asia*, Cambridge University Press 2008, p.137;

46 Mallikarjun, *Indian Languages and the digital divide*, in Language in India, April 2004, p.10

47 *ibidem*

ing the majority language principle, the "fathers of the Constitution" had to enshrine also the protection of the minority languages, while multilingualism or bilingualism was affirmed at the federal level. In practice, the single States differed widely with respect to the implementation of the Constitution's general language policy targets. The present structure of India in fundamentally monolingual federated States, with one or more link-languages for supranational communication, appears to be similar to the linguistic construction of the European Union, which was formed in a bottom-up process from a compound of nation-states.

"The provision of federalism in the Indian Constitution are designed to protect the rights of linguistic communities. By giving effect to the reorganization of state boundaries along linguistic lines, it enables such communities the right of self-governance" Castellino and Dominguez observe.[48] But the Parliament retains the right to demarcate new states. In India's constitutional setting often the 'national' prevails over the 'federated units', despite the precise demarcation of powers between the state and the Centre, contained in various lists of competences annexed to the Constitution. The constitutional provisions relating to the use of the language in legislation at the State level largely mirror those relating to the official language at the central level, with minor variations. State legislatures may conduct their business in their official language, Hindi, or for a transitional period English, and members who cannot use any of these have the same rights to use their mother tongue with the Speaker's permission. The authoritative text of all laws must be in English, unless the Parliament passes a law permitting a State to use another language. If the original text of a law is in a different language, an authoritative English translation of all laws has to be provided.

The State has the right to use its official language in public administration, and in general, neither the Constitution nor any central enactment imposes any restriction on this right. However, every person submitting a petition for the redress of a grievance to an officer or authority of the State Government has a constitutional right to submit it in any language used in that State regardless of its official status. This is a fundamental act of respect vis-à-vis the multilingual composition of the population of each State. In addition, the Constitution grants the central Government, acting through the President, the power to issue certain directives to the government of a State in relation to the use of minority languages for official purposes. The Indian President may direct a State to officially recognise a language spoken in its territory for specified purposes and in specified regions, if a substantial proportion of

48 Joshua Castellino and Elvira Domínguez Redondo, *Minority Rights in Asia, A Comparative Legal Analysis*, Oxford University Press 2006, p. 99

its speakers demand it (Article 347 of the Constitution). Similarly, States and local authorities are required to endeavour to provide primary education in the mother tongue for all linguistic minorities, regardless of whether or not their language is official in that State. The President has the power to issue directions he deems necessary to ensure that they are provided these facilities.[49]

Since the 1980s the creation of new States has continued, and does not seem to be completed even after the establishment of Uttaranchal, Jharkhand and Chattisgarh in 2000. Several States in the Northeast have been carved out from existing States in order to prevent secessionist claims and movements (Manipur, Nagaland, Meghalaya, Tripura and Mizoram). Allegations that the divisions of the Union along linguistic lines could jeopardise the unity of the Federation have not come true, rather the formation of new states has stabilised the existing federal system. On the other hand, the Centre has always been very determined in rejecting any attempt at secession and, in order to come to terms with sub-national self-determination movements, in some cases has created new States. Several self-determination movements have been curbed by military means (Kashmir, Nagaland, Mizoram, Punjab).

The State official languages have become more prominent in public life and in the life of a major part of the population. Their use in all media has increased drastically, establishing them as languages with high prestige. "... in almost all States a sort of linguistic convergence towards the majority language is in progress, which may gradually reduce the number of speakers of minority languages. This may even, in due course of time kill the minor languages in the Hindi speaking States."[50] Even after the reorganization of India's subdivision in linguistic States, those States are far from being monolingual or linguistically homogeneous. Conversely, the existence of minority peoples who account for some million speakers within a State did not automatically lead to the creation of a new State unit reserved for them. The new States were meant to create administrative and political units, which would comprise the bulk of a people or linguistic community on its traditional territory. The minor linguistic communities within this framework, however, would have needed a sub-state legal-political framework in order to be taken into account.[51] In most cases this did not happen.

---

49 See Jayaran, B.D./Rajyashree K.S., *State Official Language Policy Implementation*, Central Institute of Indian Languages, Mysore 2000, p. 1-28. This issue is more specifically dealt with in chapter 4.

50 *ibidem*, p. 309

51 See R. Srivastava, *Linguistic Minorities and National Language*, in: Florian Coulmas

A woman of the Pnar community in Rymbai (Jaintia Hills, Meghalaya)

The political organisations and movements' capacity to pressure the central institutions was of major importance in the process of linguistic reorganization. The Union and the States had to find ways to accommodate such linguistic minorities, which included at least some forms of recognition of the official use of their languages. The Constitution provides the possibility for a State to declare a minority language to be official in part of its territory or in the whole State, provided the President retains that this accords with the wishes of a substantial proportion of the population of a State speaking that language (Article 347 of the Constitution). Only few States adopted regulations to recognizing minority languages as official languages for a section of their territory. We will return to a discussion of the safeguards that apply to the rights of linguistic minorities in chapter 4.

(ed.), *Linguistic Minorities and Literacy: Language Policy Issues in developing Countries*, p. 99-114, Mouton De Gruyter, Berlin 1984

Chapter 3

A typology of the linguistic minorities in India

3.1 Definition of minority languages

Generally, minority languages in most countries of the world are defined only by the criterion of numerical inferiority with regard to the majority language spoken in that State or the State's official (titular) language. Moreover, a minority cannot occupy a dominant position. A further salient feature of a minority is the willingness to preserve distinct qualities, as captured by the UN's definition: "The term minority includes only those non-dominant groups in a population which possess and wish to preserve stable, ethnic, religious or linguistic traditions or characteristics markedly different from those of the rest of the population."[52]

In the Indian context, defining linguistic minorities by numerical strength alone is not appropriate. Such a numerical definition renders all the languages spoken in India "minority languages". Even Hindi (or its dialects and variants), which is the official language of India spoken as a mother tongue by more than 40% of India's population – today about 430 million, occupies a relative minority position nation-wide. In turn, the minority languages of India generally share the features "non-dominant" and "different from the rest of the population." Moreover, this definition points out that a language receives its minority status due to the minority status of the community within the State to which it belongs. It allows a language to be labelled as a minority language if the community using it is numerically large or in a majority at the State level, but non-dominant.

Thus, if on the one hand the minority status of a language depends on the territory of reference (Union, State), on the other hand factors like the political, economic and cultural power of the language must also be considered when attributing minority status. English, for example, is the mother tongue of just 178,000 Indian citizens (the "Anglo-Indians", figures according to the census 1991), but the role of English in daily life can hardly

52 Capotorti in 1978 with regard to Article 27 of the ICCPR gave the following, widely used definition: "A minority is a group numerically inferior to the rest of the population of a State, in a non-dominant position, whose members – being national of the State – possess ethnic, religious or linguistic characteristics differing from those of the rest of the population and show, if only explicitly, a sense of solidarity, directed towards preserving their cultures, traditions, religion or language." See: Thomas Benedikter, *A Short Guide to Minority Rights in Europe*, EURAC, Bozen 2008, p.8

be put on the same level with the language Nissi/Dafla spoken by 173,000 people in Arunachal Pradesh.

The Indian Constitution recognises the concept of linguistic minorities, but is silent regarding the definition of the term. Articles 29 and 30 comprise the right of children of minority communities to be taught in their mother tongue, but they do not indicate any definition of what is a "mother tongue" and under which conditions this right can be claimed. Hence the judiciary had to define it for the purpose applying Article 30 of the Constitution:
"A linguistic minority for the purposes of Article 30 (1) is one which must at least have a separate spoken language. It is not necessary that the language should also have distinct script for those who speak it to be a linguistic minority. There are in this country some languages which have no script of their own, but nonetheless those sections of the people who speak that language will be a linguistic minority entitled to the protection of Article 30 (1)."[53]
Some Indian institutions thus assume that a linguistic minority is automatically defined when their mother tongue differs from the regional language of the area or that state.[54] But such a concept would be both theoretically unfounded and practically insufficiently precise, as it would include every language different from the regional official language, including the languages of newly immigrated individuals and communities. A further indication on this term is given by the Supreme Court of India, which in 1958 presented a parameter for defining a minority language as "the language of the minority community, a parameter which is applicable only at the State level as there is no linguistic group in India which can claim the majority status on federal level".[55] Thus the linguistic majority-minority question, unlike the religious issue, is considered in reference to the State only: "Since India is divided into states on the basis of the language of the majority of the people of a given region, it was deemed that 'linguistic minority' could only be construed in the context of a particular state. The jurisprudence is consistent on this question: 'If...the state has to be regarded as the unit for determining 'Linguistic minority' vis-à-vis Article 30, then with 'religious minority' being on the same footing, it is the state in relation to which the majority or minority status will have to be determined."[56]

53 Wisdom of the Supreme Court (AIR 1971 S.C. 1987)

54 See NCLM, 42th report, p.14, at: http://nclm.nic.in

55 Chaklaer S., *Linguistic Minority as a Cohesive Force in Indian Federal Process*, New Delhi, Associate Publishing House, 1981, p. 14

56 Joshua Castellino and Elvira Domínguez Redondo, *Minority Rights in Asia, A Comparative Legal Analysis*, Oxford University Press 2006, p. 68, quoting T.M.A. Pai Foundation and others versus State of Karnataka and others, WP (Civil), no 317/1993 (31.10.2002), para 76

Nevertheless, apart from judicial and semi-official definitions, further criteria should be included in order to render a typology of linguistic minorities in India useful for analysis and for conceptualizing language policies. Relying on a concept developed by Pandharipande[57] minority languages can be defined on the basis of two major features:

a) Their functional load

b) Their functional transparency in the various domains of society

Minority languages are typically those that carry a relatively lower or marginal functional load and transparency. The concept of "functional load" in this context refers to the ability of languages to successfully function in one or more social domains. The load is considered to be higher or lower on the basis of the number of domains it covers.

Table 7 - The hierarchy of functional load

+ functional transparency	+ number of domains	High functional load	Example: English and official regional languages
+ functional transparency	- number of domains	Higher functional load	Sanskrit and Bazaar Hindi
- functional transparency	+ number of domains	Lower functional load	Attrition of minority languages: minority languages used along with dominant languages
- functional transparency	- number of domains	Low functional load	Attrition situation: dominant languages displace minority language

Source: Rajushwari Pandharipande, Minority matters , p. 20

The higher the number of domains, the higher the functional load. For example, in India English covers almost all major public domains such as media, business, education, national and international communication, science and technology. In contrast, the tribal languages control only one (rapidly diminishing) domain, that of home, whereas regional languages cover at least four domains: home, education, public administration and to some extent media and interstate communication.

"Functional transparency" refers to the autonomy and control that the language has in a particular domain. If a language A is the only language

57 See Rajeshwari Pandharipande, *Minority matters: issues in minority languages in India*, in: International Journal of Multicultural Societies, Vol. 4, No.2, UNESCO 2002

used to perform a particular function in a particular domain, then language A can be said to have "functional transparency" vis-à-vis that function. In contrast, if the same function is performed by more than one language, the languages involved are said to be non transparent (but opaque) as to that function. A language with a higher functional transparency can be said to have a higher functional load compared with a language that does not have functional transparency. For example, the only language used for science and technology in India is English. Therefore English can be said to be transparent as to this function. Similarly, regional minority languages (in their own regions) are almost exclusively used at home, and therefore command functional transparency in that domain. Some that are presently spoken exclusively at home, however, also gradually begin to be accompanied by the dominant language when children begin schooling in that language. This parallel use of two languages (minority and dominant) even in private and community life reduces the functional transparency of minority languages, indicating an increasing threat to lose their last domain.

The question of maintenance and shift of languages is related to the scheme above. Can we assume that a high degree of functional load is a necessary as well as a sufficient condition for the maintenance of a language? The answer is as follows: a language with a higher functional load has a better chance of survival than a language with a lower functional load. For example, the regional languages with a higher functional load are more likely to be maintained in India than the tribal languages with a very low functional load. Nevertheless, a language with a higher degree of transparency (and low number of domains) has a better chance of survival than a language with a high number of domains, but low transparency.[58] Thus, transparency is higher if the language does not share functions with other languages.[59] In other words, if it is perceived as the most appropriate language to carry out that particular function, the language is considered to be "transparent to the function". Sanskrit, for example, is most transparent in expressing Hinduism, while such regional languages as Telugu or Kannada are most transparent to their function as State languages. Similarly, English is transparent as to the function of "modernity". Transparency depends directly on the functional load of a language.

Multilingualism is a part of the hierarchy. The less important a language is, the more languages the mother tongue speakers of that language have to learn and to speak if they move out of the limited area of usage of their mother tongue. Minority languages hold a lower position within the given

58 R. Pandharipande, *Minority matters,* p.20
59 *ibidem*, p.2

hierarchy of languages and thus are driven to „multilingualism by necessity"..

In summary, two key factors are important in determining the minority character of a language: numerical inferiority and a lesser functional load and transparency. The concept of "functional load" provides an appropriate and sufficient criterion for defining minority languages. As Pandharipande puts it: "...all the above definitions of minority languages have one feature in common: minority languages (regardless of whether they are numerically a minority or not) carry a marginal functional load, or none of all, in the public domains of society. Thus, English, though numerically a minority, cannot be called a minority language as it carries a heavy functional load in the public domain (education, business, international and intra-national communication, technology etc.). In contrast, Kashmiri, a majority language in one State, is viewed as a minority language because it does not carry a heavy functional load in the public domain of the society within which it is located. The tribal languages are numerically minority languages and only in some cases carry a marginal functional load in the domains of education, business and inter-group communication."[60]

This concept is also dynamic: wherever, due to social, economic and political factors, the functional load of a language is reduced, a language is pushed into a minority position. On the contrary, where it is uplifted by adding new domains (e.g. in education), the minority position can be reduced. This definition also implicitly assumes that a stable or increasing functional load is conducive to language retention, while a decreasing functional load leads to language attrition. It also predicts that a minority language can acquire the status of a dominant language if its functional load increases in the public domain.[61] Thus the numerical criterion has to be integrated with two additional features: "non-dominance" and "difference from the rest of the population of a State". In India, in almost all cases, minority languages are both numerically inferior and have no official power or extended functional load. Exceptionally they are numerically superior in a given region or State, but lack official power as Kashmiri in Jammu and Kashmir, Khasi in Meghalaya, Nagamese in Nagaland, Mizo in Mizoram, and some tribal languages in Arunachal Pradesh. Some additional types of minorities referred to India's linguistic landscape will be introduced later.

60 *ibidem*, *Minority matters*, p.6
61 *ibidem*, p.7

3.2 The importance of scripts

With regard to the availability of a script India's linguistic scenario may be summarised in this way:

- Languages with a longstanding written tradition
- Languages that have only recently acquired a script
- Languages without a written equivalent
- Languages/dialects that once had a written tradition, but subsequently dialectilized.

The number of scripts in India's linguistic landscape are many, but basically consist of three main kinds, namely derivatives of Brahmi, Arabic and Roman, resulting in 10 major scripts: Nagari, Perso-Arabic, Gurumukhi, Gujarati, Bengali-Assami-Manipuri, Oriya, Telugu-Kannada, Tamil, Malayalam, Roman. In a few cases of alphabetisation, entire new scripts were invented to write languages, and some languages continue to be written in more than one script. A script is currently in use for approximately 50 of the total of 114 languages registered in the official census.[62] Certain unwritten, purely spoken languages show a high degree of refinement in their oral tradition and prove more important than the written languages in certain contexts.[63] In India, apart from the 14 different scripts in use for the scheduled and some non-scheduled languages, the following scripts are used for other minority languages:

Table 8 – Scripts of minority languages (other than the 14 official)

Name of script	Name of the State/UT	Name of communities
Baital Nagari	Rajasthan	Jaga/Brahm Bhatt
Balti	Jammu and Kashmir	Broq-pa
Bodhi	Himachal Pradesh, Ladakh (Jammu and Kashmir) Sikkim	Beda, Bodh Bodh, Champa, Gara, Mon Bhotia
Burmese	Tripura	Mag/Magh
Hingna	Arunachal Pradesh	Khamba
Meitei-Mayak	Manipur	Meitei
Mon	Arunachal Pradesh	Khampri

62 Survey of the Registrar General of India, Government and ICRB, 1988

63 S.S. Bhattacharya, *Languages in India – Their Status and Function*, in: Itagi/Singh (eds.), *Linguistic Landscape in India*, CIIL Mysore, 2002, p.64

Ol Chiki	Bihar West Bengal	Santal Santal
Takri/Tankri	Himachal Pradesh	Gaddi Rajput, Pajira, Seok
Tana/Thana	Lakhshadweep	Manikfan, Raveri, Thakru, Thakrufan
Tibetan	Arunachal Pradesh Himachal Pradesh Sikkim West Bengal	But Monpa, Dirang, Monpa Kalaktang Monpa, Monpa Lishpa, Zakhring/Meyor, Khampa, Bhotia, Lepcha, Sherpa
U-Chhen	Sikkim	Tibetan
U-Med	Sikkim West Bengal	Druk-pa/Dukpa, Tibetan Druk-pa/Dukpa

Source: Mallikarjun, Multilingualism and the digital divide, Language in India, 2004

Minority languages that recently adopted a script largely favoured Devanagari. Some of the non-scheduled languages have adopted other major scripts, as these have the advantages of being well-established scripts with technological equipment already in place. Tulu, for example, is written in Kannada script, Bodo in Devanagari, Bishnupriya Manipuri in Bengali script, and so on. Some linguistic minorities have sought to revive their traditional script. The linguistic group Sourashtra in Tamil Nadu is using its own script as well as modified Tamil script. There are attempts to revive Meitei Mayek for Manipuri and Maithili script for Maithili. Roman script, under the influence of the missionaries, has been the favourite among the tribal peoples in the Northeast, as well as in Konkani in Goa. The third response has been to create a new script, as illustrated by the example of Ol Chiki for the Santhali language. Santhali, as some other Adivasi languages, is dispersed over several States and is written in different scripts in distinct areas, which complicates usage and standardisation. Sanskrit is written in many scripts, but has a very peculiar role in Indian culture. Finally, in India the majority of all spoken languages are still without a script.

Two cases may be emblematic in the debate over adopting a new script. The Assamese script was being used for the minority language Bodo in Assam. The conflict between Bodo speakers and Assamese regarding sharing socioeconomic advantages in state development became associated with Bodo speakers' opposition to the Assamese script. The script issue assumed central importance in the conflict and lead to violence. Ultimately the prominent members of the Bodo community were persuaded to accept the Devanagari script as an alternative solution, though there are still some Bodo speakers who want to use the Roman script.

The other case, concerning Santhali speakers, is more complex. Santhali speakers are found in four states: Bihar, Assam, Orissa and West Bengal. If one were to respect the principle that the script of the regional official language should be adopted, Santhali would have to be written in four scripts. Some groups among the Santhali speakers favor adopting one of the three scripts of indigenous origin. Again in terms of social divisions and religious affiliations, some Santhali speakers want to adopt Roman script and others favour Devanagari. The choice of one script would help in the process of social mobilisation and group solidarity and promote the use and development of the Santhali language. This alternative has been suggested by the NCLM. However the governments of Assam, Bihar, Orissa and West Bengal have objected to this suggestion for administrative, socio-economic and educational reasons. Thus, if the situation remains as it is, any concerted efforts to spread the use and development of Santhali language by Santhali speakers through different States will be extremely difficult.[64]

Concerning literary production, a distinction has to be drawn between a literary production in the true sense and written communication. In 2001, the Indian Sahitya Academy (National Academy of Arts) registered 22 languages used for literary purposes. At least 50 languages, however, are written for diverse purposes and show a varying number of publications. By the absolute number of publications available, India's languages can be divided into four groups:

Less than 100 publications	100-3.000 publications	3000-10.000 publications	More than 10.000 publications
All other languages	Bodo/Boro Dogri Lushai/Mizo Khasi Thado Hmar Ladakhi Manipuri/Meitei Garo Gorkhali/Nepali Konkani Tulu Santhali	Oriya Punjabi Assamese Urdu	Hindi Bengali Marathi Tamil Malayalam Telugu Gujarati Kannada

Source: S.S. Bhattacharya, Languages in India – Their Status and Function, in: Itagi/Singh (eds.), Linguistic Landscape in India, CIIL Mysore, 2002

64 See Dua, p. 160-161, and also the interesting Portal of the Santhals (including a newsletter in Ol Chiki) at: http://wesanthals.tripod.com/

According to these figures only a dozen Indian languages show a significant printing production. If English on the one hand is a welcome tool of international or inter-State communication in India, its elitist character has created some communication problems between social classes. In 1979, English written print-media fell behind Hindi for the first year, both in terms of printed copies and number of printed products. Nevertheless, English remains the most important means of intra-India intercultural communication. In India the number of books and scientific journals published in English are equal to the number of all publications in Indian languages put together. About 50% of India's book production is in English and far more publications are imported.

3.3 Tribal peoples: a group of its own?

In 2001, the members of so-called "scheduled Tribes" (ST) made up for 7.08% of India's total population (about 71 million in 2001), but by far not all still speak a tribal language. Tribal peoples are a minority in most Indian States, except in some States of the Northeast, where absolute majorities or relative majorities of the population belong to the "tribal population" and show a high rate of language retention. They were distinct for their status as the lowest group identity on the country's socio-economic spectrum. The proportion of India's ST within the total population increased until 1981, though later this proportion shrunk slightly. Nevertheless in absolute numbers the tribal peoples are still growing considerably. Tribal peoples constitute 50% or more of the total population in as many as 285 taluks.[65]

Table 9 – Scheduled Castes (SC) and Scheduled Tribes (ST) on India's total population

	In million persons				In % of the total population			
	1961	1971	1981	1991	1961	1971	1981	1991
scheduled castes	64.4	80.0	104.8		14.7	14.6	15.8	
scheduled tribes	29.9	38.0	51.6	71	6.8	6.9	7.8	7.08%

Source: Rajendra Pandey, Minorities in India – Protection and Welfare, APH Publishing Corp., New Delhi, 1997, p. 80 (figures of the Economic Intelligence Service, Bombay)

65 D.P. Pattanayak, *Multilingualism and Mother-Tongue Education,* Oxford University Press 1981, p. 79

The first attempts in modern India at recognizing these specific ethnolinguistic group of peoples originates in the Presidential notification of 1950.[66] The "notified tribal languages" are: Abor, Adi, Anal, Angami, Ao, Assuri, Agarva, Bhili, Bhumij, Birhor, Binija/Birijia, Bodo including Kachari, Mech, Chang-Naga, Chiri, Dafla, Dimasa, Gadaba, Garo, Gondi, Ho, Halam, Juang, Kabui, Kanawari, Kharia, Khasi, Khiemnungam, Khond/Kandh, Koch, Koda/Kora, Kolami, Konda, Konyak, Korku, Kota, Korwa, Koya, Kurukh/Oraon, Lushai/Mizo, Mikir, Miri, Mishmi, Mru, Mundari, Nicobarese, Paite, Parji, Rabha, Ranghkul, Rengma, Santhali, Savara, Sema, Tangkhul, Thado, Toda, and Tripuri/Kokborok. It has to be mentioned that many of the 623 Scheduled Tribes[67] have definitely lost their traditional native language by adopting one of the major languages spoken in their area, district or State of residence. "As per the all India average, about 50% of people in the ethnic groups do not have an ethnic mother tongue, but normally have the dominant culture and language of the area or the language of another dominant group as their mother tongue."[68]

If we apply Pandharipande's criteria for defining minority languages – based on the categories of functional load and functional transparency – on India's tribal languages, we may realize that these 90 odd languages occupy the most vulnerable and weakest position among India's linguistic minorities, as they do not dominate nearly any domain other than family life and intra-group communication.

3.4 A typology of minority languages

India is a mosaic of major and minor linguistic groups and communities. Different kinds of linguistic minorities can be distinguished at different government levels (State, district, taluk). On the one hand, the numerical criterion (size of a speech community) is not sufficient to describe the minority situation in India. On the other hand, no simple criterion of language dominance can be applied in India as different languages are dominant in different domains in typically multilingual environments. Therefore, both the size of the speech community and the functional load, indicating the structure of dominance of a language, must be taken into account to explain the

66 See Joshua Castellino, *Minority Rights in India*, in J. Castellino/Elvira Domínguez Redondo, *Minority Rights in Asia, A Comparative Legal Analysis*, Oxford University Press, 2006, p. 74

67 „Scheduled Tribes means such tribes or tribal communities or parts of or groups within such tribes or tribal communities as are deemed under article 342 to be Scheduled Tribes for the purposes of this Constitutions“ (article 366 Const.).

68 See D.P. Pattanayak, *Multilingualism and Mother-Tongue Education*, 1981, p. 83

Garo girls in Tura (Meghalaya)

status of a minority language within India's multi-layered multilingualism. According to estimates, approximately 120 million Indian citizens occupy these linguistic minority positions.

1. Relative and absolute minorities

The concept of a "relative minority" refers to the existence of a "kin-state" using the language of linguistic minority as an officially recognized language. Whenever the language of a linguistic minority is spoken as official language in another state, it is a "relative minority", whereas a minority language is "absolute" when no other State has accepted its language as official, whether it is scheduled or not. Based on these criteria, Pandharipande distinguishes three groups of minority languages:

1. Non-dominant minority status in one or more home states ("absolute minorities")[69]
   a) Tribal languages
   b) Non-tribal languages
2. A language reduced to minority status in a State where it forms a numerical minority, that also constitutes a majority in other States

69 Such languages in no State form a majority and have a reduced functional load vis-à-vis the Regional official language in most of the public domains.

("relative minority")

3. Languages distributed across various States: Sindhi, Urdu, Sanskrit

2. Scheduled and non-scheduled languages

The inclusion of a language in the list of languages of the 8th Schedule of the Constitution yields a form of official State recognition. In 2009, 22 languages are holding this status. They are not necessarily principal languages of any State (as e.g. Santhali, Bodo, Maithili, Dogri, Kashmiri), nor do they require a precise geographical area of diffusion (no link to a specific territory as Urdu, Sindhi and Sanskrit). The speakers of scheduled languages constitute 97% of India's total population.

India's languages by scheduling

<table>
<tr><td colspan="3">114 languages (registered by census)</td></tr>
<tr><td colspan="2">22 scheduled languages (97% of all speakers in 2003)</td><td>92 non-scheduled languages (3% of speakers in 2003)</td></tr>
<tr><td>scheduled languages official in at least one state: 14</td><td>scheduled languages official in no state: 8</td><td>Non scheduled languages (very few co-official on district or local level)</td></tr>
<tr><td>957 mil. speakers (2001)*</td><td>39 mil. speakers (2001)*</td><td>24 million speakers (1991)
31 million speakers (2001)**</td></tr>
<tr><td colspan="3">Out of 114 languages 88 are "tribal languages" (including Santali and Bodo, the only scheduled tribal languages) with about 31 million speakers</td></tr>
</table>

* Urdu (51,5 million speakers in 2001) here is counted under "official language in at least one state", as it is the official language of Jammu and Kashmir. In reality the mother tongues of 80% of the population of that state are Dogri and Kashmiri. 50 million Indian citizens using Urdu as mother tongue are living in all other States as a minority, where Urdu only in a few cases is co-official.

** No figures for the total speakers of non-scheduled languages of the census 2001 are available. By estimate they should be 31 million, as in 2001 India's population reached 1,027 million.

Being scheduled not automatically bring about a clearly defined set of individual or collective rights for the speakers of that language. It is not yet clear what kind of rights on the constitutional and State level can be legitimately be derived from such recognition. Nevertheless, most States recognise other scheduled languages different from the regional official languages spoken on their territory as minority languages with a widely dif-

Table 10 - The numerically most important linguistic minorities in each State/UT (2001)

In bold: "absolute" linguistic minorities - Source: NCLM, official leaflet 2008

State/Union territory	ling. majority	%	first ling. minority	%	2. ling. minority	%	3. ling. minority	%
Andhra Pradesh	Telugu	84.77	**Urdu**	8.36	Hindi	2.77	Tamil	1.33
Arunachal	**Misi/Dafla**	19.91	**Adi**	17.94	Nepali	9.39	Bengali	8.19
Assam	Assami	57.81	Bengali	21.67	**Bodo/Boro**	5.28	Hindi	4.62
Bihar (+Jharkhand)	Hindi	80.86	**Urdu**	9.89	**Santhali**	2.95	Bengali	2.92
Goa	Konkani	51.52	Marathi	33.36	Kannada	4.64	**Urdu**	3.41
Gujarat	Gujarati	91.49	Hindi	2.94	Sindhi	1.70	Marathi	1.37
Haryana	Hindi	91.00	Punjabi	7.11	**Urdu**	1.99		
Himachal	Hindi	88.87	Punjabi	6.28	**Kinnauri**	1.19		
Jammu&Kashmir	Kashmiri	52.29	**Dogri**	24.39	Hindi	17.32	Punjabi	2.84
Karnataka	Kannada	66.22	**Urdu**	9.96	Telugu	7.39	Tamil	3.84
Kerala	Malayalam	96.56	Tamil	2.12				
Madhya Pradesh	Hindi	85.55	**Bhili**	3.35	**Gondi**	2.24	Marathi	1.94
Maharashtra	Marathi	73.34	Hindi	7.81	**Urdu**	7.26	Gujarati	2.55
Manipur	Manipuri	60.43	**Thado**	5.64	**Tangkhul**	5.45	**Mao**	3.89
Meghalaya	**Khasi**	49.54	**Garo**	30.86	Bengali	8.36	Nepali	2.77
Mizoram	Mizo	75.11	Bengali	8.57	**Kokborok**	3.83	**Lakher**	3.33
Nagaland	**Ao**	40.04	**Sema**	12.38	**Konyak**	11.37	**Angami**	6.06
Orissa	Oriya	82.75	Hindi	2.40	Telugu	2.10	**Santhali**	2.09
Punjab	Punjabi	92.22	Hindi	7.29				
Rajastahn	Hindi	89.56	**Bhili**	5.13	**Urdu**	2.17	Punjabi	1.90
Sikkim	Nepali	63.09	**Bhotia**	8.20	**Lepcha**	7.34	**Limbu**	6.64
Tamil Nadu	Tamil	86.71	Telugu	7.12	Kannada	2.16	**Urdu**	1.86
Tripura	Bengali	68.88	**Kokborok**	23.50	Hindi	1.66	**Mogh**	1.01
Uttar Pradesh	Hindi	90.11	**Urdu**	8.98				
West Bengal	Bengali	85.99	Hindi	6.08	**Santhali**	2.73	**Urdu**	2.14
Andaman Islands	Bengali	23.05	Tamil	19.07	Hindi	17.63	Telugu	11.75
Chandigarh	Hindi	61.07	Punjabi	34.72				
Dadra NH	**Bhili**	55.03	Gujarati	21.91	Konkani	12.32	Hindi	5.05
Daman and Diu	Gujarati	91.01	Hindi	3.59	Marathi	1.24		
Delhi	Hindi	81.64	Punjabi	7.94	**Urdu**	5.45	Bengali	1.29
Lakshadweep	Malayalam	34.47						
Pandichery	Tamil	89.19	Malayalam	4.75	Telugu	4.31		

fering degree of legal attributes. The non-scheduled languages comprise all those languages not included in the 8th Schedule that are generally qualified by leading linguistic and State institutions (Census authorities) as languages. In 2008 there were 92 such languages.[70] Most of the non-scheduled languages are neither used in education nor in public administration.

3. Notified tribal languages versus non-notified tribal languages

Fifty-eight out of about 90 tribal languages of India were notified as tribal languages by a Presidential Order published in the Gazette of India, Part II, section 1, dated 13 August 1960.[71] The criteria for such a distinction are not understood, but the distinction itself is not very relevant, as the majority of the notified tribal languages do not enjoy any special public attention, recognition or promotion.[72]

4. Languages with and without a literary tradition

The recognition of an Indian language under the 8th Schedule largely required evidence of a literary tradition, which most of the non-written languages could not demonstrate. Apparently, languages in India are not qualified based on their comprehensive potential, but largely on their cultural performance in history. The absence of a literary tradition is one of the reasons States advance for denying education in "non-literary languages".

5. Languages by the number of speakers

The merely quantitative criterion still plays a very important role. Languages with fewer than 10,000 speakers are not even registered in the general census and are included in an undifferentiated and unrecognized category of "other languages." In 2001, 566,000 people spoke such a language as their mother tongue. The numerical criterion again denies the potential for the development and possibility of preservation of these languages and, without officially stating as much, writes them off.

6. Old and new linguistic minorities

This criterion, quite important and often discussed in the European discourse regarding ethnic, linguistic and national minorities, plays no major role in India so far. But with increasing flows of migrants moving from one State to another within the Indian Union, triggered by inequalities of economic growth and diverging labour market opportunities, the issue of the cultural-linguistic impact of internal migration is rising. This type of linguistic reshaping of the population triggered several harsh political conflicts. This lead to the emergence of the concept, currently under debate, of

70 For the complete list see chapter 1.

71 For the complete list see section 3.3.

72 National Commissioner for Minority Languages, 42d report, p.14, at: http://nclm.nic.in

"autochthonous minorities and "newly immigrated minorities," which refer to the historical time period of an ethno-linguistic group's settlement in a given territory. The issue of how many generations must pass before an immigrated "new minority" can legitimately claim to be considered an autochthonous minority is debated on an academic and political level.

The cases of the languages of the States of Arunachal Pradesh and Nagaland as well as the UT of Dadra Nagar Haveli are quite particular, as their indigenous languages are not declared "State official languages", although these languages are in relative or absolute majority position in the respective state.

3.5 New minorities? Language rights and internal migration

Internal migration in India has had a growing impact on the linguistic composition of the resident population of some States. The internal migration flows from poorer to richer regions, as well as immigration from neighbouring countries has brought about not only political turmoil and social change, but also cultural alterations. New migrants do not arrive in communities, but individually. All over India they have some access to the cultural means of their linguistic group and – to some extent – can receive education in private institutions run in a minority language medium – a fundamental right enshrined in the Constitution. Many continue to preserve their "language loyalties", but must also learn the language of the new social environment, which in most cases is the regional official language of the State of residence.

India has no public register of the resident population and no obligation for individual migrants to register. As the census inquires about birthplace, but not residence, it is rather difficult to filter out reliable data about internal domestic migration flows. However, in every major Indian city there is a considerable number of migrant workers, coming from all parts of India. Nevertheless, there is still no mass migration from the rural areas to the cities, and the majority of India's population still lives in rural areas. Little research is available about the cultural and linguistic impact of migration.

Major political conflicts arose between members of indigenous peoples speaking autochthonous languages and Indian citizens newly emigrated from other States (Assam, West Bengal, Tripura, Nagaland), particularly the migration of workers from West Bengal and Bangladesh to India's Northeast and from Nepal to Northern West Bengal. In the 1980s, the political movements of the Nepali speaking inhabitants of the District of Darjeeling (West Bengal) demanded the recognition of Gorkhali/Nepali under the 8th Schedule Const. and the formation of a new federated State of India with the name of Gorkhaland. Finally, an Autonomous Gorkha Hill Council was conceded (capital Darjeeling) and in 1995 Nepali was inserted in the 8th Schedule of the Constitution.

In countries that accept full freedom of movement and internal multilingualism, internal migration raises some serious problems for autochthonous peoples. In particular, uncontrolled migration can put pressure on the protection of minority languages through political provisions. The principles of free migration and the protection of local languages are conflicting goals. Generally, in India linguistic minority rights are not linked to the "autochthony" of a language. Rather, the States are free to adopt new co-official languages at the local or district level, in accordance with the proportion of speakers of that language within the total population in that part of the State. The changing linguistic composition of the resident population gives rise to claims for new linguistic group rights or for the application of the linguistic minority rights enshrined in the Constitution – from education to public administration. In several cases the recognition of a language formerly spoken by newly immigrated people as an official language is demanded. These languages can then be declared co-official in the district or part of a State. They consequently assume greater importance, as the States are free to declare new co-official languages or "languages used in administration". Theoretically new States can also be carved out from existing ones and new autonomous districts can be formed.

The language of India's armed forces has also been of some importance to the process of linguistic integration. India has a professional army, which by number of employees, is the largest federal institution as well as a national symbol of the utmost importance. Hence the prevailing language regulations of the Indian army should not be disregarded. The Indian Army uses a type of command language based on simplified Hindi/Urdu mixed with some English, and written in Roman characters. This tradition is a legacy of the British colonial rulers, who chose the most widespread language used by their Indian soldiers, while the officers added English and the Roman script. After independence this tradition was maintained.

Bilingual information boards Karbi-English in Karbi Anglong (Assam)

Chapter 4

Constitutional safeguards for linguistic minorities

4.1 India's Constitutional provisions regarding linguistic matters

The Constitution of India, in its preamble, pledges to establish a sovereign democratic republic and a new social order wherein all citizens would have "justice, socio-economic and political liberty of thought, expression, belief, faith and worship; equality of status and of opportunity; and to promote among them fraternity sharing the dignity of the individual and the unity of the nation". To implement these overarching values Part III of the Constitution (articles 12-35) contains a Bill of Rights enshrining fundamental rights.[73] As the preamble states, these rights arise out of the "original

73 For the full text of the Constitutional provisions in linguistic matters see the annex, part 2.

freedoms" that are both the necessary attributes and modes of expression of human beings and primary conditions for community life within an established legal order. These are comparable to the "natural and inalienable" rights described in the American Declaration of Independence and the "Fundamental Rights" contained in the Lisbon Constitutional Treaty of the EU. These fundamental rights include the right to freedom of speech and expression (Article 19 (1a)) and the protection of interests of minorities (Articles 29 and 30). Article 29 (1) stipulates that "any section of the citizens residing in the territory of India or any part thereof having a distinct language, script, or culture of its own shall have the right to conserve the same." A salient point must be emphasized with regard to Article 29: the substantive content of minority rights is focused on language and culture, while religion is excluded as the article makes no mention of religion.[74]

The Constitution regulates languages in different articles, distinguishing among the use of official languages and the language of legislation and administration and the provisions for the protection of minority languages. Here the most prominent provisions will be briefly outlined:

a) Official use of language at the Union level

Article 343 Const. recognises Hindi in Devanagari script as the Official Language, and "for a period of fifteen years from the commencement of this Constitution, the English language shall continue to be used for all the official purposes of the Union for which it was being used immediately before such commencement". However "... Parliament may by law provide for the use, after the said period of fifteen years, of (a) the English language ... or such purposes may be specified in the law".

Article 351 Const. also considers it the duty of the Union to promote the spread of the Hindi language, to develop it, and to enrich it by assimilating the forms, style and expressions in Hindustani and other languages in the 8th Schedule, etc.

Article 120 Const. provides for the use of Hindi and English to transact business in Parliament. However, if a person cannot adequately express himself in Hindi or English, the Chairman of the Council of States or Speaker of the House of the People may permit him to address the House in his mother tongue.

The Indian Constitution is to be found at: http://www.oefre.unibe.ch/law/icl/in01000_.html

74 See Joshua Castellino and Elvira Domínguez Redondo, *Minority Rights in Asia, A Comparative Legal Analysis*, Oxford University Press 2006, p. 76-77

b) Official language at the State level

Article 345 Const. empowers the Legislature of the State to adopt "any one or more of the languages in use in the State or Hindi as the language or languages to be used for all or any of the official purposes" of the concerned State. Nevertheless, it provides for the continued use of English for the "purposes within the State for which it was being used before the commencement of the Constitution", until the Legislature of the State provides otherwise by law.

Article 210 Const. provides for the use of the Official Language, the language of the State, Hindi, or English. However, if a member cannot adequately express himself in any of these languages he may address the House in his mother tongue.

According to Article 348 (3) Const., in cases in which a State has prescribed any language other than English for use in Bills or Acts passed by the Legislature "a translation of the same in the English language published under the authority of the Governor of the State in the Official Gazette of that shall be deemed to be the authoritative text".

With regard to inter-State communication, Article 346 Const. stipulates that the language authorised for use in the Union for official purposes shall be the official language for communication between the State and another State and between a State and the Union. If two or more States agree that Hindi language shall be the official language for communication between such states, that language may be used for such communications.

c) Linguistic Minorities

The Constitution of India includes no definition of linguistic minorities. The Supreme Court defined minority languages as separate spoken languages, even if the language does not have a separate script or has no script at all. Thus, although the Constitution does not mention the "non scheduled languages" and thus does not explicitly recognise them as minority languages, it does contain a general form of safeguard of the smaller languages to protect them from discrimination. In Article 29 the Constitution provides explicit guarantees for the protection of minorities:

Article 29(1) *Any section of the citizens residing in the territory of India or any part thereof having a distinct language, script or culture of its own shall have the right to conserve the same.*

(2) No citizen shall be denied admission into any educational institution maintained by the State or receiving aid out of State funds on grounds only of religion, race, caste, language or any of them."

Having articulated the right of minority peoples to maintain their own language and culture, the Constitution also includes the right of religious and linguistic minorities to provide education in their own language. Article 30 Const. details this right, alongside protection against discrimination in receiving government grants for education:

Article 30 (1) *All minorities, whether based on religion or language, shall have the right to establish and administer educational institutions of their choice.*

(1a) In making any law providing for the compulsory acquisition of any property of any educational institution established and administered by a minority, referred to in clause I, the State shall ensure that the amount fixed by or determined under such law for the acquisition of such property is such as would not restrict or abrogate the right guaranteed under that clause.

The state shall not, in granting aid to educational institutions, discriminate against any educational institution on the ground that it is under the management of a minority, whether based on religion or language.

The second clause enables linguistic minorities to claim state aid for running their educational institutions. This final clause does not prevent the States from adopting provisions for educational standards for all schools, but it states a clear right concerning the medium of instruction.[75] These constitutional articles can be seen as minimum requirements for protecting minority languages in primary education, although no positive legitimation is provided, but only a prohibition of discrimination. However, "protection under Articles 29 and 30 Const. does not mean that the state must recognize that language. There need to be a common thread that binds these provisions, which is lacking."[76] There is no right mandating that linguistic minorities be provided with educational institutions using their mother tongue as medium language.

According to Article 41 Const. the State is responsible only for education until age 14, and granting school education at the high school level under this article is possible only "within the limits of its economic capacity and development". But the constitutional commitment to grant general

75 Minority institutions, however, cannot refuse admission to members of non-minority community. Admission refused solely on the grounds of religion, race, caste, language, or any of these is a clear breach of artcile 29 (2), though preference given to minority candidates is acceptable within certain limits. See Joshua Castellino and Elvira Domínguez Redondo, *Minority Rights in Asia, A Comparative Legal Analysis*, Oxford University Press 2006, p. 78

76 Nikhil Nayyar, *State and language – The 8th Schedule*, New Delhi, 1995, p. 173

tuition-free education, or to grant everyone free school attendance at the secondary level has not been achieved so far. Basically an individual young citizen's right to higher education is left to the economic capacity of his or her family.

Article 347 Const. provides that if there is a demand from a linguistic minority, the President can invite the respective State to recognize their language as a co-official language, but it remains open what "substantial" means and who precisely is entitled to make this kind of demand.

Art. 347 *Special provision relating to language spoken by a section of the population of a State.*

> *On a demand being made in that behalf the President may, if he is satisfied that a substantial proportion of the population of a State desires the use of any language spoken by them to be recognised by that State, direct that such language shall also be officially recognised throughout that State or any part thereof for such purpose as he may specify.*

This Article facilitates the use of minority languages for official purposes. It declares that a state should be recognized as monolingual only where one language group constitutes about 70% or more of the entire population and that, where there is substantial minority constituting 30% or more of the population, the State should be recognized as bilingual for administrative purposes. It further declares that the same principle should hold good at the district level. It is not uncommon in India to find areas in which minority languages reach a majority language position locally, such as in:[77]

- The Rajasthan-Bhili region, Kandesh and Northern Bihar, all having different varieties of Hindustani;
- The Himalayan region, with Pahari in Uttar Pradesh, Hindi in Himachal Pradesh, Nepali in Darjeeling, Sikkim and northern West Bengal
- South Assam, with Karbi and Dimasa in the Autonomous Districts and Bengali in Cachar
- The North of Jammu and Kashmir with Ladakhi and Balti
- Jammu with Dogri and Hindko.
- The Chota Nagpur Plateau extending into Jharkhand and Orissa

In addition to these general safeguards, the Indian Constitution includes a section titled "Special Directives" in which language and education issues beyond the simple protection for minorities are explicitly addressed. Article 350 Const. guarantees the right of all people to use a language they understand in "representations for redress of grievances". Two articles were

77 See Rakesh Bhatt/Ahmar Mahboob, *Minority languages and their status*, in: Kachru/Kachru/Sridhar, *Language in South Asia*, Cambridge University Press 2008, p.139

Members of the Kinnauri minority in Kinnaur (Himachal Pradesh)

added to the 7th Amendment to the Constitution, made in 1956, addressing linguistic minority issues:

350 A *Facilities for instruction in the mother tongue at the primary stage*

It shall be the endeavour of every State and of every local authority within the State to provide adequate facilities for instruction in the mother tongue at the primary stage of education to children belonging to linguistic minority groups; and the President may issue such directions to any State as he considers necessary or proper for securing the provision of such facilities.

350 B *Special Officer for linguistic minorities*

(1) There shall be a Special Officer for linguistic minorities to be appointed by the President.

*(2) It shall be the duty of the Special Officer to investigate all matters relating to the safeguards provided for linguistic minorities under this Constitution and report to the president upon those matters at such intervals as the President may direct, and the President shall cause all such reports to be laid before each House o*f Parliament, and sent to the Governments of the States concerned.

It should be noted that the NCLM has only an advisory capacity and no judicial or decisional authority. He cannot force any recommendation, rather he receives the complaints and transmits them to the Parliament and the President in his yearly report. The NCLM was created in 1957 "with a view to ensuring effective enforcement of the implementation of the various Constitutional provisions relating to minorities, whereas the Minority Commission was created in 1978 which has now been given a statutory status in 1992. The Commission addresses to the various problems faced by the minority communities and tries to seek redress of their grievances."[78]

The Indian States are entitled to regulate minority rights within the limits given by the Constitution, and can therefore impose restrictions on minority rights. Nevertheless, the core powers of administration must not be adversely affected. State regulations must respect the principles of utility, necessity and proportionality. Whenever the States do not obey these principles, the citizens concerned may seek legal remedy with the State High Courts and the Supreme Court to enforce their fundamental rights (including minority rights). [79]

4.2 The implementation of constitutional safeguards and the 8th Schedule

How have the constitutional safeguards been implemented so far? Most States have fulfilled their duty under Article 350 (A) Const. to provide primary education in the mother tongue of linguistic minorities very reluctantly, while others have not complied at all. This constitutional provision requires India's education authorities to assess the demands of linguistic minorities and to open separate sections of schools or distinct schools if certain minimum numbers of interested pupils are reached (the 10:40 ratio, 10 pupils per class, 40 pupils per school). No results concerning such assessments could be found in the scholarly literature, as there are no sta-

78 S.P. Massey, *Minority Rights: the Constitutional Vision*, p.56; for a presentation of the NCLM see the annex, part I, and his website at: http://nclm.nic.in

79 "Furthermore the Constitution empowers the High Courts in each State through Article 226 to issue writs, directions or orders for the enforcement of fundamental rights and for any other purpose. The power conferred on the High Courts by this Article is not in derogation to the power conferred on the Supreme Court under Article 32 of the Constitution. The duty of High Courts for providing protection to the fundamental rights of the people is in no way less than that of the Supreme Court. High Courts cannot decline jurisdiction simply because it is the duty of the Supreme Court to enforce fundamental rights." See S.P. Massey, *Minority Rights: the Constitutional Vision*, p.55

tistics regarding requests from parents and linguistic minority groups nor are there detailed statistics in primary schools on whether and how many minority children have an "absolute minority" language as the medium of instruction. But a renowned scholar of linguistics observes: "The formula 10:40 pupils per class and school of minority children for threshold to form separate classes or schools in mother tongue medium language did not work. The parents themselves mostly opposed it as they do not want to separate from the mainstream. The children should get a job later. This is the simple reason. Language skills including the mother tongue turns out to be a resource only if there is a link to jobs, to its utility on the labour market."[80]

At the secondary stage of education the mother tongue formula has been applied for use as the medium of instruction to an even lesser extent. This stage provides more advanced education to enable students to follow a vocation after leaving school and also prepares them for higher education in universities. According to the TLF, the languages used at this stage should be the modern Indian languages mentioned in the 8th Schedule of the Constitution as well as English. "Thus one needs not be surprised", holds S. P. Massey, "when the 5th All India Educational Survey identifies that 'only the major 16 languages recognized by the Constitution are used as media of instruction in a large number of States and Union Territories and most of the remaining languages display a localized pattern confined to one or the other State or Union Territory. Thus other Indian languages used in primary or upper primary stage like Maithili, Kokborok, Dogri, Ao, Angami, Sema do not continue as medium at the secondary stage. Also Santali, Khezha, Tripuri, Bodo, Garo, Mizo, that were used as medium of instruction at the secondary school stage during the 3d All India Educational Survey, also dropped out as media of instruction at this stage, leading to the conclusion that, as we go up on the educational ladder, the number of languages used as media of instruction goes declining."[81]

"In the use of languages in administration too", states B. Mallikarjun,[82] "the 8th Schedule has played the role of the controller of recognition of languages. There are many districts where a majority of the population of the district in daily life uses a language other than the official language of the State, and since in such areas 'the language of the minority group should be recognized as an official language in that district in addition to the State

80 From an interview with Omkar N. Koul, Shillong, 20 March 2009

81 S.P. Massey, *Minority Rights: the Constitutional Vision,* p. 72

82 See B. Mallikarjun "*The 8th Schedule Languages – A Critical Appraisal*", in: *Language and the State – The 8th Schedule*, New Delhi 1995, p. 72

official language' the minority is entitled to such a recognition. Recognition for this purpose may, however, be given ordinarily only to major languages of India specified in the 8th Schedule of the Constitution. Though this goes contrary to the Constitutional provisions, this almost bars any other language from being recognized as an official language." Thus, when considering the degree of implementation of Constitutional safeguards concerning minority languages in the public administration two issues have to be distinguished:

1. First, the issue of whether minority languages have been accorded official or co-official status on the sub-State-level (district, tehsil, municipality etc.), where persons/speakers of such languages constitute 60% or more of the population;
2. Second, whether a range of cases is established in which the administration has to interact with the citizen concerned in the minority language (e.g. the translation and publication of important rules, regulations, notices, etc. into all languages, which are spoken by at least 15% of the total population at district or sub-district level; the receipt of and reply to representations in minority languages)

Again, no statistics and figures could be found in the scholarly literature and Government institutional reports concerning the implementation of these provisions in districts or sub-districts.

The implementation of Article 347, which provides that if there is a demand by a linguistic minority the President can invite the respective State to recognize their language as a co-official language, has been very limited. Just five States and one Union Territory have established one or some co-official language in some regions: Assam in Cachar (Bengali) and Bodoland (Bodo), Karnataka in some regions (Malayalam, Tamil and Telugu), West Bengal in three subdivisions of Darjeeling (Nepali) and Orissa in Ganjam/Koraput (Telugu). Tripura has recognized Kokborok as a second official language State-wide, and the UT Pondicherry has named all neighbouring languages as co-official.

At this point, the issue of official recognition itself appears to be the key for further linguistic minority demands to enjoy the rights safeguarded by the Constitution. As explained in Chapter 1, the Constitution neither comprises a definition of such minorities, nor provides a specific procedure for the recognition and listing of recognized minorities. The 8th Schedule is ambivalent in this regard and does not prevent minority languages from being recognized at State level. The Indian Parliament's Minorities Commission Reports, while considering the requests of different languages for inclusion in the 8th Schedule, have stated that:

a) Art. 344 and 351 do not confer any special status or privilege to speakers of these languages
b) It is not the case that the 15 languages (now 22) mentioned in the 8th Schedule of the Constitution are the only recognized languages
c) A language is conferred no benefit or harm by virtue of its inclusion in or exclusion from the 8th Schedule. The Government is endeavouring to encourage the development of the cultural and literary heritage of all languages irrespective of their inclusion in the 8th Schedule
d) No mention has been made of the 8th Schedule in the provisions of the Constitution relating to the safeguards for linguistic minorities
e) The non-inclusion of a language in the 8th Schedule does not preclude the speakers of such languages from the benefits provided for linguistic minorities
f) No additional benefits or safeguards are available to linguistic minorities whose languages are not scheduled
g) The inclusion of further languages in the 8th Schedule leads to the unending demand for addition of more and more languages, and
h) The number of languages in the country is too large for inclusion in the 8th Schedule

Nevertheless there are some privileges reserved for the scheduled languages, which lead various language movements to press for the recognition of their language. "A language gets not only a different status after its inclusion in the 8th Schedule, but also certain specific privileges. It becomes a modern Indian language. These languages get opportunities which other languages are deprived of. Automatically they become eligible along with English to get the benefit of assistance to authors, publishers producing books to serve as textbooks, discipline-oriented supplementary reading materials and reference books of an acceptable standard."[83]

Languages included in the 8th Schedule are also important because they are only languages admitted for the "Union Public Service Commission Civil Services Examination". Nevertheless, the main examination is only conducted in English and Hindi. As Hindi is the official language of the Union, and English is the associate official language, most of all-India level employment opportunities require a minimum competence in Hindi and English at the entry point. However, the knowledge of the State Official Language should not be a prerequisite for recruitment to the State services. A test of

83 See B. Mallikarjun, *The 8th Schedule Languages – A Critical Appraisal*, in *Language and The State: Perspectives On The Eighth Schedule*, Creative Books, New Delhi 1995, p. 75

proficiency in the State Official Language can also be held after selection and before the end of the period of probation. Moreover, a candidate should have the option of using English or Hindi as medium of examination for State Services, as an alternative to the official language of the State.[84]

Other privileges reserved for the languages of the 8th Schedule are literary awards restricted to these languages only and some financial aid and support projects from the Union Ministry. The Department of Education (Ministry of Human Resource Development) offers programmes for the promotion and development of languages and defines Indian languages as "languages as specified in the 8th Schedule of the Constitution, including their recognized dialects and other recognized tribal languages." But the latter languages rarely benefit from such promotion, and in such cases it is only a "token show of 'non-discrimination' among Indian languages".[85] Absolute minority languages do not receive sustainable assistance for language status and acquisition planning, concludes Mallikarjun in his critical appraisal of the 8th Schedule: "The main language development activities for expanding their functions are planned in scheduled languages with States only, whereas language development for non-scheduled languages is normally for their preservation. In the natural process, the majority of them may not be developing or expanding the range of their registers. In Karnataka, the majority of Tulu and Kodagu speakers become bilinguals in Kannada. So the regional language functions as their language for absorption and expression of modern knowledge. These languages do not find any need to expand their vocabulary and registers for expression and dissemination of contemporary knowledge."[86]

84 *ibidem*, p. 75
85 *ibidem*, p. 70
86 *ibidem*, p. 79

Scheduled languages: 22

Dialects of scheduled languages: 67

Non scheduled languages (mostly „tribal languages“): 92

Dialects of non scheduled languages (mostly variants of tribal languages): 149

The hierarchy of India's languages

Examining the relative advantage and disadvantage in position of the Indian languages, four groups emerge in order of decreasing advantage:

1. Hindi
2. Other scheduled languages with a State
3. Scheduled languages without a State
4. All other non-scheduled languages.

Therefore addressing the concept of language recognition seems to be unavoidable in order to avoid advantages to some and disadvantages to others, while formulating language policy.

4.3 Are the constitutional safeguards sufficient?

First, it must be acknowledged that the Constitution makers did not overlook the issue of minority languages, perhaps to emphasise the unity of the country. Rather they enshrined a minimum standard of protection in various articles. The Indian Constitution, although recognizing individual and collective rights of minorities, does not define a minority or provide criteria to do it, nor does it provide a list of recognized minorities. Thus, a linguistic minority simply is considered to be each group that has a distinct language in a numerically inferior position at the State level. The Constitution offers two major tools for protecting the rights of minorities, be they of religious or ethno-linguistic nature. These are: on the one hand, the strategy of protection from state discrimination, mostly focused on religious groups and communities; on the other hand the Constitution makers explicitly recognised group (collective) rights of linguistic minorities in order to maintain their separate identity, though restricted to the cultural area. The emphasis of the Constitution's approach to linguistic minorities clearly lies in non-discrimination, not on affirmative action.

While the Constitution does not explicitly provide for a recognition and protection of all linguistic minorities, it prohibits discrimination on linguistic grounds and recognizes the fundamental right of minorities to maintain their language. It allows for some language status planning at the State and local level and requires active public commitment of the States, at least in the domain of education. The right to education in the mother tongue, be it a majority or minority language, is limited to the level of primary education, whereas both religious and linguistic minorities are free to run private schools that cover the high school level as well. As there is no explicit constitutional right to education in the mother tongue in tuition free public schools up to level XII, achieving the general provisions though concrete State education policies becomes even more important. But how is that ensured at present? It is also relevant that the States, in granting aid to educational institutions, shall not discriminate against such schools on the ground that it is under the management of a minority, whether based on religion or language (Art.30).[87]

Education is generally a State subject, but minority rights in education are a 'concurrent subject', which gives the Union a right to interfere in the States' education policies. How can States that do not comply with their duties under the Constitutional safeguards for linguistic minorities be obliged to do so? Although the Centre has the power of co-ordination and the duty to safeguard the fundamental rights of linguistic minorities it does not intervene in State education policy regarding the right to education in one's mother tongue. There is no particular legal machinery offering the possibility for individuals or groups to take legal action to enforce the rights enshrined in Article 29 and 30. Ultimately, it is debatable whether these rights also contain a recognition of minorities' right to cultural and educational autonomy.[88] But, alas, the Centre does not recognize this right.

87 In 1978 by the 44th Amendment Act an amendment was made in Art. 30 of the Constitution and Clause IA was added which empowered the State to acquire the property of a minority educational institution. However, it provided that the amount of compensation given must be such as would not abrogate or restrict the right guaranteed under Article 30 Const.

88 The provisions for autonomy are contained in article 244 of the Indian Constitution with article 399 and 400 dealing with the relationship of the central administration in these issues, including a description of the control of the Union over the administration of Scheduled Areas (Article 339) and the appointment of a commission to investigate the conditions of backward classes (Art. 340).

A Bodo woman in Kokrajhar (Bodoland, Assam)

As far as higher education in minority languages is concerned, the Constitution implicitly delegates the responsibility to private or community initiatives, instead of establishing a State duty to provide education services with its resources. Instead, access to public aid is granted by the Constitution, though the Constitution imposes no conditions and constraints with regard to the very nature of instruction in such minority schools. Instead, most emphasis is placed on the prohibition of any discrimination of any student in admission to such schools on the ground of language, religion, caste etc.[89] This provision is particularly contradictory in the Indian reality, as it is

89 See Iqbal Ansari, *Minorities and the Politics of Constitution Making in India*, in D. L. Sheth/Gurpreet Mahajao (eds.), *Minority Identities and the Nation State*, Oxford University Press, 1999, p. 125; "With regard to the prescription of the compulsory learning of the majority language in schools run by linguistic minorities without any choice to learn their language, the Supreme Court has held that it violates the fundamental right for equality before the law. (Art. 14 Constitution). Thus minority schools have to meet both requirements: the preservation of the culture, language and religion as demanded by the families of minority students, and avoiding discrimination in the access to other interested students, not belonging to this group. The minority schools maintain a basic freedom of decision on the purposes of the special institutions. While the State can not prescribe the medium of instruction, but the schools has to meet educational standards of "modern higher education".

well known that linguistic minority communities and families face structural economic hardships (e.g. tribal communities). They are exposed to strong pressure, exerted by the economy and labour market, not to devote major time and effort on education in minority languages, but to focus as much as possible on the dominant languages in order to safeguard the opportunities of their children.

Art 29 (2) seems to contradict the very sense of Article 29 (1) (the right to preserve one's language), and of Article 30 (the right to establish and run schools). In fact, under this Article the Constitution does not stipulate that the educational institutions, maintained or supported by the State, should teach or employ the minority language if a school has students speaking that language. Again this provision dodges the overall objective of preserving a minority language and culture. Wealthier sections of the linguistic minority groups rather aim to have private English medium language schools, which are usually more costly and expensive. Poorer sections of the linguistic minorities, for whom no public school in minority language can be established as there is no such State duty enshrined in the Constitution, are the victims of the absence of a public (State) duty to provide higher education in minority language.

In the scholarly literature no case has been reported in which linguistic minorities claimed to establish and run "a college of their choice" in a language not recognized within the 8th Schedule of the Constitution.[90] Obviously, such initiatives would not have obtained any recognition by the authorities, as no university on the national level would have offered the examinations. In addition, such schools would have to meet the requirement of obtaining appropriate textbooks and didactic materials. If such schools would choose a scheduled language, official recognition by the competent State Ministry would be possible, as this college could turn to an University in the State in which the chosen medium language is the official State's language in order to grant the final examinations. These legal constraints do not enable the establishment of schools with (absolute) minority languages as a medium. While Article 30 assigns the initiative in educational matters to the minority communities, Article 350 (A) requires an initiative of the State to safeguard

---

See Iqbal, p. 125

90 See Horst Friedrich Rolly, *Bildungsrecht und Bildungspraxis religiöser und linguistischer Minderheiten in Indien*, P. Lang Verlag, Frankfurt 2002, p. 222. In India the colleges of the secondary level are obliged to meet the requirement of the 3-languages-formula, if they benefit of the grant-in-aid of the respective State. Generally no school can renounce on such financial aid. A language other than the regional official language can be chosen as medium language, but the requirements of the examinations have to be met, which are conducted in a centralized form for all India.

the interests of linguistic minorities: "It shall be the endeavour of every State and every local authority within the State to provide adequate facilities for instruction in the mother tongue at the primary stage of education to children belonging to linguistic minority groups; and the President may issue such directions to any State as he considers necessary for securing the provision of such facilities."[91] But again, no precise conditions are specified under which minority members are entitled to demand a primary school run in their mother tongue.

Apart from education, the Constitution contains safeguards for minorities in the field of public administration, including the recruitment of public employees. Article 347 of the Constitution, referring to minority languages in administration, endows the President with the power to direct in appropriate cases that the minority language should be officially recognised for use in administration throughout a state or any part thereof for such purpose as he may specify:

- Where at least 15% of the population on municipal level belongs to a linguistic minority, most important public documents have to be issued in the minority language;
- If at least 60% of the population of a district speak a minority language different from the regional official language, this language would be declared "additional official language".

The implementation of the latter provisions is likely to be widely avoided. India comprises 330 districts (comparable with provinces or regions in Europe), but very few have adopted such a regulation, although often many more than 60% of the inhabitants speak a language different from the State's official language. Additionally the results regarding the provisions on bilingualism in official documents, as reported by the NCLM, are not very satisfactory. Almost no arrangements have been documented for the translation of languages of "non scheduled minority language groups", due to the lack of staff, facilities and financial means.[92] Finally, the minimum percentages set for minority presence to attribute linguistic rights in the public sphere are questionable.

Finally, Article 350 B of the Constitution establishes a National Commissioner for Linguistic Minorities. This Commissioner, who represents an organ of the Union, has the task of overseeing the fulfilment of linguistic minorities' rights, whereas no State institution performs this role. In his yearly reports

---

91 H.R. Dua, *Language Planning and Linguistic Minorities*, p. 138, quoted by C. Groff, at http://www.sil.org/asia/ldc/parallel_papers/cynthia_groff.pdf

92 See NCLM 39th, 41st and 42d report, at: http://nclm.nic.in

to the President and the Parliament, the NCLM regularly complains not only of many cases of discrimination, of legal and political shortcomings and violations of State or Federal law in linguistic matters, but also of his own rather powerless function. Indeed, the NCLM only can receive complaints and collect information, but he has no powers to directly intervene in political affairs and procedures or to act as a judicial institution.[93] According to his own words[94], the NCLM "despite his status as a constitutional authority, enjoys no authority and state governments do not even supply the required information to him. The reports of the NCLM, though tabled in the Parliament, are not discussed and do not receive attention as they hardly contain up-to-date information. The Conference proposes that the post should be abolished and replaced by a "National Commission for Linguistic Minorities" with quasi-judicial authority." In his 42d report, the NCLM also invited the Government, to devolve powers of civil courts on the Commissioner in addition to proposing a standing Commission for resolving the problems faced by linguistic minorities.

93 See the recent reports on the website of the NCLM at: http://nclm.nic.in

94 *ibidem*, 42d report, 2004, p.5

Chapter 5

The States' language policies and the protection of linguistic minorities

5.1 A brief genesis of the States' language policies

The linguistic reorganisation of States succeeded in bringing together the majority of the speakers of the major (and scheduled) languages in one or more States that may legitimately be called "home states" of those languages. According to Table 10, most of the languages upon which the reorganisation of the States was drawn, comprise a majority of the population ranging between 70 and 95%. With the reorganisation along linguistic lines these languages were also established as "official languages" and the "language of the law," and thus acquired a new political stance and dominance in many social or public domains. After this re-organisation the official language policy of the States aimed to enlarge the respective linguistic domains and to achieve a major linguistic homogenisation.

Nevertheless, the Indian States were not and are not "nation states", comparable with the European states. For many centuries they were home to a plurality of languages, religions and cultures, and thus it was normal to have a considerable number of people speaking languages other than the dominant language of the State. For this reason establishing a majority language as the only official and thus dominant language in every public domain was more difficult a challenge as it may have appeared, as it triggered resistance from both the "relative minorities" who speak a language that is official in another state; and more immediately from the "absolute minorities" who do not have any other "state of reference" in any part of the Indian territory to rely on for support.

The historical experience in the hundreds of princely states before independence had been the selection of one language only as the official language, which was not necessarily the majority language, but the language of the respective ruling elites. Later the language of the colonial regime brought about cultural domination and social discrimination. There was a time when English in India was used even at the Panchayat level (local administration). This not only created a conflict between the customary laws and the body of law sought to be imposed from outside, but also created many distortions. It denied the people advice and consent in the process of governance and thus stopped the implementation of a participatory democracy.

Table 11 - Numerically significant minority languages in each State (in 1991)

State/Territory	Numbers of speakers	%	State/Territory	Number of speakers	%
Andhra Pradesh			*M. Pradesh*		
Telugu	56,375,755	84.8	Hindi	56,619,090	85.6
Urdu	5,560,154	8.4	Bhili/Bilodi	2,215,399	3.3
Hindi	1,841,290	2.8	Gondi	1,481,265	2.3
Arunachal			*Maharashtra*		
Nissi/Dafla	172,149	19.9	Marathi	57,894,839	73.3
Nepali	81,176	9.4	Hindi	6,168,941	7.8
Bengali	70,771	8.2	Urdu	5,734,468	7.3
Assam			*Manipur*		
Assamese	12,958,088	57.8	Manipuri	1,110,130	60.0
Bengali	2,523,040	11.3	Thado	103,667	5.6
Bodo/Boro	1,184,569	5.3	Thangkul	100,088	5.4
Bihar			*Meghalaya*		
Hindi	69,845,949	80.9	Khasi	879,172	49.5
Urdu	8,542,463	9.9	Garo	547,690	30.9
Santhali	2,546,655	2.9	Bengali	144,562	8.1
Goa			*Mizoram*		
Konkani	602,626	51.5	Lushai	518,099	75.1
Marathi	390,270	33.4	Bengali	59,092	8.6
Kannada	54,323	4.6	Lakher	22,938	3.3
Gujarat			*Nagaland*		
Gujarati	37,792,000	91.5	Ao	169,837	14.0
Hindi	1,215,825	2.9	Sema	152,123	12.6
Sindhi	704,088	1.7	Konyak	137,539	11.4
Haryana			*Orissa*		
Hindi	14,928,409	91.0	Oriya	26,199,346	82.8
Punjabi	1,170,255	7.1	Hindi	759,016	2.4
Urdu	261,880	1.6	Telugu	502,102	1.6
Him. Pradesh			*Punjab*		
Hindi	4,595,615	88.9	Punjabi	18,704,461	92.2
Punjabi	324,479	6.3	Hindi	1,478,993	7.3
Kinnauri	61,794	1.2	Urdu	13,461	0.1
Karnataka			*Rajasthan*		
Kannada	29,785,004	66.2	Hindi	39,410,968	89.6
Urdu	4,480,038	10.0	Bhili/Bhilodi	2,215,399	5.0
Telugu	3,325,062	8.2	Urdu	953,497	2.2
Kerala			*Sikkim*		
Malayalam	28,096,376	96.6	Nepali	256,418	63.1
Tamil	616,010	2.1	Bhotia	32,593	8.0
Kannada	75,571	1.2	Lepcha	29,854	7.3
Tamil Nadu			*Tripura*		
Tamil	48,434,744	86.7	Bengali	1,899,162	68.9
Telugu	3,975,561	7.1	Tripuri/ Kokborok	647,847	23.5
Kannada	1,208,296	2.2	Hindi	45,803	1.7
West Bengal			*UttarPradesh*		
Bengali	58,541,519	86.0	Hindi	125,348,491	88.0
Hindi	4,479,170	6.6	Urdu	12,492,297	9.0
Urdu	1,455,649	2.1	Punjabi	661,215	0.5

Source: Census of India 1991 (figures for Jammu&Kashmir not available; in 2000 three new States were established: Jharkhand, Uttarakhand and Chhattisgarh, but no figures available yet)

After independence and the re-organization of the States along linguistic lines, the regional elites were again allowed to impose the respective majority language as the only official language, only restricted by Article 347 Constitution, which allowed the recognition of minority languages as associate official languages on the State or district level. Accordingly, if a "substantial proportion" of the population of a State spoke a language different from the official one, their speakers could claim to be recognized as second official language. On the district level, if the speakers of a minority language reach at least 60% of the total population, they can claim some linguistic rights in the public administration. But the result of this general principle for the States' language policies has been rather modest, as shown by the officially recognized minority languages in 2001:

Table 12 - Official/officially recognized languages (2001)

No.1	State	Official Language	Other officially recognized languages (regional or State level)
1.	Andhra Pradesh	Telugu	Urdu, Oriya
2.	Arunachal Pradesh	English	-
3.	Assam	Assamese	Bengali, Bodo
4.	Bihar	Hindi	Urdu
5.	Chhattisgarh	Hindi	-
6.	Goa	Konkani	Marathi, Kannada
7.	Gujarat	Gujarati, Hindi	-
8.	Haryana	Hindi	Punjabi
9.	Himachal Pradesh	Hindi	Punjabi
10.	Jammu&Kashmir	Urdu	-
11.	Jharkhand	Hindi	-
12.	Karnataka	Kannada	Malayalam, Tamil, Urdu, Telugu
13.	Kerala	Malayalam	English, Tamil, Kannada
14.	Madhya Pradesh	Hindi	-
15.	Maharashtra	Marathi	-
16.	Manipur	Meitei/Manipuri	-
17.	Meghalaya	English	Khasi, Garo
18.	Mizoram	English	Mizo
19.	Nagaland	English	-
20.	Orissa	Oriya	-
21.	Punjab	Punjabi	-
22.	Rajasthan	Hindi	-
23.	Sikkim	English	Nepali, Lepcha, Bhotia
24.	Tamil Nadu	Tamil	-
25.	Tripura	English	Bengali, Kokborok
26.	Uttarakhand	Hindi, English	Urdu
27.	Uttar Pradesh	Hindi	Urdu
28.	West Bengal	Bengali	Nepali

A Rajbongshi in Cooch Bihar (Northern West Bengal)

Only the emergence of identity assertion movements led to the recognition of such sub-regional languages. Thus Andhra Pradesh has recognised Urdu and Oriya among others as sub-regional languages, West Bengal has recognised Nepali, Karnataka recognized Tamil and Telugu, Kerala recognized Tamil and Kannada, Goa Marathi and Kannada as co-official languages etc.. The Indian Constitution does not specify the official languages to be used by the States for their official functions and leaves each State free to adopt any language used in its territory, Hindi or English its own official language. This language need not be one of those listed in the 8th Schedule and several States have adopted official languages that are not listed, as Kokborok in Tripura, Mizo in Mizoram, Khasi, Garo and Jaintia in Meghalaya and French in Pondicherry (a Union Territory).

When the States' language policies are discussed, terms like official language, language used in administration, lingua franca, common language, regional languages and provincial languages are frequently used. In India, some discussions in academic circles and most discussions in the media treat official language, lingua franca, national language and common language as synonyms. But each one performs different functions in society. The 'Official Language' and the 'Language used in Administration' in the Indian context have to be well distinguished. An example can be cited to illustrate this point. Though the Official Language Act of Andhra Pradesh of

1966 recognizes Telugu as the Official Language for use in its territory, it also permits the use of English, Urdu, Kannada, Tamil and Oriya in certain specified situations and regions for administrative activities. Hence these latter are the "Languages used in administration in Andhra Pradesh", though only Telugu is the Official Language of the State. Precisely speaking,

- Official Language is "a language used for legislative, executive and judicial purposes";
- Lingua Franca is "a language which is used habitually by people whose mother tongues are different in order to facilitate communication between them",
- Regional Language is "a language which is used as a medium of communication between people living within a certain area who have different mother tongues",
- Vernacular Language is "a language which is the mother tongue of a group which is socially or politically dominated by another group speaking a different languages",
- and National Language is "the language of a political, social and cultural entity."[95]

At the central level, considerable progress has been made to implement the Constitutional directive to make Hindi the national official language. However, the progress has been slow because of pressure from the English lobby and the regional language lobbies. Hindi has not been able to forge a partnership with the regional languages and provide them with leadership to replace English as official language and language of law at different levels. It has not worked out procedures for balanced Centre-State communication, nor has it stored out its internal problems in developing a standard taking into account different regional Hindis. In summary, Article 351 of the Constitution has been observed only partially.[96] The main instruments setting out the language policy on the State level were the States' Official Language Acts.[97]

5.2 The Union and States' Official Languages Acts

The Indian Constitution does not specify the official languages to be used by the States for official functions, and leaves each state legislature free to

95 E. Annamalai, *Language Use in Administration and National Integration*, at: http://www.languageinindia.com/index.html, p. 30. Therefore a language of a minority in one country is not be considered a vernacular language if it is an official language in another State or country.
96 *Ibidem*, p. 31
97 For this issue see B.D. Jayaram and K.S. Rajyashree, *State Official Language Policy Implementation*, CIIL, Mysore June 2000

adopt Hindi or any language used in its territory as its official language or languages. The language need not be one of those listed in the 8th Schedule, and several states have adopted official or co-official languages which are not listed in the 8th Schedule, such as Kokborok in Tripura, Mizo in Mizoram, Khasi, Garo and Jaintia in Meghalaya, and French in Pondicherry. With regard to the official languages of the States, Chapter II of the Constitution of India affirms:

Article 345. Subject to the provisions of articles 346 and 347, the Legislature of a State may by law adopt any one or more of the languages in use in the State or Hindi as the language or languages to be used for all or any of the official purposes of that State:
Provided that, until the Legislature of the State otherwise provides by law, the English language shall continue to be used for those official purposes within the State for which it was being used immediately before the commencement of this Constitution.

Article 346. The language for the time being authorised for use in the Union for official purposes shall be the official language for communication between one State and between a State and the Union. Provided that if two or more States agree that the Hindi language should be the official language for communication between such States, that language may be used for such communication.

Article 347. On a demand being made in that behalf the President may, if he is satisfied that a substantial proportion of the population of a State desire the use of any language spoken by them to be recognised by that State, direct that such language shall also be officially recognised throughout that State or any part thereof for such purpose he may specify.

The constitutional provisions regarding the use of official languages in legislation at the State level largely mirror those relating to the official language at the central level, with minor variations. State legislatures may conduct their business in their official language, Hindi or (for a transitional period, which the legislature can extend if it so chooses) English, and members who cannot use any of these have the same rights to use their mother tongue, with the Speaker's permission. The authoritative text of all laws must be in English, unless the Parliament passes a law permitting a state to use another language. If the original text of a law is in a different language, an authoritative English translation of all laws must be prepared. The state has the right to regulate the use of its official language in public administration, and in general, neither the Constitution nor any central enactment imposes any restriction on this right. However, every person submitting a petition for the redress of a grievance to an officer or authority of the Federal government has a constitutional right to submit it in any language used in that state, regardless of its official status.

Proceeding from this fundamental legal setting, the policy followed by the Union Government and some of the States relating to the use of a language or languages in their administration is reflected in the Official Languages Acts, which express the different approaches followed by the Union and the States to regulate the language rights on the respective government levels.[98]

Union

The Official Languages Act, 1963, enacted to 'provide for the languages which may be used for the official purposes of the Union, for transacting the business in Parliament, for Central and State Acts and...'; makes provision for: the continuing use of English in addition to Hindi for all official purposes of the Union for which it was being used immediately before the Act was passed, and for the transaction of business in Parliament; the use of English for communication between the Union and a State which has not adopted Hindi as its official language; and for communication in Hindi to be accompanied by its English translation if the receiving State of the concerned communication has not adopted Hindi as the official language. Even if a State has not adopted Hindi as the official language, it can communicate with the Union or a State that has adopted Hindi as its official language in Hindi. Communications are to be in English or Hindi for communication between one Ministry and another, one Ministry and Company etc., of the Central Government, and between any Corporation or Company etc., of the Central Government. The Hindi communications shall be accompanied by English translation. Both Hindi and English shall be used in resolutions, general orders, etc., in administrative and other reports and official reports laid in the Houses of the Parliament; contracts, agreements executed by the Central Government.

The Resolution adopted by both the Houses of the Parliament on January 18th, 1968 regarding the use of language in administration said that "... it is the duty of the Union to promote the spread of the Hindi language and to develop it so that it may serve as a medium of expression for all the elements of the composite culture... A more intensive and comprehensive programme shall be prepared and implemented by the Government of India

98 See E. Annamalai, *Language Use in Administration and National Integration*, at: http://www.languageinindia.com/index.html, p. 32

Subodh Hansda, a leader of ASECA-organisation for the education of Santals, wife, son

for accelerating the spread and development of Hindi, and its progressive use for the various official purposes of the Union..." Concerning languages of 8th Schedule, "it is necessary in the interest of the educational and cultural advancement of the country that concerted measures should be taken for the full development of the languages". To protect the interests of the people in matters relating to the public services of the Union, compulsory knowledge of either Hindi or English shall be required at the stage of selection of candidates for recruitment to the Union Service or posts, and all the languages included in the 8th Schedule of the Constitution and English shall be permitted as alternative media for the All India and higher Central Service examinations after ascertaining the views of the Union Public Service Commission on the future scheme of the examinations, the procedural aspects and the timings.[99]

All single States of India have adopted a provision to regulate the official State language, which also sometimes contains special provisions for linguistic minorities.[100]

99 See E. Annamalai, *Language Use in Administration and National Integration*, at: http://www.languageinindia.com/index.html, p. 34

100 *ibidem*, p. 35

Andhra Pradesh[101]

The 1964 Legislative Assembly Bill of Andhra Pradesh[102] recognized Telugu as the Official Language of Andhra Pradesh. Accordingly Telugu may be used by Notification for:

(i) Bills introduced, amendments, Acts passed by the Legislature, or in ordinances promulgated by the Governor;

(ii) Orders, Rules, Regulations and By-laws issued by the State Government under any law of the Parliament or Legislature;

(iii) Appeals, affidavits, judgements or documents, awards, etc., in the courts or tribunals;

(iv) The medium of instruction in schools, colleges and other educational institutions.

And "until the State Government otherwise directs by notification under section 3 first the English language shall continue to be used for these official purposes within the State for which it was being used immediately before the commencement of this Act; and second the English language may continue to be used for the transaction of the business in the Legislature of the State".

The Act also has made special provision for the use of Urdu or any other language or languages in addition to Telugu in certain areas of the State for specific purposes. The notification issued on May 25th, 1967 in pursuance of the above-cited act makes provision for use of Oriya, Tamil, Kannada, Marathi and Urdu languages in specific regions for specific purposes in addition to Telugu. Telugu was introduced in certain Departments at Taluk level in 1966, with the aim of gradual implementation. It was then extended to all offices of the Government at District level in 1976. Telugu was also introduced for certain purposes at Secretariat level in the three sections of the Official Languages wing of the General Administration Departments. The State has also recognised Urdu as the second official language in the Telengana region.

Assam

According to the Assam Official Language Act of 1960, the Official Languages are: Assamese in the Brahmaputra Valley Districts, Bengali in the Cachar District, and English in the Autonomous Districts of Assam State. In the newly established "Bodo Autonomous Hill Council," Bodo has been declared the official language, along with Assamese. In 2003, Bodo was also

---

101 B.D. Jayaram and K.S. Rajyashree, *State Official Language Policy Implementation*, CIIL, Mysore June 2000, p.151

102 Published in Gazette Extra-ordinary on December 7th, 1969

included among the scheduled languages of the Constitution.[103]

Bihar

In Bihar, Hindi is recognized as the Official Language. The Bihar Official Language (Amendment) Act, 1980, declared Urdu to be a second Official Language for specified areas and purposes. Hence, in addition to Hindi, Urdu is recognized as second official language in 15 districts for the following purposes:

i) Receipt of applications and memoranda in Urdu and replies thereto in the same language;
ii) Acceptance by the Registration Officer of registration of documents written in Urdu;
iii) Publication of important government rules and notifications in Urdu;
iv) Publication of important government orders and circulars of public importance in Urdu;
v) Publication of important government advertisements in Urdu;
vi) Translation of Zilla Gazette in Urdu and its publication; and
vii) Display of important signboards in Urdu.

Gujarat

The Gujarat Official Language Act came into existence in 1960, and declared Gujarati and Hindi in Devanagari script to be the official languages of the State. Then a phased program was formulated beginning in 1965 to achieve progressive widespread use of official languages in every field and at every level of the administration. A series of necessary steps were taken for its implementation , such as establishing various institutions as well as issuing several notifications and directives.[104]

Jammu and Kashmir

The Jammu and Kashmir State is very flexible in its official language policy. Urdu is the official state language and is used only in the lower levels of administration along with English. English is widely used in the mid and higher levels of administration. Neither Kashmiri nor Dogri, the languages spoken dominantly in the Kashmir valley and Jammu area respectively, have a place in the official language policy and are not used in administration. They have very limited roles in education and mass media too.

103 B.D. Jayaram and K.S. Rajyashree, *State Official Language Policy Implementation*, CIIL, Mysore June 2000, p.161

104 Ibidem, p. 168

Karnataka

The 1963 Mysore Official Language Act recognizes Kannada as the Official Language of the State. It makes provision for continued use of English for official purposes and for the transaction of business in the Legislature. As per the Notification No.GAD 55 Pol 71, dated 26th June 1972
"if the population of linguistic minority in any Taluk is not less than 15 percent:
(i) Petitions shall continue to be accepted in the minority language concerned and replies given in that language as far as possible;
(ii) Hand-outs and publicity materials shall continue to be given in such a minority language;
(iii) Government Notices shall continue to be published in such a minority language".[105]
According to the official language policy of Karnataka, all the work in the government offices is done in Kannada. English is used in correspondence with other states or central government organisations located outside the state of Karnataka. Proficiency in Kannada is required at all levels.

Kerala

Taking effect beginning November 1st, 1965,[106] the Government of Kerala ordered that Malayalam shall be the Official Language for some of the officers in the Panchayats, Municipalities etc. With effect from May 1st, 1966,[107] authorized the use of Malayalam as official language was extended to office of Prison, Education, Survey and Land Records, etc. The 1969 Kerala Official Languages (Legislation) Act recognized Malayalam and English as the official languages of Kerala.[108] They are the languages to be used for all or any of the official purposes of the State. The Act has also made special provisions for two linguistic minorities of Kerala, while the remaining minorities must use English or the State's official language.
Accordingly:
(a) The Tamil and Kannada minorities in the State may use their respective languages for their correspondence with the State Government in the Secretariat and the Heads of Departments and also with all the local offices of the State Government situated in those areas which are declared by the Government to be linguistic minority areas for this purpose, and the replies sent in such cases shall also be in their respective minority languages and

105 B.D. Jayaram/K.S. Rajyashree, *State Official Language Policy Implementation*, CIIL, Mysore June 2000, p.154-155

106 See the Gazette O(P) No. 647/65/PD, dated 19th October 1965

107 See theG.O.(P) No.159/66/PD dated 19th April 1966

108 B.D. Jayaram and K.S. Rajyashree, *State Official Language Policy Implementation*, CIIL, Mysore June 2000, p.140-143

(b) The linguistic minorities other than Tamil and Kannada in the State may use the English language for their correspondence with the State Government offices and in such cases the replies sent to them shall be in the English language'.

Madhya Pradesh

The 1957 Madhya Pradesh Official Language Act recognizes Hindi as the Official Language in the Devanagari script for "all purposes except such purposes as are specifically excluded by the Constitution and in respect of such matters as may be specified by Government from time to time". The Madhya Pradesh Rajbhasha (Anupurak Upabandha) Adhiniyam, 1972, makes provision "for the publication of authoritative texts in Hindi of laws passed originally by the State Legislature in English..." The 1972 Madhya Pradesh Official Languages (Amendment) Act inserts a clause for "The form numerals to be used for the official purposes of the State shall be the Devanagari form of numerals: provided that the State Government may, by notification authorize the use of the international form of Indian numerals in addition to the Devanagari form of numerals for any of the official purposes of the State". In order to avoid difficulties resulting from a sudden switch over to Hindi from English, the use of English was also permitted in some matters. However, the scope of the use of English was minimised beginning August 25th, 1977. Hindi was made compulsory except in (a) Prescriptions, Post-mortem reports in medico-legal cases, and (b) Correspondence (including agreements) with newspapers transacting their business in English.

Maharashtra

The 1964 Maharashtra Official Languages Act reads: "Marathi shall, as from the appointed day, be the language to be used for all official purposes referred to in the Article 345 of the Constitution, as respects to the State of Maharashtra except such purposes as the State Government may, by rules issued from time to time in the Official Gazette specify, and Hindi may be used as the Official Language for such expected purposes".[109] And ".. the English language may, as from the appointed day, continue to be used, in addition to Hindi and Marathi, for the transaction of business in the Legislature of the State". Marathi in Devanagari script is used here and it is supposed to be used at all levels of administration. It is largely used in the District and lower levels of administration, whereas English continues to be used in the higher levels of administration.

Orissa

The 1954 Orissa Official Languages Act recognizes Oriya "to be used for all

---

109 B.D. Jayaram and K.S. Rajyashree *Ibidem*, p. 164

or any of the official purposes of the State of Orissa". The 1963 Orissa Official Language (Amendment) Bill makes provision for the continuing use of the English language "in addition to Oriya for transaction of business in Legislature of the State of Orissa". In the Orissa border district bordering Andhra Pradesh "... State Government have issued a notification which makes Telugu the Court language besides Oriya in some of these areas".[110]

Punjab

Punjabi is the official language in this State. It is extensively used in the lower level of the administration. The offices at the district level follow the official language policy very strictly. However, in the higher levels of administration English continues to be used to some extent.

Rajasthan

The Rajasthan Official Language Act was passed in 1956. In 1957, a notification made the use of Hindi mandatory for all purposes in the following government departments and offices at specified levels, except where the use of English was unavoidable:

i. Panchayat – up to Chief Panchayat Officer
ii. Municipalities – up to the Manager of local bodies
iii. Educational Directorates – up to inspectors of schools
iv. Co-operatives – up to the Registrar of co-operatives except for the files maintaining correspondence with Apex banks
v. Temples – up to the commissioner of temples
vi. Sub-sections of departments of law in public administrations

In 1957, another notification extended the use of Hindi to the Department of Revenue, except for the legal procedures of the Revenue Board. In 1965, Hindi was also made mandatory for the legislature and its committees. Under this provision, all the matters brought before the legislature and its committees by the heads of the departments must be written in Hindi.[111]

Tamil Nadu

The 1956 Madras Official Language Act recognizes Tamil as the Official Language of the State. Additionally, "the English language shall continue to be used for all the official purposes of the state for which it was being used before the commencement of the Act...".[112] With the aim of gradual implementation of the use of Tamil in administration, in 1958 about 1700 small Government offices were advised to use Tamil. Gradually the same policy has spread to other departments and offices. At present, the entire

110 *ibidem*, p.157
111 *Ibidem*, p. 172
112 *Ibidem*, p.147

District Administration conducts business mostly in Tamil. At the Secretariat level there has also been a significant shift towards the use of Tamil in all the departments.

Uttar Pradesh

In Uttar Pradesh, Hindi is the Official Language. The Uttar Pradesh Ordinance No.20 of 1982 provides for the use of Urdu in addition to Hindi for the following purposes:

- i) Entertaining applications in Urdu presented by members of public.
- ii) Receiving documents in Urdu presented for registration, with a copy in Hindi.
- iii) Publication of important Government rules, regulations and notifications.
- iv) Publication of important Government advertisements, etc.
- v) Translation of the Gazette in Urdu.

West Bengal

Bengali is the official language of West Bengal. It is used widely in lower levels of administration and along with English also in higher levels of administration. The official language policy is not followed strictly in the State. The 1961 West Bengal Official Language Act recognizes "(a) in the three hill sub-divisions of the district of Darjeeling, namely, Darjeeling, Kalimpong and Kurseong, the Bengali language and the Nepali language, and (b) elsewhere, the Bengali language shall be the language or languages to be used for the official purposes of the State of West Bengal...".[113] The 1964 West Bengal Official Language (Amendment) Act makes provision for the "continuance of English language for official purposes of the State and for use in the State Legislature". The Language Act of 1961 was amended in 1973 through the West Bengal Official Language (Amendment) Act, which inserted Section 3A stating that "the Nepali Language may, in addition to Bengali language, be used for

(a) rules, regulations and bye-laws made by the State Government under the Constitution of India or under any law made by the Parliament or the Legislature and

(b) notifications or orders issued by the State Government under the Constitution of India or under any laws made by Parliament or the Legislature of West Bengal, as apply to the three hill sub-divisions of the district of Darjeeling, namely, Darjeeling, Kalimpong and Kurseong".

In the States of Manipur, Meghalaya, Nagaland, Arunachal Pradesh, Sikkim

113 Ibidem, p. 160

and Mizoram, and in the Union Territories of Chandigarh, Dadra and Nagar Haveli English is the Official Language, along with other local languages. In Mizoram the additional official language is Mizo, in Tripura Bengali and Kokborok, in Meghalaya Garo and Khasi, in Sikkim Lepcha and Bhotia.
There is a well-defined official language policy of the central government. All the central government offices located in the Hindi speaking States (Bihar, Haryana, Himachal Pradesh, Madhya Pradesh, Uttar Pradesh, Rajasthan, Uttarakhand and Delhi) have to use Hindi at all levels in administration. In the Region B (Jammu and Kashmir, Gujarat, Punjab, Maharashtra and the Uts of Chandigarh, Andaman-Nicobar Islands) they are supposed to use Hindi along with English wherever required, and in all other states they are supposed to use only English. The central government officers and staff are supposed to acquire certain level of proficiency in the administrative use of Hindi. In practice the official language policy is not followed strictly as English continues to have a significant role in administration.[114] The recruitment to different types of posts is made on the grounds of educational eligibility, which includes language proficiency too.

Article 347 of the Constitution offers the legal key for a stronger presence of minority languages on local or district level. It gives a "substantial proportion of the population of a State the right to submit a demand to the President in order to be recognized as official language either on State or on regional level".[115] When comparing the "absolute" linguistic minorities (92 non-scheduled languages) with the existing co-official languages, very few have been recognized through Article 347 Const., mostly because their speakers are the most important speech communities in the concerned States (Kokborok in Tripura, Mizo in Mizoram, Khasi and Garo in Meghalaya). Looking at the figures of the numerically strong minorities (see table 10, "relative minorities"), the rate of recognition is very scarce. Among the three numerically major minorities there are 11 tribal languages in 8 States, but – except Khasi and Garo in Meghalaya and Mizo in Mizoram - none of their languages have been recognized as official languages – not even at district level. In addition, the presence of such major "relative minorities" as Bengali in Assam, Sindhi in Gujarat, Kannada and Telugu in Tamil Nadu, Hindi in West Bengal and Orissa, Punjabi in Rajasthan, did lead to an official recognition.

In case of recognition of a minority language at the State level, the most common regulation refers to the right of minority members to interact with

114 Omkar N. Koul, *Language, Education and Communication*, 2005, p. 48/49

115 The full text of all constitutional articles referring to language rights is given in the annex.

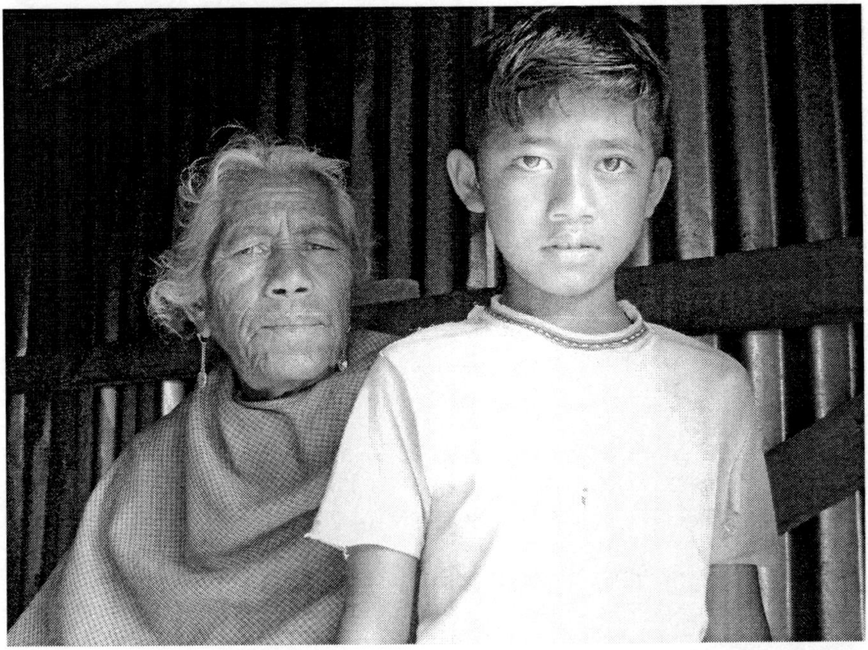

Khasi in Sohra (Meghalaya)

the authorities in their own language, referred to individual purposes, e.g. filing petitions or letters. This can be considered merely a first step to a bilingual administration or "equal linguistic rights" in the public sphere. Only the general public use of all officially recognized languages marks a high standard of "official bilingualism", but it is not known how many districts, tehsils (taluk) or municipalities are implementing such a scheme. The second issue is the implementation of the TLF with regard to linguistic minorities and the right to education in the mother tongue. Whereas the former issue will be dealt in detail in chapter 7, there are no State data available on the latter issue.

5.3 What is the impact on minority languages?

The reorganisation of the Indian States on a linguistic basis has brought about a great degree of homogenisation and the languages of the respective majority populations have become official languages. Firstly, this has been helpful in limiting the historical dominance of English as the language of public affairs (legislation, judiciary, administration). Consequently, a major number (13-15) of Indian languages could be further developed to occupy some more domains such as legislation, education, administration, media, and business. Most of these State official languages are still excluded from functioning as interstate link-languages, as languages for university education, science and technology, and for international communication. On the other hand, due to the implementation of the official language policy and other general social and political developments, the "functional load" of the absolute minority languages is being progressively reduced.[116] The lack of functionality of many minority languages in States with traditionally dominant (English, Hindi) and emerging dominant (official State) languages has lowered their status and reduced their usage and importance. How can minority language speakers maintain their languages in this new context? The number (or share) of the speakers can hardly be increased, but the functional load of their languages can. The functional load of a language can sometimes only be improved by changing the general conditions of language policy in the territory where it is spoken. If the functional load is increased, this promotes the longevity of a language, whereas a reduction of its functional load causes decay and attrition.

Generally minority speech communities are reacting in four ways:

a) Language movements against the official policies of imposing one dominant language
b) Segregation from the "mainstream communities"
c) Assimilation with the larger majority language communities
d) Adoption of multiple strategies

In India most linguistic minorities did not actively react, but underwent a slow process of language attrition and assimilation, under the pressure of dominant languages in their traditional areas. In particular, the smaller tribal languages succumbed to such processes, as indicated by the decreasing language retention ratio among tribal peoples.[117] The lack of educational facilities such as textbooks, teachers, schools with the tribal language as the medium of instruction, lack of a standard language (and script), and, most importantly, the marginalisation or exclusion from the major domains of the public sphere have severely curtailed the sustenance of tribal languages. Minority language speakers in Diaspora commonly adopt multiple strategies - using minority languages at home and the dominant language at school and for other public domains. These languages have a stable cultural and linguistic base elsewhere that provides more constant support for their retention.

Apart from such defensive strategies, there are two major strategies to

116 Pandharipande, *Minority matters*, p.9

117 See the following chapter 6 on tribal peoples.

improve the situation: devising a script and providing for the codification or standardisation of the language. First, minority languages need to be written in order to be used in education, administration and media. A script also serves as the expression of a separate identity, with religious and emotional significance. Secondly, there are too many varieties of minority languages. Thus three alternatives are given to minorities: to choose one variety as the official one, to accept all varieties, or to blend all varieties and form a new one. But there is lack of institutions that can decide such issues. Problems also arise in vocabulary expansion and in the development of suitable forms of discourse. In particular, different sources of vocabulary expansion have created conflicting currents of opinion not only in the case of quickly developing major Indian languages but also in the case of minority languages. There is likely to be an increase in minority languages borrowing from the regional languages or from Hindi and English. On the other hand, if the minority language planners place too much emphasis to the native resources for lexical expansion, they widen the gulf not only between the spoken and written forms of the language, but also between the minority language and the majority language. These are typical issues of language status and acquisition planning. Such programs are generally missing from the Indian States' official language policy. Empowering minority languages does not appear to be a priority on their agenda.

Chapter 6

The languages of India's tribal peoples

6.1 India's indigenous peoples: an overview

The term "tribe" has been used since the British rulers introduced it in 1872 to apply to a few select communities. Tribes or indigenous peoples, in India also called "Adivasi", do not form a homogeneous socio-cultural category. Some scholars consider a clear distinction between tribal and non-tribal is impossible[118]. The tribes exist outside the Hindu caste system. The concept of "Adivasi, equivalent to indigenous people, has now become part of the common consciousness of these peoples as an "expanded identity, cutting across tribes bearing different names, speaking different languages or dialects. It also goes beyond groups and communities listed in the Constitution as scheduled tribes."[119]

As per Article 342 of the Constitution, certain tribes are "scheduled" by the President and Parliament. In the 2001 census 84.32 million persons were classified as members of Scheduled Tribes (ST), equal to 8.32% of India's total population.[120] In the Schedule of the Constitution of 1950 212 tribes were included and thus officially recognised as STs. In the amendment of 1974 there were nearly 300 tribes. Currently 623 communities recognized all over India, but not half of the members of these scheduled tribes still speak a tribal mother tongue.[121] Estimates of the actual number of tribes living in India go as high as 635. There are many ethnic groups that claim the status but have not been officially recognized as STs under the Constitution. Also, in some States an ethnic group may be recognized, while it is not in the neighbouring State. From a ethnological perspective the official list cannot be considered authoritative.[122]

There is a quantitative and qualitative difference in the socio-political and economic status across tribes in the Northeast, the Himalayan borders and in other parts of the country. Some of the tribes, like the Gonds, Santals,

---

118 Anvita Abbi, *Tribal languages*, in: Kachru/Kachru/Sridhar, *Language in South Asia*, Cambridge University Press 2008, p.153

119 Virginius Xaxa, in: Christian Erni (ed.) *The Concept of Indigenous Poeples in Asia – A Resource Book*, IWGIA Document No. 123, Copenhagen/Chiang Mai, 2008,p. 326

120 See: Nilsson/Erni, Country Profile India, in: Christian Erni (ed.) *The Concept of Indigenous Poeples in Asia – A Resource Book*, IWGIA Document No. 123, Copenhagen/Chiang Mai, 2008, p. 371-372. The most updated report on India's tribal peoples can be found in: AITPN, The State of India's Indigenous and Tribal Peoples 2009, New Delhi 2009, at: http://www.aitpn.org/Reports/Tribal_Peoples_2009.pdf

121 Anvita Abbi, *Tribal languages,* p.154

122 Nilsson/Erni, Country Profile India, p. 371

Oraon or Bhils have large populations of several million people. Others, like the Onge or the Great Andamanese are on the brink of extinction. Geographically, India's tribal populations are concentrated in three major zones:

1) North East India comprising the sub-Himalayan regions Assam, Arunachal Pradesh, Meghalaya, Nagaland, Mizoram, Manipur and Tripura (11%);
2) Central and East India comprising Madhya Pradesh, Bihar, Andhra Pradesh, Jharkhand, Chhattisgarh, Orissa and West Bengal (the central tribal belt with 85%)
3) Southern India (3%)

The highest ethnic diversity is found in the seven northeastern States where 220 distinct groups have been identified.

Map 2 - Tribal peoples of India's Northeast

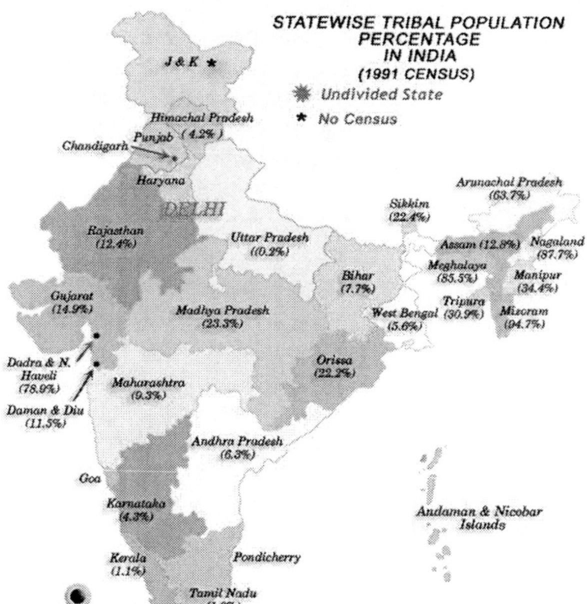

Source: Braj B. Kachru/ Yamuna Kachru/S.N. Sridhar, Language in South Asia, 2008

The tribal people in India are stratified, from highly sophisticated tribes to tribes that live in abject poverty. Due to the ecological conditions, geographical outlay of the hills, valleys and plains, and the poor means of communication and infrastructure, for long periods of history the tribal people settled in isolated villages and based their livelihood on hunting, fishing, food gathering and shifting cultivation supported by a barter economy. They are peoples with lively ancient customs, oral traditions, music, songs and dances. They follow animistic beliefs, or worship ancestors with shamanistic practices and rituals. In India, like in most other countries of the world, tribal peoples have been pushed to the most inhospitable areas and still are displaced by the construction of dams and other infrastructure, mineral mines, industrial areas. Non-tribal settlers in search of agricultural land often penetrate the traditional tribal areas, depriving the original owners of their land and cutting them off from their special relationship with nature.[123] Tribal peoples are among the poorest of the country. The STs have the highest poverty rate of the three scheduled groups (ST, SC and OBC). 52.17% live below the poverty line, while among the SC it is 48.14%, among other people 31.29%. The dismal situation is reflected in the health and nutritional status of tribal villagers. Especially where access to forest products to supplement their diet and to provide additional income is not possible anymore – either because the forests have been destroyed or their rights of access are being denied – under-nourishment and malnourishment is widespread.[124] As 89% of the labour force among STs is working in agriculture, almost nine tenth of tribal families rely on natural resources for their livelihood. The tribal members within the Indian society occupy the lowest rank of the social hierarchy, along with the other lower and scheduled castes

Nevertheless, due to increasing contacts with the non-tribal population and the Christianising of some important regions, accompanied by higher education, the tribal societies underwent a certain "modernisation" and social and cultural transformation. Previously, living isolated from the cities and major villages, many tribal communities could maintain their languages due to their isolation from the mainstream population, which did not interact with them on a daily basis. But in the fifty years since India's independence in 1947, it has become necessary for tribal communities to interact with the

---

123 The main features and the general concept of indigenous peoples in India is concisely explained by Virginius Xaxa, *The Concept of Indigenous Peoples in India*, in Christian Erni (ed.) *The Concept of Indigenous Peoples in Asia – A Resource Book*, IWGIA Document No. 123, Copenhagen/Chiang Mai, 2008

124 Nilsson/Erni, Country Profile India, in: Christian Erni (ed.) *The Concept of Indigenous Poeples in Asia – A Resource Book*, IWGIA Document No. 123, Copenhagen/Chiang Mai, 2008, p. 372

mainstream population because of the following changes:[125]

a) Mechanisation of the professions of farming, fishing, tanning of leather etc.
b) Deforestation and urbanisation of villages and
c) The policy of state governments to promote education in these communities (through the TLF), which has accelerated the learning of the dominant regional language among tribes.

As a result, the majority of the members of tribal communities have already shifted to the regional dominant language of their area in almost every functional domain. The functional domain of their own languages, if maintained at all, is restricted to home and intra-group communication. Moreover, the majority of the tribal languages still do not have a script. Khubchandani[126] shows that due to the lack of script, the paucity of teaching materials and the small number of speakers a large number of tribal languages are facing attrition. The shift to regional dominant languages concerns most of the smaller tribal communities, whereas such numerically bigger groups or peoples as the Santhali in Bihar, Orissa, West Bengal and Jharkhand, the Bhili and Gondi in Madya Pradesh and Maharashtra suffer a lesser degree of language shifting.

It is important to note that among the tribal population of India customary laws are still in force, alongside formal Indian law. Custom, according to Pandharipande, is a "socially prescribed mode of behaviour carried by tradition and enforced by social disapproval by its violation. The customs of social control in tribal societies in different parts of India are divergent and need to be codified with reference to their customary laws, which is based on the experiences of a tribe's respond to the ecology of the environment and social organisation of the tribe."[127] The customs of tribal groups living in the Himalayas, those on the hills, those on the plains, and itinerant tribes are diverging. The advent of Christianity and other foreign religions, quicker transport systems, the establishment of schools and the introduction of new technologies have resulted in social change, thus weakening traditional customary laws.

The North-eastern States of Nagaland, Mizoram, Arunachal Pradesh, Meghalaya, Manipur, Tripura, Madhya Pradesh, and Jharkhand have the highest density of tribal population. Or rather, the majority of the peoples of the

125 Rajeshwari Pandharipande, *Minority matters: issues in minority languages in India*, in: International Journal of Multicultural Societies, Vol. 4, No.2, UNESCO 2002, p.12

126 Lachman Khubchandani, *Tribal Identity: a Language and Communication perspective*, Indian Institute of Advanced Studies, Shimla 1992

127 Pandharipande, *Minority matters*, p. 13

Northeast are socially, ethnically and linguistically different from the rest of India. "The difference between the tribal populations of the Northeast and those of Jharkhand lies in the nature of the language contact and linguistic convergence. The latter are in closer contact with speakers of Dravidian and Indo-Aryan languages than those of the Northeast. Consequently language shift has taken place in a larger number and at a faster pace here than in the Northeast."[128]

The tribal populations of South India speak different languages of the Dravidian family. As a result there is a high rate of bilingualism; the literacy rate of these peoples is also higher than in the rest of India.[129] For example, speakers of Gondi, a Dravidian language, spoken in the middle of the Dravidian speech community of Telugu, a major scheduled language, are known to shift to Telugu in high numbers. South India does not present a homogeneous picture of language maintenance and language shift. Only about 20% of tribal members live in Western India, where they are mostly surrounded by communities of scheduled languages such as Gujarati, Marathi, Hindi and the Hindi-variant Rajasthani. In the Nicobar and Andaman Islands, some thousands of tribal members have been surviving in almost total isolation for 20,000 years. They are under severe threat from ongoing colonisation and immigration from the mainland of India.

6.2 Tribal languages

Languages spoken by these scheduled tribes are considered "tribal languages", but there is no linguistic definition of tribal languages, so as they are seen merely as smaller linguistic communities: "The tribal languages of India are not a special kind of languages which could be linguistically characterized as a homogeneous group, except as languages of a special kind of people who are historically, geographically, politically, socially and culturally different from other people."[130]. The term "tribe" is not used by any other South Asian country. Each of the 4-5 language families of India has its own tribal languages and specific speech areas. Out of 92 non-scheduled languages, 88 are tribal. 96% of the non-scheduled languages registered on the census are "languages of tribes".

128 Anvita Abbi, *Tribal languages, in: Kachru/Kachru/Sridhar, Language in South Asia,* Cambridge University Press 2008, p.161

129 *ibidem*, p. 161

130 E. Annamalai, 1997b, p.22, quoted by Anvita Abbi, *Tribal languages*, in: Kachru/Kachru/Sridhar, *Language in South Asia*, Cambridge University Press 2008, p.153

Members of the Zou community of Mizoram

Although some of the "tribal languages" are spoken by more than a million people, just two (Santhali and Bodo) have so far been accorded the status of a scheduled language. The tribal languages and their variants stand at the bottom of India's hierarchy of languages.

Out of the 92 non-scheduled languages, the majority are languages of scheduled tribes. Fifty-eight have been scheduled as "tribal languages"[131]: Abor, Adi, Anal, Angami, Ao, Assuri, Agarva, Bhili, Bhumij, Birhor, Binija/Birijia, Bodo including Kachari, Mech, Chang-Naga, Chiri, Dafla, Dimasa, Gadaba, Garo, Gondi, Ho, Halam, Juang, Kabui, Kanawari, Kharia, Khasi, Khiemnungam, Khond/Kandh, Koch, Koda/Kora, Kolami, Konda, Konyak, Korku, Kota, Korwa, Koya, Kurukh/Oraon, Lushai/Mizo, Mikir, Miri, Mishmi, Mru, Mundari, Nicobarese, Paite, Parji, Rabha, Ranghkul, Rengma, Santali, Savara, Sema, Tangkhul, Thado, Toda, Tripuri/Kokborok. The criteria for such distinctions are not understood, but the distinction itself is not very relevant, as most of the tribal languages listed do not enjoy any special attention, public support or promotion. Bodo and Santhali were the first "tribal languages" to be included in the 8th Schedule of the Constitution in 2003.

131 By a Presidential Order published in the Gazette of India, Part II, section 1, dated 13 August 1960

As linguistic heterogeneity is a part of tribal life whenever tribes enter in contact with other groups, several tribal groups have evolved one common lingua franca or contact language for inter-tribal communication (as Sadari/Sadani, Halbi, Chhattisgarhi). A new hybrid contact language emerged in Nagaland with Zeliangrong (Zemi+Liangmei+Rongmei), which is used along with Nagamese as a new form of umbrella language.

A growing number of members of indigenous tribes do not speak their own traditional language anymore, although they declare themselves to be members of one of the "scheduled tribes" (ST). Although 7.08% (71 million) of India's population is "tribal", only about 3.8% (39 million) speak a tribal language or indicate that language as their "mother tongue", which shows a dramatic process of transition towards dominant languages.[132] Tribal communities in several parts of India are on the way toward assimilation with the surrounding or neighbouring dominant cultures. In Orissa, for instance, there are 62 tribal communities, but only 22 tribal languages have survived. In the name of national integration they are "called to join the mainstream".[133] Vernacular languages with affinities to Hindi, whether "tribal" or not, have been absorbed into Hindi in the official census.

Still, most of the tribal languages are non-written languages, which hampers their constitutional recognition. In recent years, revealed scripts, rediscovered scripts or newly developed scripts were introduced for tribal languages, such as Ol Chiki for Santhali (see also Table 8 in Chapter 2). Nevertheless, many tribal languages are facing extinction due to the apathy of their users and the absence of any public support for language development.[134] The intensity of the linguistic assimilation with major regional languages among tribal communities varies from State to State, reflecting different pressures for the maintenance of and shift in ancestral languages, as is shown in the following table. "Tribal languages", states Pattanayak, "are seldom taken into consideration by planners whether they plan development or education. In fact, the Indian languages as a whole have not been debated in the Constituent Assembly or the Indian Parliament."[135]

---

132 See D.P. Pattanayak, *Tribal Languages in Education*, p. 47

133 For Orissa this process is described by Smita Sinha, *Linguistic Human Rights in Tribal Education in Orissa*, in Language in India, May 2005

134 *Ibidem*, p.48

135 D.P. Pattanayak, *Tribal Languages in Education*, p.51; and Lachman Khubchandani, *Tribal Identity: a Language and Communication perspective*, Indian Institute of Advanced Studies, Shimla 1992, p. 15

Table 13 – Language retention among tribal peoples (1971, 1981)

States	Tribal population 1971 (mil.)	Tribal language speakers	Language retention ratio 1971	Tribal population 1981 (mil.)	Tribal language speakers (mil.)	Lang. reten. ratio 1981
India	38,015	18,420	49%	53,818	22,34	42%
Bihar	4,933	3,844	78%	5,811	4,094	70%
Madhya Pradesh	8,387	3,420	41%	11,987	3,420	34%

Source: L. Khubchandani, in: Itagi/Singh (eds.), Linguistic Landscaping in India, CIIL, Mysore 2002

Hybrid varieties, such as pidgin languages, are often used among tribal peoples, but are largely discouraged in formal education and neglected in literacy programmes. Moreover, there is a cleavage between the urban population and tribal peoples living in rural areas over the very content of education. The high standards promulgated in mother tongue textbooks are often not understandable or irrelevant to tribal people: "Such school standards may be quite unrelated to the facility in communication. No wonder, as mother-tongue textbooks in many tribal languages are originally written in English and then translated in local languages as authors in the local languages are not available."[136] The result is that many literacy programmes often lead to a total break with the rural culture, and tribal societies, by and large, find it difficult to relate the structure and content of education to their way of life. Many tribal children fail to continue school beyond initial classes as the difference between the 'school' language and the 'home' language increases and sometimes becomes insurmountable. "Many literacy drives in rural areas particularly among the tribes, though conducted under the banner of non-formal education, in essence were charged with the mission of churning out 'certified' literates, who could be sucked into the hegemonic network of the neo-rich 'non-tribal' literates."[137]

Why do tribal language occupy such a weak position? In addition to numerical inferiority and the absence of autonomous areas, the sense of inferiority and an awareness of their low social status discouraged many tribal mem-

136 D.P. Pattanayak, *Tribal Languages in Education*, p. 40

137 L. Khubchandani, *Tribal Identity*, p.41; And he adds: "..the urban tribals seldom consider it a privilege to speak their mother tongues. On the contrary, ignorance of the tribal languages is regarded as an enhancement of status and prestige. In speaking Hindi, the regional contact language, they feel superior in comparison to other fellow tribals who cannot speak it. A very low percentage of urban tribals is monolingual in its use of ancestral languages. Ethnolinguistic minority status induces a negative attitude toward language loyalty. A gradual adoption of a non-tribal language as mother tongue presents a classic case of language shift. Generally, these symptoms are diagnostic of potential language death."

bers from declaring their mother tongues in the census. The low prestige of their languages is inducing them to shift their language loyalty claim.[138] Thus, there are strong convergence areas in India, such as Jharkhand, Madhya Pradesh, Bengal, Orissa, Chhattisgarh, wherever tribal areas are surrounded by speakers of non-tribal languages. In India there has been no co-ordinated general language status and development planning for tribal languages. Hence, both the standardization of those languages and the preparation of written textbooks and literary products generally has been retarded, if not neglected at all. Literacy programs among tribal members, largely carried out in a dominant regional language and through enrolment in the education system, show a remarkable ambivalence: on the one hand they lobby for education and literacy among tribal peoples so as to integrate them into mainstream society, on the other hand they enhance mother tongue loss. Indeed, the language retention ratio is decreasing from census to census, and probably at present just half of the 80 million Indian citizens belonging to scheduled tribes still retain their traditional language.

6.3 Tribal literacy

The literacy ratio among tribal peoples all over the country is lower than the total literacy ratio in the single States. According to the 1991 census, the literacy rate among scheduled tribes is 29.6% against a national average of 52.2%. In 2001, general literacy in India reached 65.2% (rural areas 59%, in urban areas 80%), whereas data on the tribal literacy has not been published yet. 63.8% of the children of families belonging to scheduled tribes dropped out of the school at primary level; 79.35% dropped out in middle school and 86.27% in secondary school (Census of India).[139] The literacy levels of tribal girls is lamentably low. The drop out rates of tribal children in primary schools is about 80%, but educational research does not yield any precise information on these developments.[140] Nevertheless,

138 Anvita Abbi, *Tribal languages*, in: Kachru/Kachru/Sridhar, *Language in South Asia*, Cambridge University Press 2008, p.163

139 In his 42d report the NCLM writes: "The literacy rate itself is misleading. Familiarity with the writing of the language is considered sufficient for a person to be considered as literate. If we consider the statistics of the persons who have completed the senior secondary (class XII), the disparity will be even more evident. In my visits to various districts, I have been confronted with the figures of how the children have studied up to the level till the education was in their language. In my last report, I have cited the case of a veterinary doctor, who went away to Andhra Pradesh to continue his studies in Urdu (which was not available in his district Berhampur, Orissa) and when he came back, he was denied admission to MBBS course for he had not studied in Oriya and had to perforce become a veterinary doctor." See www.nclm.nic.in

140 Pattanayak, *Tribal Languages in Education,* p. 56

in the last four decades since 1961, the tribal communities have recovered very strongly. Whereas in 1931 the census of India showed a literacy rate of 0.1%, in 1981 this had increased to 16.3%, to 29,6% in 1991. In the North-eastern States of India the tribal population almost caught up with the rest of the population.[141] The literacy rate of the tribal population in Mizoram, Nagaland, Meghalaya and Manipur, which constitute a majority in these States, crossed the 50% mark. Where tribal peoples settle in cities to a significant extent, their literacy rate equals that of the rest of the population. The tribes of the Centre-east and Centre-west region of India, on contrary, show significantly lower rates of literacy.[142] The literacy rates of the most populous tribes – e.g. Gond, Oraon, Khond, Bhil, Mina – are lower than those of many tribes with smaller populations.

Table 14 – Literacy rates among tribal peoples (in 1991)

Community	State	Lit. rate	Community	State	Lit. rate
Malayarayar	Kerala	65.9	Khairwar	M. Pradesh	22.0
Mizo	Mizoram	60.0	Chaudhri	Gujarat	22.0
Kanikaran	Kerala	41.2	Bodo Kachari	Assam	20.5
Pulayan	Kerala	39.5	Kawar	M.Pradesh	14.4
Tangkhul	Manipur	35.6	Kokna	Maharashtra	14.3
Dhodia	Gujarat	31.2	Gond	Orissa	13.5
Lohara	West Bengal	30.6	Mikir	Assam	13.2
Halba	Maharashtra	29.6	Naikda	Karnataka	13.1
Khasi	Meghalaya	28.7	Mech	West Bengal	12.8
Chakma	Assam	27.3	Ho	Bihar	12.7
Lepcha	West Bengal	26.0	Dhanka	Gujarat	12.4
Kabui	Manipur	24.6	Saora	M. Pradesh	11.9
Thado	Manipur	24.5	Soligaru	Karnataka	11.8
Kuruman	Kerala	23.8	Kisan	Orissa	10.7
Bhutia	West Bengal	23.6	Mundari	Orissa	10.7
Garo	Meghalaya	23.5	Bhumij	Bihar	10.3
Marati	Kerala	22.7	Yerukula	Andhra Pradesh	10.3
Rabha	Assam	22.2	Karmali	West Bengal	10.0
Maratha	Karnataka	22.1			

Source: Khubchandani, Tribal Identity: A language and Communication Perspective, Indian Institue of Advanced Studies, Shimla 1992 p. 31-32

141 In some States this distinction is highly artificial and hardly legitimate as various smaller titular peoples of such States in the Northeast are just smaller peoples belonging to other ethno-linguistic families. The very term appears scientifically questionable in such cases.
142 Khubchandani, *Language Demography and Language in Education*, p. 38

Adult education enrolment among the scheduled tribes is reported at 14.3% against a general enrolment of 60% in the country as a whole. Despite the progress in literacy, the gap between general and tribal literacy remains remarkably high. The residential remoteness of tribes, their different professional aspirations, their distinct lifestyle and the lack of protection of their linguistic rights are among the decisive factors contributing to this situation.

Should literacy programs be initiated in the mother tongue or in the regional language? Koul observes on this regard: "India's States had huge amounts of funds for literacy campaigns for adults, but concentrated the expenditures on the State official languages. The scheme was biased from the very beginning. When the tribal peoples asked the State to be appointed with the literacy programs and funds, they were ignored. The State did not transfer any money or responsibility. On the other hand large parts of tribal peoples request[143] to be integrated, and this happens through dominant languages."

Srivastava points out the negative consequences of initiating literacy programs in a second language.[144] There are three major obstacles for promoting literacy in tribal languages. First, tribal education raises specific difficulties for literacy education. In the absence of a common standardized written language, tribal communities use different scripts (for example the Santals and their original script Ol Chiki). Then there are many tribal languages that have no script at all. "This problem in India is due to the fact, that several tribal languages as Bhili, Oraon, Kurukh are spread over different states and thus could not achieve any unity in standardizing their language."[145]

Second, the tribal communities are predominantly rural communities, which is reflected in the usage of the language and its major domains. Literacy materials are produced with very little practical village content and this hardly strengthens the motivation for learners.[146]

---

143 From an Interview with Prof. Omkar N. Koul, IILS, Shillong 20 March 2009

144 R. Srivastava, *Linguistic Minorities and National Language*, in: Florian Coulmas (ed.), *Linguistic Minorities and Literacy: Language Policy Issues in developing Countries*, p. 99-114, Mouton De Gruyter, Berlin 1984

145 *Ibidem*, p. 100

146 "On the one hand the creation of reading material is not encouraged or no funds are allotted for its production and, on the other hand, the lack of material is cited as the reason for not using the language. This was the experience in Sourashtra language in Tamil Nadu. It was said, that Sourashtra does not have a script, much less a book. The Sourashtra people produced a book for use at the primary level of education and submitted it to the Govern-

Nepali mother-tongue students of the Notre Dame-College in Darjeeling (West Bengal)

Third, there is a remarkable difference between the home language of the tribal peoples and the school language. Even when a major part of a tribe is bilingual in the dominant regional language, there is a major gap between the spoken and the written official version. The gap in the literacy rates is often due to a general low State expenditure in the education facilities for scheduled tribes.[147] Finally, the problem remains that the communities can use these tribal languages exclusively for intra-group communication and for very limited domains. Tribal members are often not convinced of the usefulness of such teaching programs. This all results in the large difficul-

ment for production. Nothing has happened for the last two or three decades". See NCLM, 42 report, p.15, at: http://nclm.nic.in

147 The NCLM in his 42d report stated in this regard "…it has been accepted as a duty of the State to see that every child is entitled to receive, at the cost of the State, education up to the year 14. And when we say education, we mean education in the real sense. The framers of the Constitution envisaged that the primary education will be in the mother tongue. To postpone it on the excuse, that it is costlier to do so, is going against the spirit of the Constitution. The decision appears to be that either you have it my way or not to have it at all….. The Commissioner has argued in a previous report that the extra expenditure involved is not substantial and certainly not of the magnitude which can not be borne by the State. It is also observed that the argument is given by more prosperous states whereas smaller states are keen on achieving the goal of teaching through the mother tongues."

ties that lead to an overall low literacy rate among tribal peoples.[148]

The medium language of education is among the most relevant factors accounting for the low literacy and education levels of the tribal population. Tribal children mostly attend schools in the dominant official languages of the respective state or that offer bilingual education with a blend of native language as an auxiliary medium, replaced gradually by the respective regional language and/or Hindi/English. According to NCERT (National Council for Educational Research and Training), in the 1970s there were 80 tribal languages used as medium languages in education. That number has sharply declined since that time. "In the present context of education in India, no policy is enunciated for use of tribal languages in education. Being victims of development, many of them have become itinerants. No efforts are being made to bring the school to their door steps. Their languages are neither compulsory as first, second, or third language nor are they optional languages. They are under perceived and ignored. Their cultures are impoverished."[149] If the official expectation is that the smaller groups would melt and fuse their identities and assimilate in the dominant language and cultures, the perspective for the survival of most tribal languages is quite bleak.

6.4 Language attitudes and functional load of tribal languages

One of the major factors affecting the maintenance of a minority language is the speakers' perception of their own language. The attitude regarding language is strictly linked to the general modernisation and social integration of society. Increased social and geographical mobility, due to the growing integration of the national economy and labour market, the building up of regional and national State bureaucracies and structures (including a national army), the impact of new communication technologies, and most recently the opening-up to global exchange in economy, trade, culture and media, deeply affect the functional load of the smaller languages. In India, the labour market and professional life in the industry and the service markets is dominated by English and the regional languages, at the expense of tribal languages. The latter are used only in agriculture, forestry, hunting,

148 Rakesh Bhatt/Ahmar Mahboob, *Minority languages and their status*, in: Kachru/Kachru/Sridhar, *Language in South Asia*, Cambridge University Press 2008, p.144-145

149 Pattanayak, *Tribal Languages in Education,* p. 57. Critical on this issue also Sanjay Radhan, *Educational Deprivation of scheduled Tribes in India*, in: D.C. Sah/Yatindra Singh/Sisodia, *Tribal Issues in India*, Rawab Publications, Jaipur/New Delhi 2007, p.148-156

fishing. There is a growing gap in functional load between the tribal and other absolute minority languages and the regional official languages, let alone English or Hindi.

Abbi supports this claim: "It is sad that the Kurux and Kharia languages are quickly disappearing from most of the urbanised area of Ranchi district. This trend indicates that the urban tribes seldom consider it their privilege to speak their mother tongues. On the contrary, ignorance of the tribal languages is regarded as an enhancement of status and prestige. In speaking Hindi they feel superior in comparison to other fellow-tribal members who cannot speak it."[150] This negative attitude towards their languages has resulted in a massive shift to the dominant languages and in a drastic reduction in their use. In India, as elsewhere, languages are perceived as the decisive tool of success in a modern integrated society. Technological development, the major role of media and education, the modernisation of public administration and services, a globalising industry and the declining role of agriculture bring about new forms of competition and new criteria of individual success. When language is considered just as a means to individual economic success, minority languages are on the loosing side. Throughout history, most of the indigenous languages of North America, Australia and Russia have been replaced by the dominant national language, and the same is happening today in Brazil and Africa.

Many statements in India's political discourse clearly reveal that the protection of the languages of the tribal people were never a priority for Indian policy makers. These 'undeveloped' languages would not further the cause of science, and science and technology are considered a sign of advancement. Little effort has been made to understand the indigenous systems of science and medicine. In effect, an entire system was declared illegitimate as it does not conform to the State's Western liberal democratic notion of science and culture. It is not surprising, though deeply insulting, that the 'Report of the Official Language Commission' dismissed the tribal languages of the Northeast as 'insignificant speeches'. "One could not have asked for a more condescending attitude than what is reflected in the closing paragraphs of the report: 'We submit, therefore, that we ought to approach each of our languages in a spirit of humility and reverence, even if it be the rude unwritten speech of a tribal group."[151]
Is the loss of functional load and transparency causing the growing attrition

150 Anvita Abbi, *Tribal Languages*, in: R.S. Gupta/Anvita Abbi/Kailash S. Aggarval (eds.), *Language and the State*, Creative Books, New Delhi 1995, quoted by Pandharipande, p. 15
151 From the "Report of the Official Language Commission of the Government of India", 1957, quoted by Nikhil Nayyar, in „*The State and Language – The 8th Schedule*, New Delhi 1995

of tribal languages? The attrition of tribal languages is directly related to their reduced functional load,[152] but also to the conditions of settlement and the general context. In the case of internal migration, a growing phenomenon in India, languages are generally lost within two generations. On the other hand, tribal languages could retain some functional domains when tribal communities settle in a more isolated form. As they are not used in any major public domain of prestige, they face a loss of functional load, transparency and reputation vis-à-vis their own speakers. At best, a process of "folklorisation" begins, and languages are only used for unimportant domains. Languages are endangered when their functional load is reduced, but are maintained when the functional load is retained or even increased. With each loss of a domain, there is a loss of vocabulary, discourse patterns and stylistic range. It is easy to see how languages would eventually die, simply because, having been denuded of most of their domains, there is hardly any subject matter left for people to talk about, and hardly any vocabulary to do it with. The education system could play a crucial role in maintaining tribal languages' core domains, but the school cannot tackle the issue alone.

Among the tribal communities who still communicate entirely in their languages are the Mizos, the Arunachal tribes, the Andaman Islanders and Nicobarese. They are closely followed by the Nagas, Santals, and other groups in the mid-Indian tribal belt whose affinity with their traditional tribal languages is very strong.[153] An overwhelming proportion (90-100%) of the tribal population in a number of districts in the Northeast (Karbi Anglong and North Cachar Hills, Garo, Khasi and Jaintia Hills, Tuensang District of Nagaland) retain their own tribal languages. The proportion of speakers of a tribal language is equally high among the tribes living in Alwar, Bharatpur, Sawai Madhopur, Jaipur and Tonk (mostly Minas) as well as in Khota, Dungapur and Banswara (mostly Bhils). Over 90% of the tribals of Amaravati and Betul districts declare their traditional languages as their mother tongue. Likewise, tribal languages dominate in a cluster of Chotanagpur districts in Bihar and West Bengal and in certain parts of Himachal Pradesh (Chamba), Orissa (Ganjam), Andhra Pradesh (Warangal) and Tamil Nadu (Nilgiris).[154]

The regions characterized by the dominance of speakers of indigenous lan-

152 Pandharipande, *Minority matters*, p. 17

153 Aijazuddin Ahmad, Comment to Roy Burman, *The 8th Schedule of the Constitution and the Tribals*, in Gupta/Abbi/Aggarwal (eds.), *Language and the State – the 8th Schedule*, Creative Books, New Delhi, 1995, p. 162

154 Aijazuddin Ahmad, Comment to Roy Burman, p. 162

Tibetans and Ladakhi in a boarding school in Choglamsar (Ladakh, Jammu and Kashmir)

guages are generally skirted by districts where the share of speakers of the traditional languages declines to 70-90% range, which means that 10-30% have shifted to another, mostly the dominant regional language. Some 26 districts fall in this category.[155] Altogether these 54 districts (out of a total of 330 Indian districts), mostly lying in the Northeast and the mid-Indian tribal belt, account for more than two thirds of the tribal members who still retain their traditional languages. They account for one third of the tribal population of the country.[156]

6.5 Tribal peoples and education[157]

In 1981, the famous linguist D.P. Pattanayak stated: "Whether it is the sec-

155 Of these 6 lie in Bihar or Jharkhand (Hazaribagh, Ranchi, Dhanbad, Purnea, Saharsa, Monghyr); 5 in West Bengal (Murshidaba, Hooghly, Burdwan, Bankura, Midanpore); 3 in Madhya Pradesh (Jhabua, Khandwa, Bastar), 2 each in Assam (Goalpara, Cachar) and Orissa (Baudh, Kondmals, Mayurbhanj). Rajasthan (Bundi, Jhalawar); Maharashtra (Dhulia, Chandrapur); one each in Andhra Pradesh (Ananatapur): Himachal Pradesh (Kinnaur) and Karnataka (Koorg).

156 *ibidem,* p. 163

157 See also L. Khubchandani, *Language Demography and Languages in Education,* in UNESCO 2001, S. 36-43

tor, structure, mode of conveyance or management of education, unless one is clear about the goals of education in relation to the tribal community and is familiar with both the macro and micro context of the tribal societies, it is not possible to talk meaningful about tribal education."[158] This statement has not lost any of its relevance. Nevertheless, this text cannot go deeper into all latest findings about tribal societies, but must confine itself to the level of languages.

As has been said, languages spoken at home (or mother tongues) can play a crucial role in facilitating the education of children belonging to tribal communities. At present, the majority of India's tribal languages are absent as the medium of education in schools. Education, even at the boarding school level, is imparted mainly in the dominant regional languages included in the 8th Schedule of the Constitution. The sense of culture, identity and self-worth of tribal children (as of all children) is intimately linked to the possibility to use their mother-tongue. Hence, the rejection of the child's language by the school causes irreparable harm to the child's natural desire to learn as well as to the community's attitude to schooling. Equally significant are insights from recent research on the schooling of ethnic minorities that highlight the link between home languages and the general language and conceptual development of children from these communities. Research suggests that acceptance and encouragement of the first language of the child is necessary in order to promote achievement in the second language. These insights stress the necessity to adopt tribal languages as the medium of education, at least in the early stages of schooling. On the other hand, it follows that the drop-out of tribal children from school and their poor achievement may be due, at least in part, to the educational system's rejection of the linguistic and cultural resources that children bring with them.[159]

"India has failed to meet the commitment of universalizing primary education and ensuring a basic human right because of this problem of language" states a public institution of the State of Orissa[160], and the tribal peoples are certainly among those ethno-social groups most affected by the insufficient implementation of the basic right to education. In such States as Orissa, Madhya Pradesh and Jharkhand, home to a high number of tribal peoples, the nexus between language and primary education is intricate. There is

158 D.P. Pattanayak, *Multilingualism*, 1981, p. 80

159 Geetha B. Nambissan, *Language and Schooling of Tribal Children: Issues relating to the Medium of Instruction*, in: In: R.S. Gupta/Anvita Albi/Kailash S. Aggarval (eds.), *Language and the State*, Creative Books, New Delhi 1995, p. 191-192

160 Academy of Tribal Dialects and Cultures, ST/SC Development Department, *The Linguistic Survey and Mapping*, Orissa 1999

high linguistic diversification between the various tribal cultures, but no single common language. "Somebody belonging to a monolingual reality tend to consider the multilingual complexity of language as inconvenient, uneconomic and a burden, and therefore ignores the theoretical possibility to meet the social requirements for education in mother tongues."[161] This is strongly affecting tribal languages. The Indian educational system apparently has bypassed the tribal languages to a considerable extent. The number of tribal languages used as the medium language of instruction in primary schools is very low. Only because of long-lasting and vigorous protest, some tribal languages in West Bengal and Assam are now used as medium languages up to the lower secondary level. For example, Santhali in West Bengal, and Bodo and Mishing in Assam could achieve this position, but the challenges of inexperienced teachers, insufficient textbooks and a lack of public support for language acquisition planning have kept the experiment far from success.

The tribal schools in different parts of India are run by the Education Department as well as by the Welfare Department. Since the Education Departments have better facilities, their inspection is more systematic. Unlike urban schools, the tribal schools may be classified as "roadside schools" and "interior schools". Such tribal schools are not inspected for years and suffer from teacher absenteeism. Free books supplied by the Welfare Department are seldom available in adequate numbers. As a result the well to do among the tribal peoples are forced to buy books from the market. No book is written in tribal languages. There is no strategy to link the home language with the school language. Thus, the implementation of the TLF is almost impossible when the mother tongue of the speakers is tribal and does not have a script, a standard code, or literature. Eventually, "... the current concern for uniform design, structure and content of education caters to neither, confuses issues relating to the purpose and goal of education, particularly the tribal sector."[162] Education is expected to help the student develop necessary skills including the linguistic competence for participation and involvement in the administrative process and in nation building. Therefore, the plans for language use in education and in administration must be compatible with each other. If the language of education acts as a counterpoise to the language of administration, it will create tensions which may frustrate planning itself. For most tribal members, both the language of education and administration are alien. Those who are lucky to have had an education through their mother tongue up to a certain level find the doors of privilege through participation in the administration inac-

161 D.P. Pattanayak, *Tribal Languages in Education,* p. 53

162 D.P. Pattanayak, *Multilingualism*, 1981, p. 80

cessible, as the language of administration is alien. The tribal frustration concerning the process and product of planning is thus rooted in the discriminatory use of language. This explains need to upgrade the functional load of tribal languages, providing a political and administrative context of self-government with real bilingual administration, such as reinforcing the quota system for some tribal peoples in the State and Union administration. On the other hand "...also on the side of the minorities there is often a lack of motivation to preserve the language. Due to the ST-regulations part of the tribal elite can often get a public job. Then they migrate to major towns and are absorbed in the mainstream. Mostly they don't come back to the communities to work."[163]

Tribal education needs special attention for the following reasons:[164]
a) The social structure of tribal societies is different from that of non-tribal ones. Different ethnic groups have different structural problems.
b) Most of the tribal communities still have a different level of economic organization and different livelihood. Their life cycle is different from the non-tribal counterpart.
c) The tribal groups are dispersed in large, not easily accessible areas, and often live in villages made up of many hamlets. This fact makes the rational organization of schools difficult.
d) Many small tribal groups, speaking different languages and dialects, mostly unwritten, find education difficult. Both education managers and teachers erroneously consider economic and societal reasons solely responsible for low achievement. The fact that language plays a major role in the low performance of the tribal child has not been properly appreciated.
e) As there is no tradition of education in the family background for generations, and the tribal child living on the fringes of non-tribal society finds himself cognitively unequal to the non-tribal child, an inferiority complex is built into his mind right from the beginning of formal schooling. As the adults are not convinced of the benefits of formal education, and are consequently illiterate, it is not possible to escape large-scale waste and stagnation.
f) In the absence of trained SC candidates, outsiders are appointed as teachers and administrators, who without access to their languages, lack first-hand communication.

In the absence of such basic conditions it is not possible for the education department to produce teaching materials to ensure the teaching of the mother tongue, even at the primary level. Young children, who are speak-

163 From an interview with Prof. Omkar N. Koul, IILS, Shillong, 20 March 2009
164 These arguments are taken form D.P. Pattanayak, *Multilingualism*, 1981, p. 85

ers of tribal languages, tend to begin to learn the state language at the primary level of education and soon become bilingual. The use of the state language in school further causes the reduction of the domain of use of their first (tribal) language, since bilingual children tend to use the State official language (as opposed to their mother tongue) in most public domains. After a couple of generations, the language of home (of the tribal communities) is gradually replaced by the dominant state language, thus causing severe attrition of the tribal language. In contrast, those tribal children who do not go to school tend to preserve their languages. This phenomenon supports the hypothesis that a guaranteed functional load (i.e. sustained use in a domain) guarantees the maintenance of a language, while the reduction and/or elimination of functional load leads to language attrition.[165]

This kind of analysis could be done not only with reference to tribal education, but generally with regard to the role of minority languages in education. However, "...pledging for education in the mother tongue of tribal people is not equivalent to indulging to 'nostalgic romanticism' and has no compunction in making them perform in state capitals on festive occasions"[166], the kind of benevolent paternalism so well known from the Chinese approach to ethnic minorities. The attitude of the governments, which have special responsibilities for the promotion of tribal education under Article 46 of the Indian Constitution, is by and large guided by welfare considerations. But education for tribal peoples, indeed, is no issue of charity, but an issue of civil and human rights.[167]

"Tribal identity is not a matter of shame. It is true that many groups who are completely acculturated, wear it as a badge of privilege. But there is no reason to expect or demand that the tribal should either wholly retain or lose all of his culture. If the educated goes through a basically western education, but retains something what can be recognized as Indian, there is no reason why the tribal could not retain something of the tribal heritage. The education system offers little by way of tribal culture in the school curriculum. It has not recognized the triple axes of the cultural identity of a tribal in terms of 'tribalism, pluralism and nationalism' and has not evolved any strategy which will ensure a smooth transition from the home language to the school language at an early stage so as to permit him to avail of the benefits of higher studies without loss of cultural identity and individuality.

165 Pandharipande, *Minority matters,* p. 13

166 D.P. Pattanayak, *Multilingualism,* 1981, p. 86. He adds: „Others want them to be modernized and civilized, which as ‚westernization' means giving up mores, values and ways of life."

167 Ibidem, p. 86

The plea here is for ameliorative planning which will make education relevant tot he life of the tribal and help him take advantage of the mainstream education as an equal without sense of deficiency and oppression."[168]

Given this situation, the CIIL developed a program of bilingual primary education linking reading and writing of the home language with speaking of the regional language. Devoting 80% of the available time to home language and 20% to the regional language in the first years, by end of the primary school this ratio was reversed. This model achieved much success in granting sufficient competence in the home languages. Garo and Khasi people in Meghalaya are now introducing this model in primary and secondary schools. In 1976, 33 tribal languages were used in primary schools all over India, but none were used as a dominant school medium language. Generally after class 2 or 3 they become subject languages and fall into oblivion.[169] Only 6 tribal languages are used as medium languages throughout all of primary and secondary school, with only Santhali in West Bengal offered as subject of examination at the end of secondary school.[170] Other government agencies engaged in the development programmes of tribal peoples have strongly emphasized the importance of improving the schemes of tribal education.

For mother tongue education to become a reality for tribal children, concerted efforts within and outside the education system are necessary. The role of policy makers, academics, researchers, educators and teachers has already been highlighted. Tribal communities will also have to be involved in order to understand the linguistic and cultural resources that children bring to school and to identify languages that should initially be used as media of instruction. It will also be necessary to elicit the cooperation of speakers of these languages and to encourage parental and community support for education. The demand for 'quality' education in mother tongues must become part of language movements for democratic rights in general and the rights of children in particular. It will then be possible for schools to give the mother tongue of the tribal children back to them and enrich their experience of education.

---

168 D.P. Pattanayak, *Multilingualism*, 1981, p. 87

169 D.P. Pattanayak, *Tribal Languages in Education,* p. 57. The "Position of Languages in School Curriculum" in India lists Angami, Ao, Bodo, Chakasang, Chang Naga, Garo, Hmar, Ho, Karen, Kharia, Khasi, Khiemnungar, Konyak, Kuki, Lotha, Lushai, Manipuri, Mizo, Mundari, Nicobarese, Oraon, Phom, Rengma, Sangtam, Santhali, Sema, Yeimchungere, Zeliang, Gondi, Kokborok, Mishing, Rabha and Saora as educational languages.

170 D.P. Pattanayak, *Tribal Languages in Education,* p. 55

Chapter 7

Education and minority languages

7.1 The debate on the right to mother tongue education

In India's multilingual context there is a wide variation of education models in the different States as far as the medium, content, duration and even denomination of educational stages are concerned.[171] In 1980, education shifted to the "concurrent list": hence, both Union and States are allowed to initiate legislation on education. According to Article 345 Const. the States are free to choose their official language, but they must respect the fundamental right of linguistic and religious minorities to preserve their identity (Article 29 Const.) and to allow the establishment of privately run institutions for education in the mother tongue (Article 30 Const.). Education is a matter of the concurrent list and the Centre provides only guidelines, e.g. the National Curriculum Framework for School Education of 2000.

The education system of ancient India and of British colonial rule was characterised by a hierarchy of linguistic skills and medium languages, ranging from local dialects to the high-level classical Sanskrit classes. In the use of language the schools had to be tuned to the requirements of identity attitudes and purposes according to the linguistic plurality of the social context. On the one hand there were Sanskrit and Arabic/Persian speaking elites, on the other hand schools in local or regional languages for the common people. There were obvious differences in the languages used by the rulers and the ruled, but few territories had just one language for every domain.

Later, under British rule, the introduction of the "vernacular languages" proceeded very slowly, as English replaced the classical languages of the elite's education. According to the British rulers, the Indian vernacular languages should not be developed for use in education, an approach which effectively postponed their introduction in formal domains for one more century.[172]

171 See L. Khubchandani, *Language in education*, 2001, p. 30

172 *ibidem*, p.30. During the British rule three patterns of education emerged: 1. The English medium in urban centers for the education of the elite, right from the primary stage; 2. The two-tier medium, vernacular medium for primary education and English medium for the advanced stage in towns; 3. The vernacular medium in rural areas (for primary education). To be recalled also Macaulay's hard line (1835): ""...imparting Western knowledge through English and then only to a minority". By that doctrine the use of Indian languages

The highly selective education structure of colonial times was vehemently criticised by national leaders of the struggle for independence – Gandhi, Gokhale, Tagore and others – who pleaded for a universal elementary education in Indian mother tongues.

In independent India the demand for a general education system based on mother tongues as media of instruction was associated with the cultural and political resurgence of the "linguistically defined States", in addition to the democratic principle of ensuring equality of opportunities through education. However, the concept of mother tongue, a basic concept in western pedagogy, has some different connotations in India's culturally plural context. The official commissions tended to employ a wider interpretation of the concept of mother tongue education and often classified minority languages as dialects, especially if they were not written.[173]

Mother tongue identity in India is not always congruous with actual language usage, and not always identified with a particular territory as is typical in the European experience. For instance the split between Urdu, Hindi and Punjabi was more ideological than linguistic and was not related to a specific territory, meaning that the process was heavily influenced by political circumstances. On the other side, the linguistic minorities preferred a narrow interpretation of mother tongue, seeking to have their languages accepted as such, and insisting upon the right to education in their mother tongues. The Constitution, although enshrining the right to education in one's mother tongue (Article 30), gives no explicit statements about the medium languages to be used in schools. Every State Government, while respecting the principle of mother tongue schools at the primary level and the freedom to run private minority schools, is free to choose the language used as medium language of the State's schools or the languages to be taught under the TLF.[174]

---

was postponed for formal domains.

173 See L. Khubchandani, *Language Policy and Education in the Indian Subcontinent*, in: S. May and N.H. Hornberger (eds.), *Enyclopaedia of Language and Education* (2d edition), Vol. I, Language Policy and Political Issues in Education, Springer Science, New York 2008, p. 373. Especially in Northern India, it has to be taken into account that not that much language barriers between Hindi, Urdu and Punjabi were relevant for the population, but religious identity and value systems giving raise to more ideological than linguistic cleavages. The issue of mother tongue acquires a different rating.

174 For instance in Karnataka: while the Government tried to push the regional official language (Kannada), the minorities tried to find shelter in English medium schools. Also Kannada speakers choose English as second language and not Hindi. The State Committee in 1981 recommended, that Kannada should be a compulsory subject of every school and the sole first language in the secondary school, but the Supreme Court did not accept it.

As mother tongue, generally the first language acquired in infancy, is understood: "The term mother tongue means the native speech acquired in infancy, through which the child gets socialised: it claims some bearing on 'intuitive' competence, and potentially it can be individually identifiable. This term is mainly categorised by one's allegiance to a particular tradition, and it is societally identifiable."[175] The term mother tongue has been questioned through such arguments. If all minority languages without a written tradition were merely considered "dialects" (as the British did), this would be equivalent of denying equal rights to linguistic minorities on the ground of practicability and superiority, similar to the French view of treating minority languages such as Provencal and Occitan as dialects of the dominant French.

As mentioned above, mother tongue identity is retained in a manner 'not always congruous' with the actual usage of languages by a given speaker. But what are the reasons for this language switch? Largely the fact that minority languages have not developed to cover certain domains, and 'ruling languages' are much more dominant and do not give space to them.

"The heterogeneity of communication patterns in many regions of the Subcontinent, the unequal cultivation of different languages for use as medium of instruction, the demands of elegant versions of mother tongue for formal purposes, the non-availability of personnel with adequate command over the textbook language, and the switching over to another medium in the multi-tier medium system without adequate preparation are some of the difficulties faced by the learners who are initiated into education through the mother tongue medium. These ground realities have led to the re-examination of the supremacy of the mother tongue medium stretched over the entire education career."[176] The task of increasing literacy and accommodating the right to education of all citizens in such linguistically heterogeneous countries as India is always connected with a range of political, ideological and practical considerations.[177]

In the 2001 Census, by 'mother tongue' people were asked to indicate the language spoken in the household. Skutnabb-Kangas pleads for a statement

---

175 See L. Khubchandani, *Language Policy and Education in the Indian Subcontinent,* 2008, p. 372

176 *Ibidem*, p.373

177 Somebody even questions the need of literacy of minor languages: "Today there is a greater awareness to make education relevant to the environment and learner needs. Literacy in certain society forms important for the right of the individuals, but not a necessary condition of his survival and dignity." Khubchandani, p. 374

of the parents, who should assess what is or are the "family languages".[178] This text considers as mother tongue the language first learned or used within the family of a child, and in the case of mixed families the first languages used by both parents when speaking with the child. It has been proven by international research that the mother tongue is the ideal medium to ensure the balanced socio-cultural, cognitive and socio-cultural development of a child. In India, and many other cases, however, many minority languages have a limited vocabulary and higher education is not always feasible. There is a widespread opinion that pupils' participation in college and university education, in professional development and generally in social and political life would be jeopardized. Thus, many minority language speakers face the decision to forget about linguistic rights in formal education in order to acquire full fluency in the dominating languages so as to keep pace in professional life. As long as minor languages are not developed for scientific purposes, they will play a secondary role also on secondary level of school education, let alone the university level.[179]

Regarding the challenge of establishing education in the Indian mother tongues, the political elite responded that a language can become a medium if a minimum of written standardisation has been obtained. But in India, until very recent times, the majority of languages were not written, nor was a majority of the population literate. In India literacy is far from including all social groups and the rate of illiteracy, although steadily declining, still lies at 35% (2001census). Indeed, in a country with about 350 million illiterate people, the issue of the protection of minority languages is to be considered in different terms compared with industrialised countries. Illiteracy in India is distributed very unequally with regard to regions (States), social classes (castes) and linguistic communities (peoples, ethno-linguistic groups). There is a remarkable North-South differential. Kerala ranks at the top with 90% literacy rate, whereas the densely populated Hindi-speaking States of the North are well below of the average (Madhya Pradesh, Uttar Pradesh, Bihar and Rajasthan). In India, many smaller languages were not recognised as languages appropriate for education only due to the lack of a script and of standardisation. In turn, the missing role or domain as a language in education or its use as medium of instruction has prevented several languages from becoming "literary productive", which in turn has prevented their recognition as scheduled languages – a vicious cycle.

---

178 See B. Mallikarjun, *Indian languages and the digital divide*, p.12

179 Take the example of Tamil Nadu: some students go through Tamil medium schools, but they do not achieve good levels in technology courses. They can get jobs only in Tamil Nadu, not in other states. So later they have to learn the technical terms also in English.

Article 350 A of the Constitution accorded the right to mother tongue education at the primary level to all linguistic minorities, and consequently the States are obliged to provide for instruction in the mother tongue at the primary level whenever 40 pupils of that language or at least 10 pupils of one single class request it. But it was not specified to what extent or duration the mother tongue would have to be used in primary education. Thus, in practice, due to high financial and administrative costs, almost all non-scheduled minority languages are used just as "preparatory medium" in the first classes and are later excluded from being used as full media of instruction and as examination languages. Although in principle India's political elite accepted the right to education in the mother tongue, there was no consensus regarding which languages should be accepted as "mother tongues appropriate for formal education" and whether children could and also should be instructed in languages lacking a script and/or a written literary tradition.

In addition, uncountable parents, speaking a minority language and having no other choice, continue to opt for a language with more prestige that offers more professional opportunities than an education in their own mother tongue, which is deprived of a literary value. However, the Governments, supported by such institutions as the CIIL,[180] made considerable efforts to empower some non written minority languages in order to enhance the instruction of smaller or tribal languages. Often those languages were given the same script as the dominating regional official language, for the purpose of issuing textbooks. As many minority languages could not reach higher levels of functional load and significance in their written standardised form in such a short time, the results of adopting the concept of primary education in the mother tongue often did not match the expectations of their speakers. Hence, the very concept of education and literacy in the mother tongue was questioned and some experiments were abandoned after some years. It would be worthwhile to enquire whether this happened due to the free and democratic decision of a linguistic minority or due to the lack of honest political commitment of the education authorities responsible.

7.2 Some basic facts about language and education in India

The Sixth Survey (INDIA 1993) records a total of 765,000 schools in the country at the primary level (classes I-V). On average, in India there is one

180 For a presentation of the Central Institute of Indian Languages see the annexes.

primary school available for every 1,096 people. In the midst of a wide variation of school regulations in different states, elementary education has acquired a distinct pattern in choosing the following as media of instruction:

1. Dominant regional languages
2. Pan-Indian languages English and Hindi
3. Neighbouring regional languages
4. Newly cultivated languages (mostly tribal and other minority languages) as preparatory media.[181]

Dominant regional language schools account for 88% of all schools (672,000 in 1991) at the primary level. There are 17 such languages spread in States and Union territories, listed in order of the numerical strength of their speakers: Hindi, Telugu, Bengali, Marathi, Tamil, Urdu, Gujarati, Kannada, Malayalam, Oriya, Punjabi, Assamese, Kashmiri, Sindhi, Konkani, Nepali, and Manipuri. In addition, three tribal languages – Khasi and Garo in Meghalaya, Mizo in Mizoram – are also introduced as principal medium in the respective States on primary level. English is claimed as a dominant medium in the North-eastern States of Sikkim, Arunachal Pradesh and Nagaland. Nevertheless, schools with just one medium of instruction rather remained as an exception: "Though many States prefer to promote the exclusive use of respective regional languages as the medium of instruction, in practice many students experience a shift in language medium at one or another stage, depending on context, domain and channel such as: students listen to one language and write answers in another; formal teaching in the classroom is conducted in one language, but informal explanations are provided in another. This milieu promotes a good deal of code-switching and hybridisation of two or more contact languages."[182]

A few multilingual States, mostly in North-eastern India as Meghalaya, Nagaland and Sikkim, have introduced bilingual education as a state education policy, in which a developing language is used as a complementary medium, together with English, Hindi, or the regional language as the principal medium. In this context "composite" courses are developed by combining a tribal language and elementary Hindi as a single course. The 5th NCERT Survey of 1993 records nearly 7% bilingual schools at the primary level country-wide (approximately 51,000 schools out of a total 765,000). The proportion of bilingual schools is higher in urban cosmopolitan areas with more heterogeneous populations.[183] Initially the NCERT (All India Survey 1974) counted 80 languages used as media of instruction; today there are

181 L. Khubchandani, *Language Policy and Education in the Indian Subcontinent,* 2008, p.374

182 *ibidem*, p.374

183 B. Mallikarjun, *Language rights and education in India*, Language in India, February 2004

Teaching staff of the Ramakrishna-school in Nartiang (Meghalaya)

fewer than 47. Apart from the 17 prominent regional languages, quoted above, and English, the Survey records 14 additional languages utilized as partial media of instruction in bilingual schools: Maithili, Santali, Kurukh, Nicobarese, Tibetan, Limbu, Bhotia, Bodo, Kokborok and five Naga languages (Ao, Sema, Angami, Lotha, Zeliang). A large number of schools in Bihar (approximately 21,000, this is 31% of Bihar's schools) have been experimenting with Sanskrit as a partial medium of instruction. With the thrust toward modernization, schools with major languages as media of instruction have been increasing, and the number of ethnic schools (minority languages as medium) has been decreasing.

Table 15 - Number of languages taught in the schools

Stage	Third survey	Fifth Survey	Sixth survey
Total number of languages	67	44	41
Primary school		43	33
Upper primary		31	25
Secondary		22	21
Higher secondary		20	18

Source: Mallikarjun, p.14, Indian languages and the digital divide

At present, there are three major contact languages spread with varied intensity – Hindi, Urdu and English –, utilized as media of instruction throughout the country. The pan-Indian distribution of Hindi and Urdu schools, spread across 24 states out of 32, with a formidable total of nearly 324,000 schools (42.4% of all existing schools), plays a prominent role in the primary education network of the country. Hindi-medium facilities are also provided in nearly 2,900 schools located outside the north-central Hindi-Urdu-belt. Urdu has a significant presence as a minority language medium in Hindi-dominant states, with nearly 7,200 schools; it is also spread in 10 states of the Southern and Western regions (over 8,000 schools).[184]

Under the TLF, in India adopted since 1968, every child is supposed to learn three languages in its school career: its mother tongue, English and Hindi, and, whenever its mother tongue is Hindi, the child is supposed to learn another modern English language, preferably a South Indian language. This formula yet, as explained later, never was strictly applied in India's school system. Although usually three languages are taught either as medium or as subject, the kind of language and the stages of introducing them vary from State to State and one type of school to another. In some schools two languages are introduced in the first primary classes and the third one is added in class VI. In others the second language starts at class III and the third at class VI. As for absolute minority languages spoken as mother tongues the „Bilingual Transfer Model", elaborated by the CIIL, is adopted in some States: the mother tongue is used both as a subject and medium of instruction in the first three years of primary education, then the State's official language is introduced at class III as a subject followed by other two languages (mostly English and/or Hindi) at class VI. The children of minority mother tongue have to learn four languages.

In a survey of 2004, based on a representative sample of data from different parts of the country, conducted by the Indian Institute of Language Studies, New Delhi, related directly to the use of language in education and elaborating data from Tamil Nadu, Karnataka, Andhra Pradesh, Delhi, Jammu and Kashmir, Punjab, Maharashtra, West Bengal and Orissa, the following findings are reported:[185]

a) There is a general preference for the study of mother tongue as well as in English as a subject in early school education i.e. primary and middle classes. The children whose mother tongue is not taught in the schools (for example, Kolami in Maharashtra, Kashmiri and Dogri in

184 L. Khubchandani, *Language Policy and Education in the Indian Subcontinent,* 2008, p.375

185 Omkar N. Koul, *Language, Education and Communication*, Delhi 2005, p.49-51

the State of Jammu and Kashmir) opt for the state official language as a subject of study. In the non-Hindi speaking states which follow the TLF, Hindi is taught in addition to the state official language as well as English. Whereas the public/private schools introduce English as a subject from the very beginning, it is introduced as a subject at the third or sixth standard in other schools.

b) The preference for the use of English as a medium of instruction increases with the level of education. Both local languages (mostly the state official language) as well as English are preferred as the media of instruction in most of the states (though the percentages vary) in the early school education. There is a wide preference for the use of English as the medium of instruction in the secondary education and the higher education.

c) The mother tongue is preferred as the primary language for the communication at home. It is only where the mother tongues do not have roles in education and administration, parents prefer to use the school language (state official language and/or English) for talking to the children at home.

d) Appropriate to a multilingual situation, the language proficiency of the respondents reveals proficiency in more than one language (though the percentages of the proficiency vary) in all the states. Most of the respondents have listed their mother tongues/state official languages higher in proficiency. Sometimes, the proficiency of languages is not linked to the language taught or learnt at school. Some languages are learnt as a result of language contact.

e) The language attitude of the respondents appears to be directly related to their emotions. Most of the respondents like their mother tongues as ‚the best'. Sometimes, the languages of preference is linked to its use in the society. The Kolami speakers, the only ‚absolute minority language' covered by the sample, consider the state official language (Marathi) as the best. Similarly, a few Dogri and Kashmiri mother tongue speakers place English and/or the state official language at the higher level of their preference than their mother tongues.

In India there are basically 5 kinds of schools: government schools, central and sainik schools, public schools and private schools. The government schools, established by the State governments, use the respective State official languages as medium of instruction. In those States, which have adopted English as official language (Mizoram, Sikkim, Nagaland, Meghalaya, some Autonomous Districts of Assam) English is used as medium of instruction right from the beginning. The Central and Sainik schools, established for the children of central go-

vernment employees and army personnel, also use English as medium of instruction as these families are often transferred from one place to another. According to the New Education Policy of 1986 India has established the Navodaya schools as model schools of learning for rural students for equalizing the quality education opportunities between rural and urban students. In practice these schools are extending English as medium of instruction in rural areas, as ‚quality' in India often is synonymous with English.
The public schools, which in reality are privately run, cater to the needs of the children of India's upper class and use English as medium of instruction. Following this model, originally introduced by the colonial administration, private English medium schools are mushrooming all over the country, as the growing Indian middle class can afford the tuition fees.

English-medium public schools, a dominant colonial legacy, also form a vital part of the Indian education system, starting from primary education itself. After independence in 1947, English medium schools, numbering over 35,000 (4.6% of all schools), continue to be identified with urbanity, status, power and career specialisation. There are more English schools, more English teachers and learners, along with a flourishing English press, than when the British left the country. The base for English education has been expanding. English schools have become a regular feature of the education system available in almost all States. While in the past the preference for English-medium education was confined to urban populations, this trend is now extending to the countryside as well. Different types of schools have been supportive of extending English as the medium of instruction in rural areas.[186] The growing importance of English in education is also reflected by the fact that State after State is introducing English beginning in class I. At this point the NCLM raises the question: "What is the overall objective of language teaching? The significance of proficiency in more languages is out of question. But if three languages have to be studied compulsorily, which skills do students have to attain and up to which level they are allowed to study in their mother tongue?"[187]

The English medium education in India is bound to expand in the years to come. Not only is English the dominating language in the top-ranking university colleges of agriculture, science, technology, management and medicine and the exclusive medium of the so-called „Central Universities", but also a growing role of English in universities at State level which adopt English as the prevailing medium in all disciplines. Thus, a kind of „cascade-effect" for all preliminary stages of the education system can be observed.

186 *Ibidem*, p.376
187 See NCLM, 42d report, p. 13, at: http://nclm.nic.in

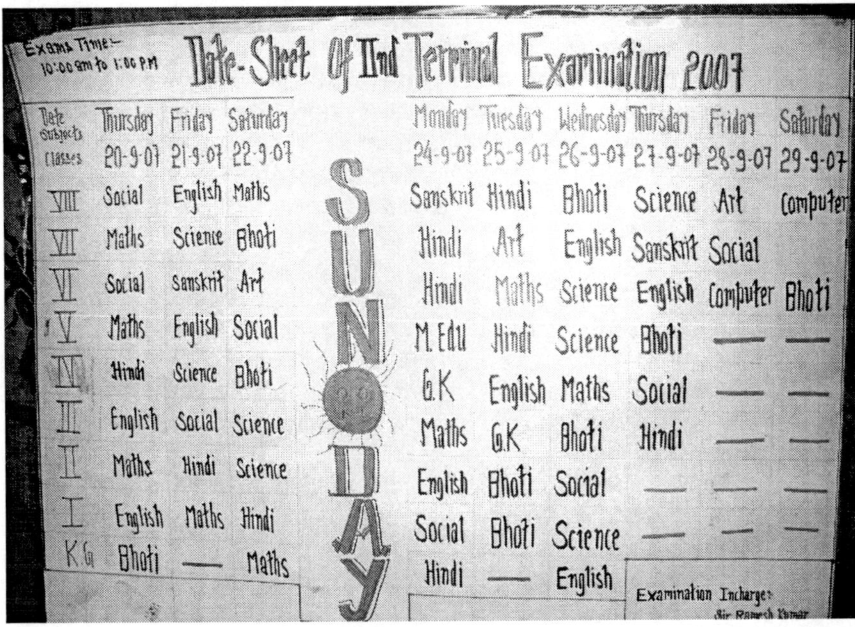

The school curriculum of a boarding school of Bhotia minority in Tabo, Spiti valley (Himachal Pradesh)

Most students who have done their secondary education in public schools or Central schools are most competitive for all Indian top level universities. Those who study through other English medium schools get admission in the State institutions of higher learning.[188] University departments run in other medium languages end up by being classified as second class institutions. The same effect can be observed with the selection for the recruitment to India's top central civil services. Though also other prominent State official languages are used as medium for examinations, English is widely preferred for some other reasons, basically for the availability of instructional materials and for the flexibility and mobility which this language offers.

This situation is likely to prevail in the future, as the number of families in the position to send their children to English medium schools is growing and the importance of English is further fostered by the globalization and its dominance in business administration, IT, international media and science and technology. „India has by and large realised the importance of English in education. Its role and function in education have undergone significant changes lately. English is no more viewed as a language of convenience

188 Omkar N. Koul, *Language, Education and Communication*, Delhi 2005, p.53

used by the British for administration, but as a vehicle for acquiring modern scientific and technological knowledge crucial for economic development. No matter how many attempts are made to arouse sentiments against the English language by projecting it as an alien language for political reasons, ist importance in education cannot be ignored. It is the market force which reigns supreme. English is accepted throughout the country as the only medium for their access to modern knowledge and will continue to be so in the years to come." [189]

Being the current „linguistic battle" in the Indian education system fought between the State official languages (not the scheduled languages as they are neither all official languages nor all used as medium of instruction) and English, the losers are – apart from other foreign languages – first of all the minority languages. Not only can almost no territory in India be found, where an „absolute minority language" is used as medium of instruction for both the primary and secondary level of instruction, but minority languages speakers are engaged in a defensive struggle for keeping their language even as a thoroughgoing subject and as medium (or as co-ordinate medium in bilingual schools) for the first classes of the primary school. The majority of India's languages is not in any form taught in schools (in 2004 37 languages out of 114 languages with more than 10.000 speakers).

7.3 A current dilemma in India's education policy

India's education policy is trying to meet the requirement of multilingualism with an enormous array of mechanisms and technical and financial means. But with regard to minority languages, the whole complex system is rather limited, as education from class I to XII (especially higher education) is granted only in the languages listed in the 8th Schedule. Accordingly, smaller, but scheduled languages with no territory of reference are accepted as medium and education languages (e.g. Sindhi, Sanskrit), whereas languages with a much higher number of speakers and links to a territory as Santhali, Gondi, Bhili are mostly restricted to an "auxiliary" role on the primary level. The Official Language Commission operating in the 1950s maintained that only the big and evolved languages with an existing literary tradition could be accepted as medium languages. To grant education in the language of every linguistic minority respecting the numerical criteria (10/40 ratio), was considered too costly and complicated.[190]

189 ibidem, p. 55

190 See L. Khubchandani, *Language, Education and Social Justice*, Poona 1986, p. 53

When the 7th Amendment of the Constitution recognized the right of linguistic minorities to education in the mother tongue under Article 350 (A), the legal context changed, but the lack of resources did not. Particular difficulties arose with the indigenous, non-written languages, for which a script had yet to be developed.[191] For many non-scheduled languages the effort to develop a script was simply seen as too high. As many such languages, in particular tribal languages, are even not standardized, it was even more complicated to establish a script accepted by all. "For example , in the North-eastern state of Assam and in Central India (Madhya Pradesh), whose tribal populations are 7% and 22% respectively of the tribal population in the country, the 22 tribes of Assam have 60 mother tongues grouped into 40 languages, and the 58 tribes of Madhya Pradesh have 93 mother tongues grouped into 38 languages."[192] Thus, the heterogeneity of the Adivasi languages was never really tackled by the education authorities and planners. Even the NCERT, the responsible body for working out the textbooks, retained those languages "uncultivated dialects with no educational importance".[193]

In 1986, the All Educational Survey of India listed 44 languages taught in schools, but 97% of all schools were working with the 15 scheduled languages as medium languages. There was a decreasing effort on the part of the authorities to support non-scheduled languages in developing their vocabulary and to assist them in modernization and standardisation. Thirteen years later, the 6th All India Education Survey (1999) stated that 41 languages were taught as school languages, and 19 were used as media of instruction at different levels. In other words, given a total number of 114 registered languages in India, 73 linguistic communities do not have any formal school education in the mother tongue at all and 95 linguistic communities do not have their mother tongue used as a medium language at any level.

What are the main problems at present? Khubchandani identifies three:[194]

- Gaps between high-brow and low-brow education
- Gaps between spoken languages and medium in school
- The mixing of languages

191 In India there are 10 major scripts (Nagari, Perso-Arabic, Gurumukhi, Gujarati, Bengali-Assami-Manipuri, Oriya, Telugu-Kannada, Tamil, Malayalam, Roman) and 14 indigenous scripts.

192 Horst Friedrich Rolly, *Bildungsrecht und Bildungspraxis religiöser und linguistischer Minderheiten in Indien*, Peter Lang Verlag, Frankfurt 2002, p. 225

193 Nambissan 1994, quoted by Rolly, *Bildungsrecht und Bildungspraxis, 2002,* p. 225

194 L. Khubchandani, *Language in education*, 2001, p. 34

In certain places, language programmes are allotted a disproportionate share of the total teaching in order to suit the climate of language privileges: "In multilingual societies, the ideal claim and the real function of a language might be at variance. One notices a wide gap between the language policies professed and actual practice in a classroom. It is not unusual to find in many institutions anomalous patterns of communication where the teacher and the taught interact in one language, classes are conducted in another, textbooks are written in a third and answers are given in a fourth language or style."[195] This practice does not appear to be equivalent to a multilingual school, which seeks to impart written fluency in three languages, while putting these languages on equal footing. Nor does it appear to solve the difficulties of the application of the so-called TLF to the speakers of minority languages.

In this context, smaller minority languages risk being used in schools only to meet formal legal requirements: "In the absence of political will, many proponents of the status quo try to walk on a tight rope. They adopt a minimalist approach to providing opportunities for mother tongue education with vague commitments and qualifying clauses which are, in turn, a result of negotiating with contradictory agendas of market forces serving the interests of the elite, and succumbing to the demands of ethnic pressures."[196] Thus, as Khubchandani concludes, the concept of many States today is to "offer some opportunities for the mother tongue education with vague commitments, on the other hand large concessions to market forces which means enforcing medium language English and Hindi and the State language."

At present, in India there is a broad consensus on the TLF to tackle the basic requirement of teaching at least three languages through the education system and to put the students in the position to cope with the country's multilingualism. Each State can decide freely under his legislation when choosing the relevant languages, their duration of instruction, and their role as subject or medium. But how can the fundamental interest of India's education policies to ensure education in three languages be brought in line with the right to education in the mother tongue?

195 *ibidem*, p. 34

196 L. Khubchandani, *Language Policy and Education in the Indian Subcontinent,* 2008, p.377

Principal and teachers of the Government primary school in Jowai (Jaintia Hills, Meghalaya)

7.4 Which medium of instruction?

Which languages are used as media of instruction at the higher secondary level in each State and UT? India can be divided in four groups based on the number of languages used as medium on this stage.[197]

a) The four-language media group
Four languages are used in Andhra Pradesh, Assam, Gujarat, Jammu and Kashmir, Karnataka, Maharashtra, Tamil Nadu, West Bengal and the UT Andaman and Nicobar Islands and Delhi. These languages are the State official language, English and Hindi and in addition the language of the largest minority group living in the State, which sometimes has the status of a second official language, e.g. Bengali in Assam, Urdu in Karnataka, Nepali in West Bengal. In certain States the languages of contiguous States are used as educational media, e.g. Tamil and Marathi in Karnataka. The diachronic comparison shows that recently languages are deleted as medium, which are not languages of contiguous States. Generally, when languages are deleted from use, they are generally either the non-scheduled langua-

197 Omkar N. Koul, *Language, Education and Communication*, Delhi 2005, p.76

ges or the classical languages. Only in Assam some tribal languages are used for imparting higher education (Garo in Meghalaya).

b) The three-language media group

The States of Bihar, Madhya Pradesh, Manipur, Orissa, Punjab, Tripura, Kerala and the UTs of Chandigarh, Dodra and Nagar Haveli, and Pondicherry come under this group. Omkar N. Koul states in this regard: „The synchronic comparison also shows that the languages that have been discontinued as media for higher secondary education are languages whose speakers forma smaller minority. The languages that have been discontinued as media of instruction are Bengali, Oriya and Telugu in Bihar, Bengali in Manipur, Telugu and Bengali in Orissa, Urdu in Punjab, Hindi and Tamil in Kerala, and Telugu in Pondicherry."[198]

Moreover „...some tribal and non-scheduled and non-tribal languages are used as instructional media for primary and upper primary education. For example, Maithili in Bihar. Other languages like Tripuri and Mizo have been discontinued as media of instruction. As these languages are clubbed under the heading „other languages" it is not possible to say that their non-use at the higher secondary level is a case of subtraction. One can only conclude that tribal and non-scheduled and non-tribal languages are not used as media of instruction for higher secondary education." [199]

c) The two-language media group

Haryana, Himachal Pradesh, Rajasthan, Uttar Pradesh and the UT Lakshadweep Islands come under this group. The two languages are English and Hindi, in Lakshadweep English and Malayalam.

d) The one-language medium group

Interestingly the Northeastern Sattes with a high share of tribal peoples Meghalaya, Mizoram and Nagaland use just English as medium of instruction on all levels of instruction, including the primary level where in the first years local tribal languages (Mizo, Naga languages, Garo, Pnar, Khasi) are used in auxiliary function. According to the 5th survey the use of Mizo and Chakma as medium has been discontinued even for the primary education.

The trends presented above highlight the complexity in the phenomenon of medium of instruction across the four levels of education:[200]

1) The statement that less number of languages are used as media for

198 Ibidem, p. 81

199 Ibidem, p. 81

200 Koul, ibidem, p.82-83

tertiary education is a simplification of a cauldron of complexities. The number of languages used for higher education is no doubt reduced in comparison to primary education. To get a more appropriate understanding of the situation a diachronic perspective is also needed, which shows that languages used as media of instruction have remained constant in many States, have decreased in a few States, and have increased in a few other States.

2) The findings in their totality indicate that in all States and UTs except the States listed in group 4 the official State languages, Hindi and English are used as media of instruction for all the four stages of education. Usually when a State shares its border with another State speaking another language which is not Hindi, this language also finds place as a medium of higher secondary education.
3) English is the language that has been used by all the States and Uts for all the four stages of education. Hindi is the second most widely prevalent medium of instruction for all the stages of education.
4) In terms of number of schools, however, Hindi medium schools outnumber English medium schools for all the four levels of education.
5) With regard to the tribal and non-scheduled and non-tribal-languages they are not used a media of instruction for higher secondary education as indicated by the diachronic comparison. So extrapolating findings on the basis of synchronic comparison and concluding that these languages are being deleted as media of instruction is misleading. In case of these languages discussion on instructional media should focus on efforts to introduce them. One cannot talk about their discontinuation as they have never been used in such a function."

Although a slight reduction of the medium languages of instruction, the State official languages still are growing stronger and being widely used for tertiary educational stages. Thus, often the higher secondary education is becoming even tri-medial, but at the expense of the absolute minority languages.

In some few cases indigenous (tribal) languages are used in education as media alongside other languages as subjects, as Hmar, Thangkul and Khasi in Manipur, Khasi and Garo in Meghalaya, Santhali and Savari in Jharkhand. But the use of this strategy is dismal because of certain reasons like the lack of standardised scripts, the apathy of the bureaucracy and State politicians coupled with the unwillingness of some tribal people to accept the use of their language for education. In some particular cases as the one of the Santals, committed language activists have developed new distinct scripts (Ol Chiki) in order to unify culturally the tribal population spread across several states.

7.5 Can the three-language-formula cope with multilingualism?

In India, unlike many European countries, there is deep-rooted and widespread traditional multilingualism. Several languages coexist on the same territory in a complex functional pattern with changing hierarchies. In many Indian urban areas this kind of multilingualism appears to be the norm rather the exception, whereas monolingualism (with dialects and standard variants) prevails in rural areas. It is a widespread accepted conviction in India that a monolingual education, as a uniform education principle from primary up to the university level, does not reflect the country's multilingual reality and cultural needs.[201] India's magic formula to tackle the requirement of multilingualism within the education system is the "three-language-formula" (TLF), issued first in 1957 and adopted in almost all States. Amid sharp controversies concerning the role of different languages in formal education, a broad consensus was achieved with this formula, which provided a basis of policy for a minimum requirement of language proficiency in school education. In 1968, the National Policy on Education formally adopted the TLF. This was also entered in the Programme of Action of the Parliament in 1992. In 1966, the Education Commission recommended a liberalised version of the Formula: it expected a student to acquire sufficient control over three languages by the time he/she completes the lower secondary stage (class X). According to the National Curriculum Framework for School Education of 2000, the three languages should comprise the mother tongue (home language or regional language) plus two non-native modern languages, broadly Hindi as an official medium and a link language for the majority of people for inter-state communication, and English as an associate official medium and an interface language for higher education as well as for "sophistic" international communication. Students having Hindi as mother tongue should learn any other modern, scheduled Indian language. Thus, the TLF regulates the medium languages of instruction along the following combination possibilities:

- The first language to be studied must be the mother tongue or the regional language
- The second language:
  1) in Hindi speaking states this will be some other modern Indian language or English;
  2) in non-Hindi speaking states the second language: Hindi or English
- The third language:
  1) in Hindi-speaking States the third language will be English or a modern Indian language not studied as the second language.

201 *Ibidem*, p.378.

2) In non-Hindi speaking States the third language will be English or a modern Indian language not studied as the second language.

This results in the following combinations for the TLF according to the "Hindi-factor":

- TLF in non Hindi-speaking States: the regional language or a minority language if different from the official regional language + Hindi + English
- TLF in Hindi-speaking States: Hindi or a minority language if different from Hindi+another Indian language (preferably South Indian language)+ English.

Nevertheless, in some States only two languages are imparted[202] and the most wide-spread deviation consists in adopting English as the second language. The acceptance of learning Dravidian languages in the Northern Hindi-belt is rather low, where some Hindi-speaking States have replaced such languages with Sanskrit.[203] Generally the TLF allows for a quite broad range of options and combinations in the single State realities, and represents a compromise between major political and economic requirements. A general aim of the formula is to use regional official languages as media of instruction and to promote the learning of English and Hindi as second and third languages. But according to the reports of the NCLM these goals have been only partially achieved.

Table 16 -The 3-language-formula as implemented or approved by States (Source: K. Vishvanatham, The 8th Schedule and the TLF)

State	First languages	Second language	Third language
1. Andhra Pradesh	Telugu, Hindi, Urdu, Kannada, Tamil, Oriya, Marathi, Gujarati or composite courses of these languages (I-X)	For those who have not Hindi as first: Hindi For those who have not Telugu: Telugu Any other modern Indian language	English
2. Arunachal Pradesh	English	Hindi	Assamese

202 Example Tamil Nadu, Nagaland

203 See the annual reports of the NCLM available at: http://nclm.nic.in

3. Assam	Mother tongue or regional language	English	Hindi (for Assamese mother tongue speakers) Assamese (for non-Assamese speakers)
4. Bihar	Hindi, Urdu, Bengali, Oriya, Maithili, Nepali, English	English	Hindi (for not mother tongue speakers), Sanskrit, Bengali, Oriya, Urdu (for others)
5. Delhi	Hindi (or any other modern Indian language)	English	Hindi/Sanskrit
6. Goa	Marathi, Konkani, Urdu, Kannada, English, Gujarati	Marathi, Konkani, Urdu, Kannada, English, Hindi	Marathi, English, Gujarati, Konkani
7. Gujarat	Gujarati (or any other mother tongue)	Hindi	English
8. Haryana	Hindi	English	Punjabi, Sanskrit, Telugu
9. Himachal Pradesh	Hindi	English	Urdu, Telugu, Tamil
10. Jammu Kashmir	Urdu or Hindi	English	Urdu in Hindi medium school, Hindi in Urdu medium school
11.Karnataka	Kannada	Two other languages from the following: Urdu, Tamil, Telugu, Marathi, English, Hindi, Sanskrit, Arabic, Persian, Malayalam, Kannada.	
12.Kerala	Malayalam (for minorities Kannada or Tamil)	English	Hindi
13.Madhya Pradesh	Mother Tongue	Hindi (for non-Hindi-speakers) and Sanskrit (for Hindi-speakers)	English
14.Maharashtra	Marathi	Hindi	English
15.Nagaland	Mother tongue	English	Hindi
16. Orissa	Oriya	English	Hindi
17. Punjab	Punjabi	Hindi	English
18. Rajasthan	Hindi	English	Sanskrit, Urdu, Sindhi, Bengali, Gujarati, Punjabi, Malayalam, Tamil

19. Sikkim	English	Hindi	Nepali, Tibetan, Lepcha, Limbu
20. Tamil Nadu	Tamil or mother tongue, when different from Tamil	English or any other non-Indian language	
21. Tripura	Bengali	English	Hindi, Sanskrit, Arabic, Persian etc.
22. Uttar Pradesh	Hindi	One of languages of 8th Schedule,	English, modern European language
23. West Bengal	Assamese, Bengali, English, Gujarati, Hindi, Lishi, Malayalam, Marathi, Modern Tibetan, Nepali, Oriya, Punjabi, Gurumukhi, Santhali, Telugu, Tamil, Urdu	English, if any language other than English is first language. Bengali, if English is first language	A classical language, a modern foreign language other than English, a modern Indian language other than the first language
28. Mizoram	Mizo	English	Hindi

From the perspective of pedagogical acquisition planning, the duration of instruction of the chosen languages under the TLF should be:

1. first language: the mother tongue or regional language (duration: 10 years)
2. second language: the official language (Hindi or English) (duration: 6 years minimum)
3. third language: another modern Indian or foreign language (duration: 3 years)

The language first used depends on the definition of "mother tongue". While the TLF is not fully accepted by all States (e.g. Tamil Nadu), all agree that the regional language should be used at the secondary school level. According to Groff[204] the major difficulties in the implementation of the TLF stem from the following factors:

a) The heavy language load in the school curriculum
b) Northern schools are not motivated to teach South Indian languages
c) Southern schools, especially in Tamil Nadu, are resisting the teaching of Hindi

204 Cynthia Groff, *Status and acquisition planning of Linguistic Minorities in India*; at: http://www.sil.org/asia/ldc/parallel_papers/cynthia_groff.pdf

d) The cost of arranging instruction of the TLF

Table 14 shows how differently the TLF has been implemented in the various States, reflecting the resistance of some states to Hindi in particular. Tamil Nadu and Mizoram have renounced a third language, thus avoiding teaching Hindi.

Thus, the various States have adapted the formula in different forms for various contexts. Some limit their options to two languages plus a classical one; some others established four languages, others provide additional optional languages. "Often, however, the importance of the languages in the curriculum outweighs the actual value placed on them in instruction, and the languages are given different amounts of time and degrees of emphasis."[205] It can easily be observed that, with exception of West Bengal (Lishi, Gurumuki, Santhali) and Sikkim (Lepcha, Limbu; Mizo in Mizoram is a majority language) no other "absolute" minority languages are allowed as medium languages under the TLF. Hence, it can be stated that, with regard to linguistic minorities, the TLF tries to accommodate the interests of speakers of "relative" minority languages (the speech communities with a language official in another State), but does not include the mother tongue of minorities speaking non-scheduled languages.[206]

Looking at the educational preferences in India, it is clear that the medium of instruction preferred by most from the primary stage onward, especially for higher stages of education, is English. Those who can afford it send their children to English medium-schools and the government has also begun to comply with this demand in selected schools. There were, however, attempts, to reduce the use of English as medium at the primary level. In some contexts English is even considered the most important medium. This minimises the value of learning Indian languages, as is the case, for example, in the so-called "Central schools" (500 schools) that have bilingual instruction in English and Hindi and do not pay much regard to the multilingual character of the country.[207] This tendency causes even the use of regional languages to be disregarded, let alone minority languages. The States, however, are trying to reinforce the teaching of official and regional languages.

The educational reality of the application, as given by table 14, is rather

---

205 Cynthia Groff, *Status and acquisition planning of Linguistic Minorities in India,* p.8

206 D.P.Pattanayak, *Tribal Languages in Education,* in: Language Education in multilingual India, UNESCO, Delhi 2001, p.55

207 This recalls the effect of the widespread use of English as a second language all over Europe, which has demotivated British citizens to learn any foreign language and which has brought about a decline in many countries in learning a second important European foreign language.

A boarding school in Tashiding (Sikkim)

varied. Many States are not implementing the TLF in its true spirit. Some States implement it only for 2 or 3 years. Some States give a long list of languages from which the students can choose as the first, second and third language (e.g. Karnataka 9, West Bengal 19, Delhi 26 languages). But what facilities have these States provided to teach all these languages and in how many schools? Madhya Pradesh prescribes mother tongue "as first language". But in reality, how many children can complete how many years of their studies in their mother tongue? According to the reports of the NCLM, it appears that the TLF, except some schools run by linguistic minorities and schools at the borders of the States, is generally applied in the following simple manner:

A. In non-Hindi speaking States

First language: State language (mother tongue of the majority population)
Second language: Hindi or English
Third Language: English or Hindi

B. In Hindi speaking States

First language: Hindi
Second language: English/Urdu/Sanskrit
Third language: English/Urdu/Sanskrit

Pattern B is a gross violation of the TLF, since South Indian languages are not taught compulsorily, and English is not made a compulsory subject at least in some Hindi speaking States. Both patterns A and B violate the TLF by not teaching (in practice) the mother tongues of the students as the first languages at the primary level. This is a clear violation of Article 350A Const., which states that the primary education must be in the mother tongue of the pupil.[208]

There is also a major disparity in the implementation of the TLF between the North and the South of India, due to the kind of languages taught under this formula. In the Dravidian South, the three languages taught (regional language, English and Hindi) belong to three distinct linguistic groups and have different scripts. In Northern India (the Hindi-belt) the imparted medium languages are mostly Hindi, Urdu, English and Sanskrit. Sanskrit and Hindi have the same script, Hindi and Urdu and Hindi and Sanskrit possess a great amount of common vocabulary, and common morphological and syntactic features. This brings about a different work load, as learning English and Hindi along with a South Asian language is much more difficult as these languages belong to three different groups.[209] The Southern States are reluctant to adopt Hindi at all levels, whereas the Hindi-belt-States are neglecting the Dravidian languages. "This modification of the original TLF (the inclusion of a modern Indian language other than Hindi for the Hindi speaking States) is not based on any sound linguistic or educational theory, but a sense of equality in terms of language load. Of course, such a sense of equality is unfortunately negative. This is partly because most language planners and language engineers treat languages as objects, ignoring the fact that they do not and cannot exist without their speakers and that it is the speakers who create and solve language problems."[210]

Is the TLF responding to the needs of the speakers of "absolute" linguistic minorities? It was repeatedly stipulated that "where the mother tongue is different from the Regional or State language, arrangements must be made for instruction in the mother tongue by appointing at least one teacher, provided there are not less than 40 pupils speaking the language in the whole school or 10 such pupils in the class"[211] (this is the so-called 10:40 formula). Obviously, these States take shelter under the last clause of the above statement, stating that the class does not contain 10 pupils speaking a particular mother tongue, although this is not correct. The other reason

208 D.P.Pattanayak, *Tribal Languages in Education*, 2001, p.56

209 *ibidem*, p. 321

210 Kailash Aggarwal, *Epilogue*, in: R.S. Gupta/Anvita Albi/Kailash S. Aggarval (eds.), *Language and the State*, Creative Books, New Delhi 1995, p. 222

211 Federal provision under the general norm of Article 350 (A) of the Const.

these States may advance is the lack of funds to appoint teachers. But "... cost is not a real issue. Bilingual education is a long-term investment, but nowhere do the costs appear prohibitive. In India producing materials in local languages adds 5-10% to total recurrent cost. But the gains can be massive because of the fewer dropouts and repetitions."[212] Rather there is a lack of will and a covert ill feeling about the minority languages to be found in the minds of educational planners in these States"[213] The TLF is a hallmark of a policy, but it has no reference to mother tongue.[214]

The role of Hindi and English in education

As far as Hindi is concerned, the expectations were that Hindi will be used as a link language for contact with the people from other states, holds the NCLM,[215] assuming that Hindi may replace English as a language for higher education all over. But presently this is only a dream and the only purpose of learning the language is for common day use. The level of competence to be achieved in Hindi is limited to learning grammar and picking up enough vocabulary to interact with other persons. Naturally the study of literature, prose and poetry, is not of much relevance except as means of contextualised learning.

In contrast to Hindi, the position of English presents a different and difficult preposition. English was not considered when the linguistic rights for the linguistic minorities were decided and responsibilities listed. However, today, English has a major role in decision-making regarding language choice in education. English is replacing the mother tongue and the regional language. Seven States have opted for the introduction of English at the earliest stage, even along with the mother tongue of the students. When language policy was debated in India decades ago, only Hindi and/or regional languages were perceived to be a threat to the place of the mother tongue in the school system. Today the situation is totally changed. At that time there were violent protests against ignoring mother tongues, and today we see total submission in favour of English. No safeguards bestowed by the Constitution or policy declarations by the governments are able to shield Indian languages from the relentless onward march of English.

In fact, "English medium schools", which offer Hindi or another modern

212 UNDP-Report 2004

213 Vishvanatham, *The 8th Schedule and the TLF*, p.320

214 Pattanayak, *Tribal Languages in Education*, 2001, p. 56

215 See NCLM, 42d report, p. 18, at: http://nclm.nic.in

Indian language as a "second or third foreign language" are very trendy in India today. Private English medium schools generally are better equipped than public schools. Their quality regarding textbooks, libraries and audiovisual media is considerably better. Thus, the English medium schools, preferred by the middle and upper class families, are cutting out the government schools with regional language medium, which are deficient or poor in terms of qualification of teachers, didactical materials and technical equipments. Public schools definitely have less prestige than private schools. "The dominant classes can effectively marginalise the majority of the subordinate classes and guard against incursions across their cultural barrier by exercising their knowledge of English.

Thus, while this cultural power is symbolic, its effects remain real".[216] To counter this tendency it is necessary to strengthen the role of English in public schools, and also to give more relevance to regional languages in government service examinations. A "linguistic regionalism" in India is increasingly opposing this homogenisation and submission to the English language under the banner of economic competitiveness in a globalising market. But again, public efforts to promote Indian regional languages on University level vis-à-vis English, are facing mounting resistance from the universities, which worry about their academic prestige and image. In 1986, out of 96 universities in India, 27 were monolingual (English), 53 bilingual (English+Hindi or another Indian regional language) and 13 were multilingual. This situation is mirroring the linguistic bias towards English in the Indian educational system: English is regarded as a brand of quality; regional languages are associated with mediocrity. There is a wealth of scientific literature in English, whereas few scholars publish in regional languages and translations into English do often not equal the textbooks produced abroad.

The minority languages are the worst suffering because they were also under siege due to the growing influence of the regional official languages. They are perceived as a threat to the unity of the State. The minority languages limited to a smaller area or to a State are the most vulnerable. If this process cannot be reversed or stalled, at least steps can be taken to protect the minority languages. For this it is necessary at least to develop certain linkages in school. Languages that have no power or support for their continued use and development are bound to vanish.[217]

---

216 Timothy Scrase, *Image, Ideology and Inequality – Cultural Domination, Hegemony and Schooling in India*, New Delhi 1993, quoted by Rolly, p. 228
217 *ibidem*, p. 18

A Khasi student of Linguistics at the NEHU University of Shillong (Meghalaya)

7.6 The educational rights of linguistic minorities

The core of the fundamental rights of linguistic minorities in education lies in Article 350A Const., which reads: "It shall be the endeavour of every State and of every local authority within the State to provide adequate facilities for instruction in the mother tongue at the primary stage of education to children belonging to linguistic minority groups; and the President may issue such directions to any State as he considers necessary or proper for securing the provision of such facilities."[218] Under this principle the States are required to establish mother tongue schools in the areas where this language is spoken, as well as a differentiation of education, when a part of the pupils belong to different minority groups. As soon as at least 40 children in a school or 10 children in a class speak a language different of the language of instruction, they should have the right to instruction in their mother tongue. In reality, this task could not be met by many public education authorities due to personnel and financial constraints, or the simple

218 A useful comment is to be found in Joshua Castellino, *Minority Rights in India*, in J. Castellino/Elvira Domínguez Redondo, *Minority Rights in Asia, A Comparative Legal Analysis*, Oxford University Press, 2006, p. 87-89

lack of political will. In addition, many minority languages still lack a script, or a literary works, a grammar or text books, and this again prevents the use of more than half of India's languages in formal education on primary school level, let alone on secondary level.

In India there is no constitutional provision that imposes on the States the duty to establish public schools for linguistic minorities run in their respective languages, in conjunction with the requirements of the TLF. Rather, the initiative is left to the minority communities themselves. According to Articles 29 (1) and 30 (1) linguistic (as religious) minorities have the constitutional right to freely run their own schools and determine the medium of instruction, but only if such institutions are privately run. Institutions established by such minorities cannot be compelled to adopt Hindi or a State official language as the general medium of instruction, but the language chosen as medium of instruction has to be accepted to take final examinations. This is no hindrance for major scheduled languages, but it is an enormous hurdle for the smaller minority languages. This right was upheld in several cases before the Supreme Court.[219] For example, the State of Karnataka made Kannada a compulsory sole first language at the primary and secondary level, even in schools run by linguistic minorities. The Court shared the position of the parents, and upheld their right to select the language of instruction for children attending private schools. On the one hand, no medium language can be made compulsory for minority schools, as they have a fundamental right to conserve their language or religion; on the other hand, in practice almost all absolute minority languages are virtually excluded, as examinations are not held anywhere in these languages.[220]

The second point of leverage affecting the control of minority languages in education is money. The privately run schools not only need public recognition, but also public financial aid. "Recognition and aid are two very powerful instruments in the hands of the State to exercise control over minority educational institutions."[221] It should be mentioned that a minority institution has no fundamental right to receive recognition and aid. It could be

219 See S.P. Massey, *Minority Rights: the constitutional vision*, p. 75

220 It may be concluded that Article 30 (1) implies the right of minority communities to impart lessons to the children of its own community in its educational institutions in its own languages. "The power of the State to determine the medium of instruction must yield to the fundamental right of the minority community to impart instructions in their own language. Even though Hindi is a national language and Article 351 of the Constitution provides a special directive to the State to promote the spread of Hindi, nevertheless, this object cannot be achieved by any means which contravenes the rights of the minorities guaranteed by Art. 29 and 30 of the Constitution." *ibidem*, p. 76

221 *ibidem*, p. 78

argued, however, that the right to aid and recognition can be derived from the Article 30 (1) itself, because the right to establish and administer an educational institution must be real, and this power will be rendered illusory if a minority institution remains unrecognised and unaided. Furthermore clause (2) of Article 30 provides, though in negative terms, that the State shall not discriminate in granting aid to such institutions on the ground that it is a minority institution.
This affirmation raises the issue of the duty of the State to guarantee education in minority languages, linked to the duty to provide education for all children. Children with other mother tongues may not be discriminated against in access to such private schools run by minorities. Article 29 (2) Constitution reads: "No citizen shall be denied admission into any educational institution maintained by the state or receiving aid out of state funds on the grounds only of religion, race, caste, language or any of them."

The education policies of India's 28 States do not follow a uniform pattern with regard to requirement to adopt the TLF and the obligation to ensure at least a partial instruction in a mother tongue medium. For several linguistic minorities, the TLF has become virtually a 4-language-formula, as many states insist on the compulsory teaching of the respective regional language. "Today many education programmes are geared to facilitate the scope of communication with the prevailing socialisation values in a community. Against the background of a multiple-choice medium policy continued after the Independence, many newly-cultivated languages (mostly of tribal peoples and other minorities) are initiated just as preparatory medium at the primary stage."[222] Many States introduced an education policy based on two or more medium languages, using the regional official language as major medium, in combination with English and/or Hindi, and assigning minority languages the function of "partial medium".

Minority schools in every State use minority languages – 'relative minorities' in particular – as the medium of instruction, and the Indian link languages Hindi and English, depending upon the availability of textbooks, teachers and the linguistic preferences given in the minority community. Moreover "...education authorities have developed 'composite' courses combining minority languages and elementary Hindi as a single course."

With regard to tribal people, some States as Rajasthan, Karnataka, Meghalaya are developing different forms of bilingual education. In Bihar textbooks are prepared in major tribal languages – Santali, Kurukh, Mundari, Hi, Ho, Kharia. The Madhya Pradesh Tribal Research Bureau has also initi-

222 Khubchandani, *Language in education*, 2001, p.32

ated a few textbooks in Gondi, Bhili, Korku and Halabi. Their implementation in school education is somewhat staggered."[223] Some States are trying bilingual educational programs. Special primary schools for children of tribal groups have been established, but often inefficiencies (teacher absence, unavailability of texts, inadequate schools, alienation from home languages etc.) have been reported.[224] In 2004, 42 languages including 5 foreign languages out of 114 were used in Indian schools. In summary, this means that at least two thirds of India's 114 vernacular languages are not used as a medium or subject. Clearly, there is a certain divide between educational facilities available for relative minorities and institutions for absolute minorities.

Table 17 - The 42 languages taught as medium languages or subject (in 2004)

1. Angami	15. Kannada	29. Nepali
2. Ao	16. Kashmiri	30. Nicobari
3. Arabic	17. Khasi	31. Oriya
4. Assamese	18. Konkani	**32. Persian**
5. Bengali	19. Konyak	**33. Portuguese**
6. Bhutia	20. Ladakhi	34. Punjabi
7. Bodo	21. Lepcha	35. Sanskrit
8. Dogri	22. Limbu	36. Sema
9. English	23. Lotha	37. Tamil
10. French	24. Malayalam	38. Telugu
11. Garo	25. Manipuri	**39. Tibetan**
12. Gujarati	26. Marathi	40. Urdu
13. Hindi	27. Maithili	41. Zeliang
14. Kokborok	28. Mizo	42. Santhali

Source: CIIL Mysore - Language and culture – Chapter 7, at: http://www.ciil-ebooks.net/html/disorder/index.htm

Note: Also Karbi is used in Karbi-Anglong. Pnar (Jaintia Hills, Meghalaya) is included in Khasi. 5 of the above listed languages are foreign languages (in bold).

Although 33 languages are used as media of instruction at the lower level, only English is the medium of technical and management education and continues to maintain its dominant position in University education, while

223 As the NCLM affirms in his 42d report one of the reasons advanced for the absence of the education in the minority languages is that the costs are too high. The text books are not available, the reason cited being that with lesser number of books to be printed, it is not a profitable business. Not enough teachers are available. Their training is a difficult preposition. State funding for minority language services other than education is also frequently presented as uneconomical.

224 Pattanayak, *Tribal Languages in Education,* 2001, p.54

Hindi and regional languages are emerging media in academic life.
Apart from such efforts to establish bilingual schools for tribal children in some States, in India there are many multilingual institutions with multilingual teachers who cater to the needs of pupils with different linguistic backgrounds. Thus, although most States prefer to promote the use of the regional official language as medium of instruction, in practice the pupils experience a double or triple shift in the linguistic medium of instruction at one or another stage depending upon the context, domain and channel:
1. Passive and active media: Students listen to lectures in one language and write answers in another
2. Formal and informal media: Formal teaching in the classroom is conducted in one language, but informal explanations are provided in another;
3. Multi-tier media: elementary education is initiated through mother tongue as a 'preparatory' medium, or "partial medium", which in some European minority areas is called "auxiliary role of minority languages". When a student moves upward on the education ladder she/he has to shift to a more 'cultivated' medium.

At the university level, almost all students have to switch to English or in a few cases to Hindi as main medium. The mentioned "multi-tier-system" in the primary and secondary schools is supposed to provide the optimal preparation for switching from one medium to another. The "multi-tier-system" in several States is supposed to be transformed into official bilingual education, which in the higher secondary level regularly shows an increasing proportion of English and Hindi as medium language. If such a multilingual scheme of education at the primary and secondary level is prevailing in most Indian States, the role of languages of the "absolute minorities" appears to be under high pressure. As the normal schools are already strongly required to cater to a multilingual context (regional language+Hindi+English), little room is left to develop minority languages further than the rudimentary primary level or a purely auxiliary role. Even regional languages cannot be fully displayed as medium languages at least until the university stage. "Absolute" minorities are in dire straits. Hence, as in Europe, the educational system does not really compensate for the growing lack of functional load of minority languages, but mirrors the hierarchy of functional load of the single languages, assigning a diverse value and prestige to the regional and link languages, with dialects and minority languages occupying the lowest level of appreciation in the school curricula.

Although the constitutional requirements are the same all over India, there is great deal of diversity in the various States and Union Territories. The majority of the minority languages are not used in primary and middle schools (class I-VIII) anymore. Only the following languages are used for 10 or 11 years as medium of instruction: Ao, Angami, Lushai, Sadani, Santhali, Maithili, Manipuri (Meitei).[225] There is simply no space left for lesser-used languages in the framework of the TLF. English, Hindi and regional official languages in non-Hindi-states is required, which provides the first reason why no minority languages continue to be used as medium language of instruction after class VIII. For instance only Ho, Maithili, Mundari, Oraon, and Santhali are taught as compulsory second languages, and only Lushai, Sadani and Santhali are taught as compulsory third languages.[226] None of the absolute minority languages are used as media of university instruction. This fact automatically raises the problem that children speaking almost all minority languages in India have to switch to another medium of instruction (except 4 cases out of 92 non scheduled languages) after some classes of primary or at maximum after 8 classes of instruction in the mother tongue. The speakers of the majority of these 92 languages do not even enjoy classes at the primary level in their mother tongue. There is one obvious justification given for this rule: "Since the minority children however are required to switch from their mother tongue to another medium of instruction in higher education, care must be taken that they are not put to disadvantage in this process. They must have adequate competence in the language that they are going to adopt as a second medium. This should not necessarily mean that the teaching of this language should be pushed in the early stages of education."[227] Thus, children of linguistic minorities appear to be squeezed between the lack of proper language status and acquisition planning of the mother tongue on one side, and the requirement of the TLF in a multilingual country as India on the other.

Stumbling blocks also include the lack of textbooks and well-trained teachers, due to the shortage of financing and personnel. The CIIL in Mysore and its regional offices organized many training programs for tribal teachers and graduates. In 1968, books were produced in 60 tribal languages, as creative literature in minority languages is required to motivate children to

---

225 Dua, *Language Planning and Linguistic Minorities*, p. 148; Ao, Lushia and Meitei only, due to the fact that a significant share of the entire States of Nagaland, Mizoram and Manipur speak these languages.

226 *ibidem*, p. 149

227 In this regard Dua states: "We must clearly understand the consequences of continuing or discontinuing the teaching of mother tongues after the primary or middle stage. The continuation of the teaching of the mother tongue beyond the middle stage involves not only the burden of learning more languages by minority children, but also a higher degree of language planning and language development of minority languages. Their discontinuation may restrict their development as well as their function". *Language Planning and Linguistic Minorities*, p.148

learn in their language. The effort was and is respectable, but by far not sufficient to meet the demand. Textbooks on philosophy, history, economics, and politics were produced only in a very few tribal languages. There is a lack of teachers because there is a general gap in literacy of tribal people as well as a lack of training facilities (like courses, institutions, etc.). There are insufficient numbers of students and a lack of academic textbooks for teachers of minority languages. "The training of teachers is essential not only from the point of view of pedagogical principles for effective teaching but also for sociolinguistic reasons. It has been found that the attitudes of the teachers towards their mother tongue, their culture, the majority culture, and the pupils may have indirect implications for minority children's' proficiency in the mother tongue and bilingualism and for the maintenance of their language and culture".[228]

All efforts for minority language education depend on the attitude of both the minority and majority communities. Of course, the preservation of a language cannot work if it caters only to symbolic functions. It must be an effective medium of communication and of education. In this case "... the minority community needs not only to lend its active support to the development of educational institutions, but also to be clear which values of the community and which elements of its history, way of life, religion and culture are to be transmitted through its language. This requires evaluation and interpretation of its own culture as well as the acceptance of the majority culture and its values by the minority group."[229] If a minority does not sufficiently appreciate its own language and, due to economic and labour market reasons, attributes much more value to the surrounding majority languages, it is paving the way to assimilation. In India in several cases the linguistic minorities, too, appear to prefer English to their own languages, joining the mainstream of the country.[230]

---

228 *ibidem*, p.151; The "Linguistic Survey of Tribal Dialects and Cultures", focusing on four districts of Orissa, reported that, "India has failed to meet the commitment of universalising primary education and ensuring a basic human right because this problem of language. They expressed the need for eradicating the language barrier, which instead of serving as a 'driving force', serves as a 'depriving force'. See the Academy of Tribal Dialects and Cultures, ST/SC development Department, Orissa, October 1999. Even the linguistic minority of the Urdu-speakers are often deprived of the right to attend a primary school in their mother tongue. The Group of Minorities Education (Government of India 1991) states: "...that the denial of this rights to the Urdu minorities has contributed largely to their educational backwardness; see Cynthia Groff, *Status and acquisition planning of Linguistic Minorities in India*; p.10

229 Dua, *Language Planning and Linguistic Minorities,* p.152

230 See J.C. Sharma, *Multilingualism in India*, in Language in India, December 2001

In addition, there have been well-established traditions in the country that encourage people to learn the dominant language for purposes outside their homes and use the mother tongue in their home domain. In the states like Arunachal Pradesh, Goa, Jammu and Kashmir, Meghalaya, Nagaland, and Sikkim, mother tongue is the medium of instruction in less than 50% of the schools, whereas major languages such as English and Hindi and the other languages of the 8th Schedule occupy a place of importance even in the states in which the speakers of the non-scheduled language are in a majority.[231] In Sikkim 1.95%, Arunachal Pradesh 2.89%, Goa 14%, Jammu and Kashmir 19.45%, Meghalaya 42.03% and Nagaland 43% used the mother tongue as media of instruction at the upper primary stage. This does not mean that such local or regional minority languages, which in some States of the Northeast even form "relative majorities", are dying out. But a growing share of minority members seem to have arrived at the conclusion that it is not necessary to use their language as a medium of instruction or for a longer period of formal education in order to maintain their language. "If tribal people apprehend that the teaching through tribal languages is merely to deprive them of the benefits of knowing the regional language," states the National Commissioner for Linguistic Minorities, "there will be hesitation. There is no such hesitation in the Northeast because no such stigma attaches to it. Santhals do not fear making Santhali the medium of instruction of the primary stage. If the tribes can be assured that tribal languages are being introduced for their convenience, there is no reason why they will not adopt it."[232]

The key to overcoming the sceptical or even hostile attitude of some tribal communities vis-à-vis education in the mother tongue is to create a linguistic environment favouring the daily use of that language and extending its linguistic domains. This can occur by creating better legal conditions for that language on its home territory in different forms of local, territorial or cultural autonomy. The attitude of majority communities often is to push the policy of cultural assimilation through higher education under the pretext of social development, modernisation and national or regional integration. Mostly the efforts to preserve minority language from this point of view are considered a waste of time and money. Alternatively, if it takes a more political character, it is seen as "source of group solidarity leading to the assertion of special rights and privileges or even separate statehood by the minority community. Under such condition, the majority community may discourage the use of minority languages in education or adopt a protracted policy in the implementation process under the pretext of economic

231 J.C. Sharma, *Multilingualism in India,* in Language in India, December 2001
232 See the NCLM, 42d report 2004, at: http://nclm.nic.in , p. 16

and administrative constraints."[233]

How should the TLF be modified to suit the educational needs of linguistic minorities and how can minority languages (especially absolute minorities) be taken into account in the framework of the TLF? The TLF is relevant only from class VI-XII, in parallel with the regional official language. One solution could be offered by a simple variation of the general TLF, which is: mother tongue (mostly regional language) + Hindi + English. For minorities, the corrected TLF could be: Mother tongue + regional language (in Hindi-states Hindi) + English. As a consequence minorities would have to face just one disadvantage. In States other than those of the Hindi-belt they could not learn both national link languages English and Hindi at school. Hence, when entering the labour market or applying for employment in public service they would be confined to their own States or regions, and would be less competitive in the national labour market outside their own State, whenever fluency in both major link-languages is required. Nevertheless, higher mobility and migration cannot be the prime objective for members of a linguistic minority, if they are interested in surviving as a community with their particular cultural features in their home region. Renouncing one of the national link-languages (English or Hindi) means giving priority to a professional life in the respective regions of traditional settlement, leaving minority students to pick up Hindi outside the schools, if they wish to.[234] Instead of the general TLF, the special formula to be adopted for minority language speakers could be: mother tongue+2.[235]

In the course of time several versions of the TLF were formulated, but the linguistic needs of tribal children were no matter of major concern. The most preferred strategy was to adopt the concerned tribal language

233 Dua, *Language Planning and Linguistic Minorities,* p. 153

234 Correspondingly, members of „absolute minorities" in Europe do not face major difficulties in attending mother tongue medium schools, adding the national language as second and a international language (mostly English) as third language. Given the required public institutional support minority children even in such a context have no substantial disadvantage in general competition. As example: Basque students can attend Basque medium schools with Spanish as second language and English (or French) as third language.

235 The alternative for minority members would be a composite course in Hindi and the regional official language. This comes close to the model in which the mother tongue is not used as medium language beyond the primary school, but remains as a subject up to class X, and subsequently left out at an appropriate stage. This form of TLF for minority language speakers has two implications: minority members may develop their mother tongue for up to a sufficient level, and do not have to face an inordinately high linguistic burden (4 languages at the same time). Nevertheless, the task of developing the functional load of a language has not been sufficiently met.

as medium and the respective State language as a subject in the first 2-3 years, followed by a total switch over to the use of the regional language medium (State language). The development of tribal languages to become full fledged medium language never had any priority in Indian education policy. Multilingualism, if used as an imperative to ensure national integration, always tends to sideline minor languages. Thus, multilingual education in India has an overriding bias to the major and dominant languages. It seeks to offer all opportunities for minority language speakers to learn official and mainstream languages, whereas it never creates a legal, political and cultural framework, linked to given territories with a smaller, but dominant language, to induce speakers of major languages to learn minor languages. „The concept of multilingual education in India can be analyzed and understood by comparing it with the concept in the Western context. The bases for comparison are definition, target, rationale and the central debate regarding the concept itself. The definition of multilingual education in the Indian context differs from the definition prevalent in Western countries. In Europe multilingual education is defined as the use of two or more languages as media of education, either simultaneously or successively. In the Indian context, multilingual education refers to the use of two or more languages in education."[236]

The target population of multilingual education in India also differs form other countries. In the European setting, multilingual education is intended for ethnic minorities, often children of immigrated families. In the Indian context multilingual education is for all. Hence it encompasses the dominant language speakers, the migrants and the speakers of tribal and minority languages. But never there are minority languages included in the languages imparted in multilingual school, always are minority language speakers expected to become multilingual in majority languages. The rationale behind multilingual education is also different in the Indian context in comparison with other contexts. In the American context, multilingual education is a concession granted to the immigrants generally under legal duress. In the Indian context it is simultaneously a strategy for bringing about national integration and unity, for linking local, regional, national and international identities and for accommodating minorities. It is a strategy that has been built into the educational policy. It is a means for dealings with the multilingual nature of the country. In case of tribal population, multilingual education is a strategy for maintaining links with their heritage language.[237]

236 Omkar N. Koul, *Language, Education and Communication*, Delhi 2005, p. 93
237 Omkar N. Koul, *Language, Education and Communication*, Delhi 2005, p.94

Chapter 8

Public administration, media and minority languages

8.1 Minority languages in the public administration

Following the reorganization of the States on a linguistic basis, there was a conscious effort to reassure the linguistic minorities in the various States that their interests would be safeguarded. These safeguards are enshrined both in Constitutional provisions and in legal and political acts set by the single federated States. The use of language in administration should regulated in accordance with the Constitution and suggestions of the Language Commissions and Committees, in order to protect the interests of the linguistic minorities. Article 347 Const. is the special provision which ensures linguistic minority rights: "On a demand being made in that behalf the President may, if he is satisfied that a substantial proportion of the population of a State desire the use of any language spoken by them to be recognised by that State, direct that such language shall also be officially recognised throughout that State or any part thereof for such purpose as he may specify." Linguistic minorities in this sense are "minorities residing in the territory of India or any part thereof having a distinct language or script of their own." The language of the minority group need not be one of the fourteen languages mentioned in the 8th Schedule of the Constitution. Linguistic minority therefore means any group of people whose mother tongue is different from the principal language of the State, at the district and taluk levels, different from the principal language of the district or the taluk.[238]

At this point it has to be recalled that in Indian public law there is a distinction between the 'Official language' and 'Languages used in administration'. Each State and Union Territory, including the Union Government, has declared one or two languages as the official languages of the State, but only a few languages have been declared official languages at the district or taluk level or local level, whereas some additional languages could obtain the status of "Languages used in public administration."[239]

---

238 See CIIL Mysore, *Language and administration*, at: http://www.ciil-ebooks.net/html/disorder/index.htm

239 For this issue see also Table 6 and chapter 5.1 on official languages on State level. Also the example cited above should be briefly recalled: Though the Official Language Act of Andhra Pradesh of 1966 recognises Telugu as the Official Language for use in its territory, it also permits the use of English, Urdu, Kannada, Tamil and Oriya in certain specified situa-

The safeguards that govern the use of minority languages for official purposes are the following:

a) At district level and below (such as municipality, tehsil (taluk), etc.), where a linguistic minority constitutes 15 to 20 percent of the population, important Government notices, rules and other publications should also be published in minority languages.
b) At the district level, where 60 percent of the population in a district use a language other than the Official Language of the State, that language should be recognised as an additional official language in that district. Recognition for this purpose should ordinarily be given to the major languages mentioned in the 8th Schedule.
c) At the State headquarters, a translation bureau should be set up where arrangements may be made for translation and publication of the substance of important laws, rules, regulations, etc., into minority languages in States or districts or wherever a linguistic minority constitutes 15 to 20 percent of the population.
d) In correspondence with the public, petitions/representations received in languages other than the Official Language should be replied to, wherever possible, in the language of the petition/representation.
   The translation and publication of important rules, regulations, notices, etc., into all languages, spoken by at least 15% of the total population at district or sub-district level, is provided by special "translation bureaus", provided by the States' central administration. It is up to the discretion of the respective Governments to decide whether a notice, a rule or other official publication is so important as to be translated into minority languages.

On the other hand, the requested declaration of minority languages as second official languages in districts where persons speaking such languages constitute at least 60% of the population, is indeed a far reaching and prominent provision guaranteeing equal rights of all citizens vis-à-vis the public administration. To what extent has this provision been applied? The wording "should be" grants a certain margin of discretion for the State Governments in deciding on the recognition of local official languages. There is currently no consistent mapping of districts under this requirement to be found. The use of minority languages in the administration at district level has been largely ignored for various reasons.

The receipt of, and reply to, representations made in minority languages has been notably applied in most cases, according to the NCLM.[240] The is-

tions and regions for administrative activities. Hence, the latter ones are the "*Languages used in administration*" in Andhra Pradesh, although only Telugu is the "*Official Language*".

240 See NCLM, 42d report, at: http://nclm.nic.in

sue of pamphlets in minority languages detailing the safeguards available to linguistic minorities is important, but more important is the concrete implementation of these provisions. The NCLM complains that there is an absence of proper machinery at the State and district levels to redress grievances in matters of the protection of linguistic minorities and comments rather sceptically in one of his last annual reports: "In the beginning the concern was repeatedly expressed and whenever there was a deviation, remedial steps taken. As the system evolved, the attention wavered and all these concerns became commonplace. Gradually a slackening was noted and, needless to say, the implementation of the safeguards at present is not uniform over the various states. With the passing of time the priorities have changed. A general sense of apathy seems to have taken hold of some of the states for various reasons. Perhaps one of the reasons is the growing complexity of the administration. The harassed administrator is far too much occupied with fire fighting operations to take a look at the other issues which can be left alone to take care of themselves. At the higher level, there are other problems which are of much more urgency to them."[241]

The arguments concerning the receipt of the applications and representations in languages beyond the official languages are nearly identical. An additional point is that very often the applications, complaints etc. are written by professional petition writers who convert whatever the applicant wants to communicate into the officially accepted style and language. Not withstanding the provisions of the Constitution, several State Governments claim that no representations are received in minority languages. It is more likely that such representations and applications are simply discouraged, as indeed was alleged by some persons in Tamil Nadu and elsewhere. Even where it has been admitted that representations are received in local languages, it is said that the replies are sent in English or the regional language. "A variety of reasons," concludes the NCLM, "which appear to be more of excuses rather than explanations, are given such as lack of appropriate machinery, lack of equipment whereas actually it is lack of will."[242]

The point remains, observes the NCLM, that so far as a substantial number of people desire and describe a certain language to be their mother tongue, their wishes should be respected and they should be given the same treatment as other residents of the state. The Constitution gives them these rights and they should be respected. For example, the representations should be accepted and arrangements made to reply to them in the same language. No State Government has stated any cogent reasons for such a refusal. Later, however, "...it has been the experience of the Commissioner

241 See NCLM, 42d report, at: http://nclm.nic.in , p.22
242 *ibidem*, p. 23

that very often the safeguards are considered to be the concern of the minority welfare department and or the minority education department, whereas this should be the concern of the entire administration and of all the officers posted in such areas where the linguistic minorities reside in a large number. To cite an instance, it is the duty of the persons in charge of the buses to see that their destinations are written in majority as well as in minority languages."[243]

Representatives of linguistic minorities raised further requests to have their language accepted for official use in public administration. These requests prove how intricate the full implementation of the rights of linguistic minority in the whole public sphere would be, particularly with respect to regulating the details. There are requests for the minority language speakers:

1. At the level of the Union
   - Providing a slot for broadcasting programmes in the minority language.
   - Printing the M.O. forms, railway tickets also in the language of the minority.
   - Printing voter lists and ballot papers also in the minority language.
   - Providing a postman who can read the language written in the address of certain localities where the linguistic minorities reside.
   - Avoiding delay in delivery of mail because of ignorance of the postman of the language of the address, etc.

2. At the level of the States:
   - Receipt of applications in minority languages and reponses in the language concerned.

As the NCLM reports, some Governments are reluctant to accept such applications in all minority languages, and assert that they have difficulty in answering them in that language. Some States respond to the petitions in the language in which the people have signed, irrespective of the language used in the petition. Other States affirm that the Official State language is understood by all the residents of the State, so there cannot be any grievance. Just a few States agree to accept and respond to the petitions in the language of the minority.

- Interaction with public officers in the State and district administration in minority languages.
- Posting signboards in the offices in the language of the minority.

Some Governments take the stand that the official language is generally understood by all sections of the population. Other States post signboards in both the official language of the State and the language of the minority.

243 *ibidem*, p. 24

A signboard in the railway station of Bangalore (Karnataka)

3. At the level of the behaviour of the public officers

- Some employees, whose mother tongue is not the minority language, must also possess a working knowledge of the minority language.
- Officers in the office may know the language of the minority, but the clerks, who actually have to deal with ordinary people speaking the minority language, do not know the language of the public.
- Officials, who are posted in areas where large number of linguistic minorities reside should have knowledge of the minority community, otherwise it will not be possible for them to function properly.
- Officials, who are in the minority regions may not be considered for promotion in the same area, but officials from other areas, who do not know the minority language, are promoted and posted to minority areas.

A very important issue has not been sufficiently addressed in India's policy on linguistic minorities: the representation of linguistic minorities on the political level. Representation at the State or District level in form of committees had been requested on various occasions, but to no avail. There have also been requests for linguistic minority representation in the

Universities of the State, but these have not achieved success.
An issue of outstanding importance is the recruitment into the State Employment Services. In India, an examination must be passed for employment in public service at the Union or State level. The examination does not require knowledge of the respective State's Official Language at the time of the applicant's recruitment. The test of proficiency in the State's Official Language can be held before the completion of the probation period. This clause is intended to protect members of linguistic minorities vis-à-vis the linguistic majority candidates of the concerned State. The provisions for recruitment into State Services are:
a) Knowledge of the State Official Language should not be a pre-requisite for recruitment to State services, that is to say, superior or gazetted services. A test of proficiency in the State Official Language may be held after selection and before the end of the period of probation.
b) A candidate should have the option of using English or Hindi as medium of examination for State Services, as alternative to the Official Language of the State.
In addition to these requests there are further requests concerning the:
- Extension of time limit to pass the departmental language examination.
- Simplification or reduction in the standard of departmental language examination.
- Elimination of oral examinations in the departmental language examination.
- Appointment of a proper share of linguistic minorities.

The State governments, besides the minimal educational qualifications required for the jobs, generally follow their respective language policies in the recruitment of the staff and in their day to day work. Of course, "certain States are more rigid than others. Usually it is primarily the concerned official language, which is used in the office work. The knowledge of other languages also is required in certain cases."[244] An example: most of the office work in Tamil Nadu is done in Tamil. The correspondence with other States, central government offices and other organisations or individuals outside the State is done in English. Thus proficiency is required in Tamil and English, and therefore every public official has to have oral and written skills in those languages.

With regard to the official languages in administration, Annamalai points out a double failure in the Constitutional regulations:[245]
a) There are no definitive constraints for the States to introduce the respec-

244 Omkar N. Koul, *Language, Education and Communication*, Delhi, 2005, p. 47
245 See E. Annamalai, *The language and the state*, p.26

tive Indian language for the States' administration, legislature and judiciary. English continues to be the second official language on all levels, not only in inter-State and State-Centre-communication. "Since English continued to be the medium of education at the tertiary level (and to be a highly important medium in secondary), this provided ground for the extension of English as an official language and the delay of the exclusive use of Indian languages in administration as envisaged by the Constitution..."[246]This resulted in bilingualism in the administration through the use of the official regional language and English. Again, as with the TLF in the educational system, the public administration, at least at higher levels, must still cope with bilingualism, leaving space for additional languages.

b) Nevertheless, with the adoption of regional State languages there has been an empowerment of these "official languages". Under the Constitutional direction that Hindi was to be the official language, the role of Hindi, along with English, was improved, although there is no time frame for replacing English. Consequently, India today has two link-languages and about 12 regional official languages. This situation brought about the adoption of the three-language-formula as a general principle for the education policy in the schools. Thus, as all Indians are required to learn both the regional official and the link languages, the members of linguistic minorities (especially absolute minorities) are expected to become fluent in at least two official languages, which are not their mother tongues. This leaves very little space for such smaller languages in public administration and creates a huge pressure to shift to the "important languages" when a citizens is addressing the administration with a personal request. Conversely, for the public authorities this is an invitation to abandon any further effort to extend the domains covered by minority languages.[247] The alternative could only be a fully bilingual public administration on the local level.

According to Omkar N. Koul the problem connected with the use of minority languages in administration are mostly due to three major shortcomings:[248]

i) the non-existence of a standardized written version of a minority language
j) the non-availability of technical and printing facilities
k) the lack of investment in the development of need-based specialized

246 *ibidem*, p. 26

247 *ibidem*, p. 26.

248 See Omkar Koul, *Use of Tribal Languages in Administration.* In: O.N. Koul and J. Imtiaz (eds), *Linguistics: Theoretical and Applied*, Delhi 2004; and Omkar N. Koul, *Language, Education and Communication*, Delhi 2005, p.147-149

vocabulary and terminology.

In some cases, certain tribes or linguistic minorities use a different script from the State official language and even different from the same language as used in the neighbouring State. As far as possible it should be attempted to use the script of the major State language for encouraging their use in public administration and also in education. This would prevent the major part of public authorities of the common pretext to not use minority languages in written form, even when they are locally spoken by a majority: the availability of typing, printing and computational facilities. Software has been developed also for some minority languages (e.g. Santhali).

Most of the Indian languages have different social and regional dialects and variants. But a certain variety has to be officially recognized and widely accepted as written standard variety in order to be adopted by the State and district administration. Eventually, for the use in administration a register of technical terminology has to be developed, which not even has been finalised for several State official languages, let alone absolute minority languages. While at the Union level the „Commission for Scientific and Technical Terminology" prepared administrative terminology for Hindi, there is a lack of co-ordination with the State level. A central agency to tackle this issue in collaboration with the concerned States still has to be constituted.

Finally, India's hierarchy of government level attributes scarce importance to the district level, which in many cases show a different linguistic composition as the State they belong to. As there is no real political autonomy for districts including the matter of official language policy – apart from 14 Autonomous District Councils mostly concentrated to India's Northeast – the Official State language policy cannot be adopted to the linguistic requirements of the population-mix of those districts. Neither have the districts the necessary power to establish a specific regulation for language use in public administration nor do they have the required financial and technical means to meet such a demand.

8.2 Minority languages in the media

Mass communication in India has attained tremendous technological progress. Almost 85% to 95% of the country is covered by different media. Media written or broadcast in English are still accessible only to a small part of the population. There has been continuous objection to the variety of Hindi used in radio and television. The Sanskrit style used as standard Hindi in the government-funded media is far from the spoken varieties of

Hindi and is not easily accessible to people at large. The same is true of regional languages within their respective regions. The situation is better in the electronic media sector. TV is more restricted than radio, where a breakthrough in the use of main minority languages has been achieved. But broadcasting time is inadequate for real language planning. There is no provision for broadcasting programs in all the minority languages, nor is there sufficient radio time for the minority languages in which the programs are broadcast.

There is no complementarity between education and the use of languages in media. This is particularly the case with the minority languages in Himachal Pradesh and Arunachal Pradesh. For instance, news and programs are broadcast in Tangsa, Noote, Idu-Mishmi, Wanchoo, Nishi, Adi, Apatani and Monpa in Arunachal Pradesh and in Mahasui, Chambriali, Bilaspuri, Sirmauri, Kangri, Kulvi and others in Himachal Pradesh, but none is used in education at any level. In some cases minority languages are used in education, but not in radio broadcasting.[249]

Why is media coverage by minority languages not provided on a larger scale? "First because the control and organisation of the programs and the key personnel in their production are more likely to be drawn from the majority community than from the minority, and this implies that majority attitude and values are likely to get prominence compared to minority interests. Secondly, the news and programs broadcast in minority languages are overshadowed by programs in the majority language. A sociolinguistic survey of Himachal Pradesh shows that minority dialect speakers have less preference for programs in their mother tongue than for programs in Hindi and English."[250]

a) Print media

In India there is no bar to starting newspapers in any language or dialect, since the private sector rules this domain. It is up to the publisher and the reader to direct the choice of the languages used. There is also no bar to writing any language in any script in India. Print media in India began in1780, and in 220 years production has grown enormously. According to the 2002 Survey, newspapers and periodicals are published in 101 languages, 20 of which are foreign languages (italics), as follows:

Ahirani	German	Kurbi	Rajastani
Anal	Goani	Lakhar-Mara	Rongamei
Angami Naga	Ghorkali/Nepali	Latin	Russian

249 Dua, *Language Planning*, p. 156
250 *Ibidem*, p. 157

Angika	Greek	Lushai	Sanskrit
Anglo	Gujarathi	Magahi	Saurashtra
Arabic	Halbi	Maithili	Simite
Assamese	Haruti	Malayalam	Sindhi
Banjara	Haryanvi	Manipuri	Sinhali
Bengali	Himachali	Marathi	Sirayaki
Bhojpuri	Hindi	Marwari	Spanish
Biate	Hinustani/Persian	Meetelion	Swahili
Bihari	Hmar	Mikir	Syrian
Bishnupriya	Indonesian	Mising	Tamil
Bodo	Italian	Mizo-Lushai	Telugu
Burmese	Jaintal	Muridari	Thadou-Kuki
Chakma	Kabur	Naga	Thandoon
Chhatttisgarhi	Kanarese	Nicobari	Thankul
Chinese	Kannada	Oriya	Naga
Dogri	Kashmiri	Pahari	Tibetan
English	Khasi	Pali	Tiddinchin
Esperanto	Koch-Rajbhansi	Persian	Tripuri
Finnish	Kodava	Piate-Pau	Tulu
French	Kokborok	Piate	Urdu
Ganje	Konkani	Pitalri	Vaiphel
Garwhali	Koshli-Oriya	Portuguese	Serbo-croatian
Garo	Kuki	Punjabi	Zemi Nagan
Gaundi	Kumauni	Pushto	Zokan

Source: Mallikarjun, The Indian languages and the digital divide, CIIL, Language in India, 2004, p.15

The resources for running newspapers are hardly available to minority groups. The support from governments is meagre and inadequate, "...effective mass circulation of minority papers is a rare phenomenon. For instance, among the newspapers printed in 42 languages other than the languages of the 8th Schedule, the circulation of dailies, weeklies, monthlies, and others in 1976 did not exceed 3.000 copies each, except in the case of Manipuri, Khasi, Nepali, Konkani and Lushai."[251] One major reason is that "the educated minority speakers do not subscribe to the minority papers as their needs and interest are not catered to by the limited range of topics covered by them. The minority papers cannot cater to the demands of the educated minority speakers as they cannot compete with the papers in majority languages in terms of coverage of topics and circulation."[252]

b) Electronic media

Print-media, audio-visual media and the Internet have probably become India's most important tools for communication, and thus also for advancing language policy. Since the 1970s radio, cinema and video and TV have seen a growing presence and audience. The Government funded "All India Radio" (AIR) whose broadcasting covers the whole Indian territory and pur-

251 Dua, *Language Planning,* p. 157

252 *ibidem,* p. 158.

Monks in the monastery of Enchey, Gangtok (Sikkim)

sues as one major objective the dissemination of information and culture to illiterate people. In addition to the most important programmes in the regional languages (all scheduled languages), there are many features in Hindi and English produced for the whole country. One major problem for audio-visual media is the enormous gap between the spoken version of the major Indian languages and their official standard version. The new written Hindi based on Sanskrit had a huge problem of popular acceptance; on the other hand there is a major diglossy between the spoken and written standard language. Spoken Hindi, on the contrary, is widely diffused also in its standardised form.

Since the 1990s private TV-channels have also gained momentum. Apart from the worldwide satellite TV-networks such as BBC, MTV and CNN there is a growing number of private sat-TV-channels in Indian languages. But languages of the so-called 'absolute minorities' (e.g. tribal languages) do not have a real importance in TV.

Cinema played a major role in the countrywide dissemination of Hindi. Unexpectedly, Bollywood had and is having a much stronger impact on language learning than the Hindi-language courses probably ever had, as it is broadcast from 30 Radio stations in Hindi speaking States and territories. The Indian movie industry is unsurpassed in the developing world, giving

English an absolutely secondary role. In most of the Hindi-movies the spoken Hindi (Hindustani) is used and understood by the majority of India's population. Tamil Nadu holds the second rank in India's film industry. Tamil has a very strong presence in all audio-visual media. Some other languages such as Bengali, Marathi, and Telugu also have a growing share of the total annual production of movies.

Communication patterns in contemporary India reveal that the trends of globalisation through mass media and information technology have intensified the existing cultural diversity. TV and radio broadcasting networks in India can be considered as one of the classic examples of being multilingual to the core. The editorial centres generally anticipate the potential of multilingual audiences. Various strategies are adopted to cater to the demands of audiences and viewers in different languages in India:
a) Different slots are assigned to various languages for regional audiences. Alternate switch-over between two pan-Indian languages, English and Hindi, or a regional language is provided to cater to cross-language audiences, such as commentaries covering sports and public events and rallies etc.
b) Many live episodes, when conducted in more than one language are broadcast/telecast, very often, without bilingual corps, such as when covering proceedings of the Parliament. Very often, musical medleys are presented in a combination of mutually intelligible languages (such as Hindi, Urdu and Punjabi).
c) With increased facilities for simultaneous interpretation in recent years, there are now more occasions to provide flash summaries in another language (mostly in Hindi or English), in a somewhat unstructured manner.[253]
d) DVD, digital supports, Internet, and new information technology devices have contributed to the growing importance of distance education, which is no longer limited to higher education. Minority languages can be used on the Internet, provided they have a script. As distance education picks up momentum, the regional languages are bound to become the vehicles of education, but at the cost of smaller languages.[254]

8.3 Minority languages and the digital sector

Apart from India's various "divides", revolving around literacy, ethnicity, reli-

253 See Lachman M. Khubchandani, *Power of the Media for the Good of "Small' Languages: an Indian Experience of Enriching Diversity*, in: Foundation for endangered language (ed.), Proceedings of the 5th FEL Conference, 20-23 September, Agadir (Marocco)., p. 22-23
254 See NCLM, 42 report, p. 7, at: http://nclm.nic.in

gion, social identity, rural/urban etc., a different kind of digital divide is fast developing. While the level of literacy in regional languages is increasing due to the efforts in media and non-formal sectors, in the formal sector educational literacy in the mother tongue is loosing value in the context of computer literacy and English. A so-called "digital divide" emerged as India tries to absorb the new communication and data processing technologies, which is resulting in a disparity in access to information, skills, means and facilities. Computer penetration in India in 2004 is estimated to be 7.5 per 1,000 people, but Internet is used by just 1% of the total population.[255] The Indian languages in which the Internet search engine Google can work are Bengali, Hindi, Marathi, Tamil and Telugu. Due to this restricted number of languages, there is mounting pressure for expanding English along with the "digital languages," and both the governments and the people are moving quickly towards introducing English at the earliest level of education. For minority languages as well as for medium size scheduled languages the challenge is to keep the pace with the digitalization.

The computer in India is still the province of elites, as the "Computer technology initiative of the Union's Government not only did not percolate beyond the scheduled languages" but did not even benefit all scheduled languages uniformly.[256] Out of one thousand projects for extending the use of computer technology, nothing is known about "Digital resources for absolute minority languages." The localization of software is just one small part of the process of digital empowerment, due to the pressure to standardise languages. However it would be wrong to see a major homogenization as the only key to developing more software in smaller or minority languages. Mallikarjun warns against to high expectations, but also against passivity leaving the field to nothing but the "global language": "The IT perhaps entered India from other shores, and Indians have mastered it in many ways as providers of solutions for good profit, but they need to look within and produce stuff that will change the scene at the village, taluq, and district levels in India. Once this direction is accepted, solving linguistic issues may become a very interesting, engaging and rewarding pursuit for the young minds. Let us remember that every thing that English has, or for that matter, what Hindi is going to have, can not be or may not be appropriated by all languages, but certainly they can increase their vitality by becoming part of the IT world. At present most of them are out of the race. We need different action plans for major and minor languages of India since their technology needs are different."[257]

255 Mallikarjun, *Language and the digital divide,* in: Language in India, 2004, p.18
256 *Ibidem*, p.18
257 Mallikarjun, Digital divide, p. 20

Chapter 9

India's multilingualism and language shift among minorities

9.1 Multilingualism on the advance

India is made up of complex multilingual and multicultural societies with largely no boundaries sharply demarcating languages, castes or religions. The famous Gujarati spice merchant, settling in Mumbai, is quoted as a typical example: he speaks Gujarati in his family, Marathi in the vegetable market, Hindi with the milkman, Konkani in trading circles and rarely English on formal occasions.[258] Multilingualism is an age-old phenomenon in the Indian subcontinent, as there has been continuous migration, intermingling, and contact between many peoples and ethnic groups in the same major cities and regions of settlement. Historically, as today, many millions Indians were accustomed to switching from one language to another depending on the social context and their individual roles in society. They switched from Pali to Sanskrit, from Tamil to Sanskrit and from Ardhmagadhi to Sanskrit with ease. Bilingualism is a widespread phenomenon in predominantly oral forms (the census asks only for communication capacities). There are certainly many quality differences in the degree of multi- and bilingualism, which has still not been researched in depth. But at the same time a considerable process of language loss and assimilation is also occurring.[259]

Multilingualism is a structural must for a country with 114 living languages. The 2001 Census of India reports that 26% of India's total population is bilingual or trilingual, but among the speakers of non-scheduled languages (including almost all 'absolute minorities'), 42% claim to know at least one language other than their mother tongue. India is multilingual in two senses: each State in India is multilingual in the sense that alongside the dominant regional language there exist several minority languages, a situation somewhat similar to Europe. In addition, a steadily growing share of the population in all States and speech communities is bilingual or multilingual. Again, in Europe rather than "multilingual" a person would be qualified as "being fluent in one or more foreign languages", although the majority of the European population is still not fluent in a foreign language. The majority of India's population is not multilingual or even bilingual, although com-

258 Rakesh Bhatt/Ahmar Mahboob, *Minority languages and their status*, in: Kachru/Kachru/Sridhar, *Language in South Asia*, Cambridge University Press 2008, p.14.

259 Rakesh Bhatt/Ahmar Mahboob, *Minority languages and their status,* 2008, p. 146

manding a second language is a societal "megatrend". The following tables, showing an overall increase of 'multilinguals' among all language groups, also reflect the systematic implementation of the TLF in most Indian States over the past 30-40 years.

Table 18 - Bilinguals among major speech groups 1971, 1981, 2001

Language Group	Bilinguals speakers in %		
	1971	1981	2001 Bilinguals and trilinguals
Sindhi	43.0	57.2	63.4
Urdu	27.9	29.4	38.0
Punjabi	21.0	30.6	37.6
Malayalam	18.7	20.0	28.8
Kannada	17.1	15.2	24.0
Telugu	17.0	13.3	21.0
Kashmiri	16.0	24.2	60.0
Marathi	14.7	23.0	27.4
Tamil	13.8	19.6	18.7
Assamese	13.2	20.7	27.8
Gujarati	13.1	19.4	24.8
Bengali	12.0	5.6	13.0
Oriya	8.5	9.6	15.9
Hindi	6.4	4.8	11.0

Source: Khubchandani, Language Demography and Language in Education, in: Language Policy in India, UNESCO, Delhi 2001, p. 24

A distinction has to be made between natural bilingualism and planned bilingualism. "Perhaps what is already happening to an extent in this de facto multilingual education can become part of the answer. In place of drilling linguistic forms, the multilingualism that students are accustomed to in society could be respected and promoted in classroom."[260] That multilingualism is common in India is perhaps understated by the Census of India rates of bilingualism, calculated to be 9,7% in 1961 and rising from there to 13,04% in 1971, 13,34% in 1981 and 19,44% in 1991. The national average rate of trilingualism, presented for the first time in the 1991 Census is 7,26%. In 2001 18,72% of India's citizens were fluent in a second language and 7,22% fluent in a third language, summing up to 26% "multilinguals".

The rate of bilingualism and trilingualism varies depending on the linguistic community, but the share of bi- and multilingual people is basically higher the smaller a linguistic community is. The knowledge of one or more "foreign languages" is most widespread among the "non-scheduled languages" (mostly tribal languages). In 2001, the bilinguals among minor languages have accounted for 38.14% and the trilinguals 8.28%.

260 Rakesh Bhatt/Ahmar Mahboob, *Minority languages and their status,* 2008, p. 147

Table 19 - Number of multilingual people among speakers of a scheduled language (in 2001)

(the question was: fluency in one or two languages other than the mother tongue)

Languages	Total number of speakers	Bilinguals	% of bilinguals	% of trilinguals
Assamese	13,079,696	1,978,990	15.1	12.7
Bengali	69,595,738	5,842,675	8.3	4.7
Gujarati	40,673,814	5,394,439	1.2	11.6
Hindi	337,272,114	27,074,421	8.0	3.0
Kannada	32,753,676	5,212,152	15.9	8.1
Kashmiri*	5,000,000	1,300,000	26.9	33.1
Konkani	1,760,607	519,715	29.5	44.7
Malayalam	30,377,176	2,799,555	9.2	19.6
Manipuri	1,270,216	141,773	11.1	21.9
Marathi	62,481,681	9,205,446	14.7	12.7
Nepali	2,076,645	409,437	19.7	20.1
Oriya	28,061,313	1,894,755	6.7	9.2
Punjabi	23,378,744	3,400,361	14.5	23.1
Sindhi	2,122,848	741,797	34.9	28.5
Tamil	53,006,368	8,786,309	16.6	2.1
Telugu	66,017,615	8,168,683	12.7	8.3
Urdu	43,406,932	11,225,024	25.9	12.1

Source: Mallikarjun, Digital divide, 2004.

*The figure for Kashmiri is estimated as the census has not been carried out correctly in Jammu and Kashmir. The figures for Sanskrit appear unreliable.

The rate of bilingualism and trilingualism varies depending on the linguistic community, but the share of bi- and multilingual people is basically higher the smaller a linguistic community is. The knowledge of one or more "foreign languages" is most widespread among the "non-scheduled languages" (mostly tribal languages). In 2001, the bilinguals among minor languages have accounted for 38.14% and the trilinguals 8.28%. Looking at the issue of which language the Indians preferably choose as a second language, significantly, among the speakers of the major scheduled languages, English is more popular as a second language than Hindi. 8% speak English as their second language, 3.15% as a third language, whereas just 6.15% of Indians, not having Hindi as mother tongue choose Hindi as second and 2.16% as third language. Speakers of absolute minority languages, on the contrary, usually have to learn the regional official or dominant language first, and later the link languages as well.

9.2 What is multilingualism in the Indian context?

In India, linguistic diversity was inherited due to the composite culture of the country, which was not politically unified for centuries, merely nominally unified. So multilingualism could become an integral part of cultural habits of both the elites and of the less educated classes. Historically, bilinguals were always respected as persons able to impart their beliefs or religions in two or more languages. Furthermore bi- or multilingualism was regarded a social need.[261] Due to intense relations between ethno-linguistic areas and the intermingling of linguistic groups, the territories today delimited as federal States of India have never been linguistically homogeneous. At present not a single State or Union Territory is monolingual or without linguistic minorities, who first of all others were required to know other languages.

Apart from the linguistic minorities, who speak scheduled or non-scheduled languages different from the official State language, there is a huge variety of dialectal forms of the official languages. Amidst all this dialectal diversity, the accepted forms of such standardised official languages has emerged as "State majority languages", both for official purposes and as a propagated general language also in education due to the efforts of the "Official State language policies" of each State in the past 40 years.[262] In India there is therefore a "high level literate multilingualism", covering Hindi and English, and a "grassroots folk multilingualism". The standardisation of some minority languages or even of some of the smaller regional official languages often brings about the convention-inspired value system of small urban elites among the minority community, but not the daily spoken language. The people used to switch between different languages or between language styles spoken by the ordinary people and the language of high literature. During the period of the Moghuls many educated people mastered both Sanskrit and Persian/Arabic, and later Urdu emerged as a new Indian lan-

261 In Siddharta Gautama's age he expressed his teaching mainly in Sanskrit, which was at that time the main language of Brahmanism, but due to the importance of Pali and Ardhmagadhi he and his followers had to switch continuously between those languages. This resulted in a new style of Sanskrit called "Buddhist Sanskrit", which was understood by both the common people and the elite.

262 Srivastava writes about the Hindi region in India: "This region attests two types of bilingualism, where literacy and fluency in both languages are aimed at, but wherein first language is restricted to the topics related to the social sciences and the second language to the science subjects (monoliterate form of bilingualism) is confined primarily to the pre-school children of village schools, ...the partial type of bilingual education has been the general norm of pre-university education system. At the university level a partial type of bilingualism is practised, where in the second language replaces the first language in all subjects of formal teaching programs. See R.N. Srivastava, *Linguistic Minorities and National Language*, in F. Coulmas (ed.), Linguistic Minorities and Literacy, The Hague, Mouton 1984

guage. Multilingualism was historically largely a product of close contact and intermingling of the four language families since ancient times: the Indo-Aryan, Dravidian and Austro-Asiatic family in the major part of India, and the Indo-Aryan and Tibeto-Burmese languages in the North-eastern part of the subcontinent.

Later, from 18th century the colonial times through independence in 1947, new forms of multilingualism developed out of the new requirements of the changing political and socio-economic environment. The need for a "link-language" or inter-State communication tool, covering the whole subcontinent, emerged first in the newly independent federal India. But due to the internal dynamics between Northern and Southern India, English was not replaced. On the contrary: since India opened up to the world, the role of English was reinforced. Hence, multilingualism in India underwent a shift to the use of English in a broad range of domains, along with Hindi and some other major Indian languages. Apart from a "spontaneous bilingualism", grown out of the social milieu, there is also a sponsored bilingualism, focused on English and Hindi and running in different categories according to the institutional arrangements of the respective States. This is the typical combination of languages for the younger generation who have grown up under an educational system obeying the TLF. The modern multilingual Indian no longer looks like the Mumbai merchant: he or she is fluent in English, surfs the web in this global speech, then chats on the mobile phone with a friend from Delhi in Hindi, and switches to read the Marathi written newspaper. On the other hand, his grandparents were members of the Bhili minority in neighbouring Gujarat, but he hardly understands anything in this strange and "uncultivated" language.

Compared with Europe and its stricter link between language and territory, India's multilingualism shows some particular features. Typically, in a multilingual environment no language caters to all the needs of the participant. The choice of a language for daily communication depends on:
1. Pragmatic requirements of the situation, depending on the listener's capacity to understand and the speaker's capacity to communicate.
2. The institutional factors of identification and norm setting. Language serves as a label for status and prestige and offers clear regulations for language usage.

In India there are many multilingual environments marked by a high flexibility in the linguistic behaviour of many speech groups who speak more than just their mother tongue. In such environments many people are constantly required to communicate in various languages depending on the

Teachers of the Choeling Academy in Pelling (Sikkim)

situation and communication partners. Mother tongue identity, moreover, is not necessarily congruous with its daily actual usage, and languages generally are less rigidly identified with specific territories, as in Europe. Another specificity of India is the co-existence in single States of "official languages" and "languages used in administration" (see chapter 8.1), used along with other languages in various administration proceedings, be it for inter-state-communication or for interacting with linguistic minorities. In Andhra Pradesh, for example, Telugu is the official language, but five other languages are used for administrative activities. In the media, as in the educational system, switching from one language to another is a quite common custom.

Research on the patterns of intra-group and inter-group communication shows that the use of more languages is required for a large share of India's population. Correspondingly, the TLF applied in the educational system tries to meet this demand. "Various factors exert a major impact on this multilingualism like: the level of education, occupation, urbanity, contiguity of language border, prestige of a language. Within this heterogeneity, however, dominant and minority languages (lesser used or with lesser prestige and status) can be discerned."[263]

The linguistic plurality of the Indian subcontinent is traditionally based upon the complementary use of more than one language and more than one writing system for the same language in 'space'. Plural communities organise their multilingual repertoire through various processes of language contact.

In Northern India the use of the lingua franca Hindustani represents one such process. Bilingualism is another such process, manifesting diverse patterns characterised by socio-economic strata and the density of population (in metropolitan cities, towns, and rural areas). As proved by statistical evidence, multilingualism concerns the different speech communities in a different quantitative and qualitative extension. In other terms: smaller groups in the circle of scheduled languages (e.g. Sindhi, Kashmiri, Konkani, Manipuri, Nepali) are at a higher percentage bi- or trilingual, and speakers of non-scheduled languages (e.g. all tribal languages) are bilingual or trilingual to an even greater extent than the speakers of scheduled languages. Looking at the figures of Table 20, there is a clear correlation between the size of linguistic minority communities and the intensity of bilingualism. These results could be correlated to education development programs and processes of language planning. One example: out of the 623 tribal communities analysed under the 'People of India' (POI) project, only 123 communities (19.74%) were monolingual and the remaining 500 (80.26%) were bilingual. For tribal minority members the second language is either a minor language, spoken in the surrounding area, or a major scheduled language, mostly the regional language of the State in which they are settled.[264] The cultural-geographic pattern of settlement is a decisive factor for this kind of spontaneous "folk grassroots bilingualism". The more "introverted" a community is due to history, settlement pattern and political organisation, the lower is the pressure to learn other languages. For example: many Mizos in Mizoram still speak Lushai as the only language, but almost all younger Tulu speakers in Karnataka know at least basic Kannada.[265]

---

263 L. Khubchandani, *Language Demography and Language in Education*, in: Language Policy in India, UNESCO, Delhi 2001, p. 23

264 Rakesh Bhatt/Ahmar Mahboob, *Minority languages and their status*, in: Kachru/Kachru/Sridhar, *Language in South Asia*, Cambridge University Press 2008, p.145

265 Many operators of the census are not properly trained. The very definition of bi- or trilingualism is not clear, as tribal languages often do not even count as a languages. In the census often people are only asked whether, in addition to mother tongue, they know English, Hindi or the State official language, but not about other local languages. The same occurs with literacy.

Table 20 – Bilingualism/trilingualism of speakers of minority languages – 1991

Source: Mallikarjun, Language in India, 4-4-2004, annex (data from census 1991)

Name of non-scheduled language	Total speakers of this lan.	% of people knowing two or more lang.	Name of non-scheduled language	Total speakers of this language	% of people knowing two or more languages	Name of non-scheduled language	Total speakers of this lang.	% of people knowing 2 or more lang.
1 Adi	158,409	36.17	**34 Khezha**	13,004	39.43	67 Monpa	43,226	27.52
2 Anal	12,156	61.46	35 Khiemnunga	23,544	1.64	68 Munda	413,894	43.93
3 Angami	97,631	44.04	36 Kondh	220,783	37.09	69 Mundari	861,378	48.12
4 Ao	172,449	30.02	37 Kinnauri	61,794	60.23	70 Nicobarese	26,261	41.75
5 Arabic/Arbi	21,975	53.41	38 Kisan	162,088	57.83	**71 Nissi/Dafla**	173,791	26.22
6 Bhili/Bhilodi	5,572,308	19.31	39 Koch	26,179	39.59	72 Nocte	30,441	39.44
7 Bhotia	55,483	60.94	**40 Koda/Kora**	28,200	47.23	73 Paite	49,237	24.02
8 Bhumij	45,302	49.63	41 Kolami	98,281	60.43	74 Parji	44,001	57.52
9 Bishnupuriya	59,233	67.13	42 Kom	13,548	47.96	75 Pawi	15,346	32.04
10 Bodo/Boro	1,221,881	37.87	43 Konda	17,864	57.79	76 Phom	65,350	29.81
11 Chakhesang	30,985	40.40	44 Konyak	137,722	20.72	77 Pochury	11,231	43.83
12Chakru	48,207	27.13	45 Korku	466,073	58.94	78 Rabha	139,365	57.34
13 Chang	32,478	19.38	46 Korwa	27,485	50.28	79 Rengma	37,521	25.64
14Koorgi/Koda.	97,011	86.46	47 Koya	270,994	54.36	80 Sangtam	47,461	27.69
15 Deori	17,901	68.83	48 Kui	461,662	37.96	81 Santali	5,216,325	40.02
16 Dimasa	88,543	46.77	49 Kuki	58,263	47.45	82 Savara	273,168	44.71
17 Dogri	89,681	52.04	**50.Kurukh/Ora.**	1,426,618	53.85	83 Sema	166,157	28.78
18 English	178,598	66.99	51 Lahauli	22,027	67.85	84 Sherpa	16,105	68.17
19 Gadaba	28,158	57.59	52 Lahnda	27,386	56.10	85 Tangkhul	101,841	40.45
20 Gangte	13,695	35.40	53 Lakher	22,947	29.02	86 Tangsa	28,121	51.66
21 Garo	675,642	18.35	54 Lalung	33,746	61.52	87 Thado	107,992	37.89
22 Gondi	2,124,852	42.34	55 Lepcha	39,342	58.57	88 Tibetan	69,416	51.40
23 Halabi	534,313	24.68	56 Liangmei	27,478	53.84	89 Tripuri	694,940	44.73
24 Halam	29,322	41.89	57 Limbu	28,174	60.01	90 Tulu	1,552,259	68.89
25 Hmar	65,204	30.54	58 Lotha	85,802	36.53	91 Vaiphei	26,1855	33.94
26 Ho	949,216	31.83	**59Lushai/Mizo**	538,842	9.88	92 Wancho	39,600	23.24
27 Jatapu	25,730	63.48	60 Malto	108,148	38.43	93 Yimchung	47,227	20.78
28 Juang	16,858	51.45	61 Mao	77,810	31.45	94 Zeliang	35,079	31.45
29 Kabui	68,925	43.14	62 Maram	10,144	37.12	95 Zemi	22,634	34.10
30 Karbi/Mikir	366,229	43.68	63 Maring	15,268	61.57	96 Zou	15,966	25.60
31 Khandeshi	973,79	40.88	**64 Mir/Mishing**	390,583	51.81	97 Others	565,949	62.70
32 Kharia	225,556	66.77	65 Mishmi	29,000	43.18	Total	31,126,324	38.14
33 Khasi	912,283	12.60	66 Mogh	28,135	34.73			

Probably many millions of speakers of Hindi or Urdu, who cover the major part of the so-called "Hindi-belt", do not even perceive their bilingualism as a particular capacity. "For many people in the North Central region, Hindi-Urdu is like an 'associate' native speech and for them switching of linguistic codes from native speech to Hindi or Urdu is similar to the switching of styles in a monolingual situation".[266] Data on bilingualism is also biased by opposite factors: some believe that being bilingual includes knowledge of other languages in written form. Others know other scripts and believe they even command control of languages written in that script. Hence, what has to be questioned in the upcoming general census is also the quality of bilingualism: which criteria does the census use to qualify an individual as "bilingual" or "trilingual"? Is the multilinguistic capacity of a high share of the population also recorded in terms of proficiency? So far, the individual respondent did not need to know how to read and write a second or third language, but only needed to have a communication capacity.

One of the salient features of India's bilingualism is its complementary character with regard to the single linguistic domains covered by the two or more languages mastered. For example, one is used in the wider family context, a second in general public life ("out on the streets and markets"), a third one in all official public business (administration, contact with public officials, educational institutions, courts) and eventually a fourth one is used in communication with foreigners and Indian citizens from other States (usually English or Hindi). A typical modern Indian speaks three languages in daily practice: his mother tongue (mostly the regional official language), Hindi and English. The majority of people living in the rural areas, however, will seldom arrive at that stage, but will be able to communicate in the regional and the State official language, with a growing repertoire of Hindi due to its strong presence in media and popular culture. If an Indian citizen belongs to an "absolute linguistic minority" (non scheduled language) he is much more compelled to learn other languages, as the figures for the 1991 Census show. A member of such a speech community often masters four languages: his own family language, the regional official language of his home State, Hindi and English.

Are minority languages withering in this movement towards multilingualism? Minority languages are protected only to a certain extent. Many of them are no longer used in the schools and by far not all minority languages are taught in schools as a medium of instruction or as first languages in the primary schools. The young generation of minority language speakers is going to be multilingual.

266 *Ibidem*, p.27

9.3 Multilingualism: a resource or a problem?[267]

The new linguistic minorities, e.g. migrant people (especially in urban areas), are bound to increase due to industrialisation and freedom of mobility, and this factor will fuel multilingualism. Migrants today migrate as individuals or families, not as whole communities, but as job seekers. Communication with kin-groups is more easy now than some decades ago. There is also more media available all over India around the clock. Thus "...when families settle down and take roots in a different linguistic environment, they still continue their language loyalties."[268] Multilingualism in modern India is enhanced by three major factors: the formal education system, the media and the mobility of the people. Sharing of languages: multilingualism always had a role to play in the development of a language. People do not have to go to school to acquire two or more languages.

Are speakers of English as a second language "bilingual"? Most probably not. Due to institutional and educational arrangements, a growing number of people acquire fluency in English as a second language. This trend is also becoming popular among rural families, as the number of schools with English as medium is increasing. But the quality of bilingualism often remains unspecified in linguistic terms.

The UNDP states in his 2004 Report: "Experience around the world shows that plural language policies can expand opportunities for people in many ways, if there is a deliberate effort to teach all citizens some of the country's major languages. Very often what multilingual countries need is a TLF, as UNESCO recommends, that gives public recognition to the use of three languages:

6) One international language – in former colonial countries this is often the official language of administration. In this era of globalisation all countries need to be proficient in an international language to participate in the global economy and networks.
7) One lingua franca – a local link language facilitates communication between different linguistic groups such as Swahili in East African countries, where many other languages are also spoken.
8) Mother tongue – people want and need to be able to use their mother tongue when it is neither the lingua franca nor the international language."[269]

Multilingualism for linguistic minorities is both a necessity and a change. It requires planned acquisition and co-ordination with the mother tongue

267 B Mallikarjun, *Language and the digital divide*, in: Language in India, April 2004, p.5
268 ibidem, p. 6
269 UNDP-Report 2004, p.60

medium. Low educational attainment continues to be a major source of exclusion for immigrants, tribal ethnic groups and backward castes. In such cases, offering bilingual education not only recognises their cultural traditions, but it also enhances learning and reduces educational disparities by widening people's choices. Children learn best when they are taught in their mother tongue, particularly in the earliest years. Experience in many countries shows that bilingual education, which combines instruction in the mother tongue with teaching in the dominant national language, can open educational and other opportunities.

9.4 Language shift and language attrition among tribal peoples

In India there is a widespread attitude towards minority mother tongues as languages that are not worth being studied at school. This signals a slow language shift to major languages, starting from a restricted economically-driven view of the value of languages. This language shift is more widespread among tribal communities. Although the tribal population accounts for about 7% of India's total population, only about 35-38 million out of 71 million (2001) have retained their language. Breton[270] observed that most tribes are involved in a general process of linguistic acculturation in favour of the regional languages. Ishtiaq (1999) claims that a positive valuation of factors such as urbanization, literacy, economy and changes in the traditional work and belief systems is enhancing this language shift.

The picture is contradictory: several minority ethno-linguistic groups such as Khasi, Naga, Santals, Khonds, Garo, Bodo still show fierce language loyalty, which has found expression in cultural and political movements, e.g. the Bodos obtaining an Autonomous Hill Council in Assam. The Santhals in all four States where they are settled show considerable linguistic identity and vitality, demanding a separate province for the tribal people of Chota Nagpur within the framework of the Government of India and with Santhali and other tribal languages as medium of instruction in public schools. Bodo and Santhali are therefore forerunners of a kind of linguistic resistance movement against the prevailing cultural and linguistic assimilation of tribal cultures in modern India.

Due to increasing mobility, an ever more integrated national economy and labour market, job-oriented learning behaviour, and a uniform mass-me-

270 Roland J.L. Breton, *Languages and Ethnic Communities in South Asia* (updated edition), Sage publication, London/New Delhi 1997

The general secretaries of the Bodo Students' Union ABSU, Kokrajhar (Assam)

dia culture makes it ever more difficult for minority languages speakers to maintain their linguistic heritage. The trend points to a major language shift toward regionally dominant languages and toward the swift extinction of several smaller languages. Apparently what is going on in India today – only marginally contained by minority protection measures – is a "rationalisation of languages", or a reduction of linguistic complexity.

Bilingualism among India's tribal peoples with an amount of 50% bilingual individuals is higher than the national average. As linguists opine, bilingualism does not necessarily lead to language shift, but in the South Asian context bi- and multilingualism has been coexisting with language maintenance for centuries. However, the question arises regarding why and how tribes and other linguistic minorities may retain their languages when the forces of urbanization and bilingualism are exerting an increasing pressure to language shift. "The answer lies in the nature of the multilingualism that prevails in India, lack of educational and other opportunities to climb the social ladder as well as in the cultural and psychological attitude that the speakers of such minority language possess. The foremost factor among these is that South Asian multilingualism is of a coexisting and not of a competing nature, which allows a speaker to assign different domains to different languages. In other words, functional specialization of different languages has identified the role of the real mother tongue (the indigenous language) for intra-tribe communication. This factor has certainly helped people to retain their languages even if they claim otherwise."[271]

The second factor may be embarrassing for the Indian educational policy, as literacy programs and the education system available to speakers of scheduled languages often are not provided to tribal communities. This served to maintain the mother tongue, as literacy programs are mostly carried out in the dominant languages.

The third important reason for mother tongue retention has been "the cultural and psychological make-up of the speaker toward their languages. More than an identity marker, the mother tongue has been seen as a personal matter satisfying a psychological need, something which is outside the bounds of external intervention...Mother tongues are seen in the same light as one's food habits, one's religious beliefs and one's living habits."[272] However, a heavy to modest language shift can be observed in some areas. Almost half of the tribal languages have ceased to be mother tongues. Any language shift as reported in the table below is an outcome of various factors, among which the following are the most significant:[273]

1. Inferiority complex of the mother tongue speakers;
2. Economic benefits of learning the dominant language;
3. Facility to learn the dominant language as part of free schooling;
4. Low tolerance of the dominant language speakers towards the minority language speakers.

Table 21 clearly reveals that the linguistic situation of the tribal peoples of Central and Southern India is quite critical, whereas they are rather safe in the Northeast and in Himalayan regions. As Anvita Abbi notes "...languages start their journey to obsolescence and death when they cease to be used in homes. When either of the parents stop using their mother tongue with their children, it is a sure sign that the language has set on its path to death. This is what is happening at present among the Kurukh speakers in urban areas of Jharkhand. Children are punished for speaking their mother tongues at home. Fortunately, not all languages of Jharkhand are in the same situation."[274]

271 Anvita Abbi, *Tribal languages*, in: Kachru/Kachru/Sridhar, *Language in South Asia*, Cambridge University Press 2008, p. 165

272 *ibidem*, p.165

273 *ibidem*, p. 165

274 Anvita Abbi, *Tribal languages*, p. 166

Table 21 Language shift among tribal people in various States

Language shift in %	Indian States or Union Territories
<1%	Sikkim, Meghalaya, Arunachal Pradesh, Manipur, Mizoram, Nagaland, Andaman&Nicobar
1-10%	Jammu&Kashmir
10-20%	Bihar including Jharkhand
20-40%	Himachal Pradesh, Rajasthan, West Bengal, Assam
40-80%	Madhya Pradesh (including Chhattisgarh), Maharashtra, Orissa, Karnataka, Andhra Pradesh
>80%	Gujarat, Kerala, Tamil Nadu, Lakshadweep, Uttar Pradesh, Goa, Diu, Daman

Source: Ishtiaq (1999)

A redeeming factor is that not all tribal language speakers see their mother tongues as deprived languages. A case point is Santhali. Various movements of language loyalists in the past 50 years have revived this language. It is used as a medium of instruction in villages at the primary level as well as for the publication of magazines and journals. An independent script, Ol Chiki, has been created to write the language. Interestingly, Ol Chiki has now been adopted by some other tribal languages in order to maintain a tribal identity. Many schools in the Jharkhand area are known to use Ol Chiki for primary education despite some tribal members' resistance to learning their mother tongue in the school domain. These conflicting behaviours by tribal communities indicate a common aspiration to be a part of the mainstream while maintaining their distinct identity and way of life.

In summary, most of India's "tribal languages" are no longer isolated, but operate in increasing contact with the surrounding world speaking regionally or nationwide dominant languages. The tribal communities' reaction is twofold: a major trend is language shift, which entails abandoning their traditional mother tongue. Half of the members of tribal communities no longer speaks their original language. The other reaction to maintain the language for some functions, but to become bilingual and multilingual for others. If these languages are maintained, they do it mostly in the absence of any recognition, official status and other state or public support, relying only on markers of distinct identity and facility of intra-group communication as their source of vitality.

The case of Khasi

A minority language's missed opportunities

Almost a million people in the Northeastern State of Meghalaya and in some areas of adjacent Assam speak Khasi as mother tongue, a language belonging to the Austro-Asiatic family, related with Mon-Khmer languages in Southeast Asia.[275] The Khasi, including its variant Pnar mostly spoken in the Jaintia Hills, together with the Garo count for about 80% of Meghalaya's total population. In European terms they are a kind of "titular people" of this State, carved out from Assam in 1972. Surprisingly, after having adopted English as official language, Meghalaya only in 2005 recognized Khasi and Garo as co-official languages of the State. But the enactment rules in 2009 still have to be issued. Thus Khasi, along with Garo, seldom can be seen in Meghalaya's linguistic landscape. Even the public buildings in Meghalaya's capital Shillong with a huge Khasi majority population almost never carry an official denomination in Khasi and there are no signs of serious efforts of bi- or trilingualism displayed in the public sphere of this State.

Khasi is a language with an ancient tradition, written since more than 150 years, when the Bible was first translated by British missionaries. Although there is a standardized version of Khasi, used mainly by journalists in various daily, weekly and monthly media[276], in Meghalaya no official board or academy is in charge of language corpus and development planning. Hence, the development of school curricula for Khasi as a subject so far was done by the Department of Khasi of the University of Shillong. Khasi is taught as a subject on secondary level, but in the education system as a whole it plays a backstage role, while English reigns supreme. Mostly in rural areas Khasi is used as medium of instruction up to class VI, according to fundamental constitutional rights. But, alas, very few textbooks have been translated from English to Khasi, even fewer produced in Khasi. The language's role is exhausted with an auxiliary role as the teacher explains and ad hoc translates English textbooks to Khasi children. No doubt, as elsewhere in India and even more in the Northeast English is indispensable. But the bulk of student do not reach real proficiency in written English and this results in many young Khasi who neither can write correctly their mother tongue nor English.

---

275 Information retrieved from C.R. Marak and J.S. Shangpliang, *Growth and Development of Khasi and Garo Language*, Sahitya Akademi, New Delhi/Mumbai/Chennai/Bangalore 2008

276 In Meghalaya there are 5 daily newspapers printing 35.000 copies, 6 weekly papers and 2 monthly magazines in Khasi language.

A typical public signboard in Shillong (Meghalaya)

The situation is not better in Meghalaya's public administration. Knowledge of Khasi (or Garo) in standard written form is no formal requirement, although it is now an associate official language. The lack of appropriate terminology is the current explanation for this situation, but in 37 years of statehood obviously nobody cared about. Although government departments use also written Khasi, employees are not required to prove proficiency at the moment of recruitment: for sure no good incentive to ever learn it properly in school. This fact is not linked to multilingual origin of the employees, as due to ST quota-regulations almost all are native Khasi, Pnar or Garo. Due to the lack of State legislation on the matter, there is no real Khasi language policy, although the State is endowed with such powers. Do the politicians use their native language? In the State's Assembly Khasi can be used, but the text has to be handed over in English version one hour before the respective speech is given. The awareness of the value of the native languages seems to be blocked at a low level, with widespread symptoms of a cultural inferiority complex.

Finally Khasi is no language recognized under the 8th schedule of the Constitution, but even since Khasi was declared official in 2005 and could display a major literature and printing production, it could not obtain New Delhi's official placet. The reason lies not only with the Centre, but Meghalaya itself did not exert sufficient pressure, while the Bodos and Santhal, without a State behind, could reach that goal.

The political elite doesn't appear to attach major value to the benefits of language development. Although the Khasi speakers have "their own State", shared with the Garo, vested with legislative powers on language issues and State funds, the necessary framework yet has to be set. In Mizoram one cannot survive without knowing some Mizo, but one can perfectly live in Meghalaya without knowing any Khasi or Garo. Perhaps, Meghalaya's electorate is well up with things as they are today? Perhaps the Khasi are afraid to loose the connection with national and global developments if their native language is upgraded and given a major role? But being strong in one's own roots is no harm for opening up to the world and learn other languages.

Chapter 10

Crucial issues of India's protection of linguistic minorities

The current situation of India's linguistic minorities, highlighted above, with all its legal, cultural, social and political facets, due to its heterogeneity hardly can be evaluated in a comparative manner with European minority situations. In Europe, too, there is neither a uniform continent-wide approach to linguistic minorities nor a common legal protection standard already implemented by a majority of states. On the contrary, even more different national devices of minority protection are applied by the single European states (47, out of which at least 39 are home to ethno-linguistic minorities). If India has enshrined some fundamental provisions for safeguarding the rights of linguistic minorities in her Constitution of 1950, Europe, apart from its regional convention of human rights ECHR, in 1998 has put in force two international conventions to protect national minorities, regional or minority languages and developed further instruments of soft law.[277]

The level and quality of implementation of these provisions varies from state to state, as the protection of national or linguistic minorities is a matter of domestic law, whereas no supra-national jurisdiction by a Supreme Court can be invoked in case of violation of such provisions, unlike the mechanisms given for legal remedy for individual human rights violations under the ECHR. The latter convention was a milestone in the global efforts to establish a system of enforceable corpus of human rights including a strong section on individual discrimination. In India a different power sharing is given in this domain, but again the single States are the main political actors responsible for the protection of linguistic minorities. The normative standard of India's regulations for safeguarding the rights of such minorities, enshrined in the Union's Constitution, and the situation on the ground can be evaluated as such. But when analysing India's current language policy with a "European mind" the substantial differences of its

277 For the text of these conventions see: *The Framework Convention for the Protection of National Minorities* (CoE), available at: http://conventions.coe.int/Treaty/EN/Treaties/Html/157 *The European Charter for Regional or Minority Languages* (CoE), available at: http://conventions.coe.int/Treaty/EN/Treaties/Html/148.htm; furthermore three text of soft law: the *Lund Recommendation on the Effective Participation of National Minorities in Public Life* (1999), *The Oslo Recommenation Regarding Linguistic Rights of National Minorities* (1998) and *The Hague Recommendations Regarding the Education Rights of National Minorities* (1996), all available at the Foundation on Inter-Ethnic Relations.

linguistic landscape, the specifically Indian form of multilingualism, the very relevance of the language in identity building of individuals and groups as compared with religion, caste, home region and some other structural differences should never be overlooked.

Whereas Europe, since the constitution of the first unitary states as the United Kingdom, Spain and France and many others in the 19th century and immediately after World War I, has been shaped along the concept of the nation-state, based on the idea of "one state for one people with one language", India in history had no prevailing state formation based upon languages, but as an independent state was a legacy of the British colonial power and its territorial possession on the subcontinent. Even during the British colonisation the foreign rulers did not seek to impose their language to all Indians, but only inasmuch English as an official language served their purpose to rule the country. Before gaining independence, future State languages were a matter of political debate among the rising Indian political forces, but never were the languages a criterion to build nation states upon it. Whereas Europe went through a long phase of "nation-state-building", India, after the trauma of partition, first started as a federal polity composed of many peoples, cultures, languages and regions, and only later had recourse to language as an organisation principle of the federation. Whereas Europe since 1957 step by step is heading towards a supranational entity embracing a growing share of the continent under the banner of the slogan "unity in diversity", India always had plenty of internal diversity, but since 1947, the country was often challenged to preserve its unity. This analysis will now examine the Indian language policy vis-à-vis linguistic minorities in light of European regulations, which are designed to become a minimum standards under the current international conventions, grouped in nine single features.[278]

10.1 The importance of language in identity building

The importance of language in building up a national identity in India differs from that prevailing in Europe. India's "national cultures" (Hinduism, other religions) and link-languages (Hindi, English) act as super-ordinate cultural coordinates, which are co-exist with regional State cultures. Indian citizens who grow up, for instance, in Karnataka and speak no other language but

278 See Thomas Benedikter, *Threatened Languages and Linguistic Rights of Minorities: some Empirical Background*, in: S. K. Singh (ed.), *Rethinking Multingualism – Issues and Problems*, Eastern Publ., Guwahati 2009; and Thomas Benedikter (ed.), *Europe's Ethnic Mosaic, A Short Guide to Minority Rights in Europe*, EURAC, Bozen 2008

A Lepcha family near Pemayangtse monastery (Sikkim)

Kannada can perfectly combine their feeling of being a member of the Indian nation and a Karnataki. On the contrary, the European identity and self-perception starts from being a citizen of one of its nation-states, and only then a feeling of membership of the new European construction is embraced. The overwhelming majority of French citizens perceive themselves first of all as French and secondly as Europeans or citizens of the EU.[279] The same pattern prevails in the other European states. The national minority issue – or in India the issue of linguistic minorities - as well as the multifaceted issue of dialects brings in the third layer, which is what Europeans call the regional dimension: the home region, often home to linguistic minorities or communities which develop a strong sense of belonging to their region.[280] Apart from this dimension, about half of Europe's peoples or linguistic communities do not have their own state and thus are "absolute minorities" who speak languages which are not recognized as official in any other European "kin-state". In turn, minorities with a "kin-state", against the background of a continent deeply moulded by the concept of the nation-state, are also defined "national minorities".

279 See European Union, *Eurobarometer 63* (2005) as well as *Eurobarometer 54 Special Report*, 2001, on: Europeans and languages.

280 Region in the European understanding is equivalent to „district" in some South Asian states, as India.

In India, on the contrary, pan-Indian national cultures act as "superordinate" languages, while regional cultures behave like localised distinct languages. As the renowned sociolinguist Srivastava puts it, "...regionalised cultures like dialects usually do not detract from the wider loyalties to a nation; rather it provides the people with a sense of belonging instead of inbreeding feeling of hyphenated rootless life. It is the cultural pluralism within a multilingual framework, with a sense of super ordinate feeling of being one nation, which is the Indian identity."[281] In India the Constitution does not consider that one language is required for developing India into a nation, although Article 343 Const. envisioned that Hindi should assume this role. Nevertheless such provisions are dormant.

Indian nationalism or national identity is not tied up with just one language or one religion. The Constitution, as in matters of religion, prescribes linguistic secularism for India. This has been the case historically, and the Constitution reflects this historical fact. The acceptance of multilingualism as a basic principle of the organisation of the Union at the federal and State level has utmost political and psychological importance as the people, speaking so many diverse languages small and big, have the feeling that all languages are equally a part of the multilingual fabric of the country. Consequently, the Constitution tries to square the circle: establish national link-languages, enhance the regional official language, ensure the multilingual character of the country and safeguard the rights of linguistic minorities. It is a different matter whether these constitutional objectives are actually implemented in the present day political reality.

10.2 Minority protection in a multilingual context

Compared with India, Europe's linguistic communities are intertwined to a much lesser extent, and languages are less intermingled, while most linguistic minorities have a close and stable relationship with their traditional territory. In many such territories autochthonous (primordial) ethno-linguistic groups are living together with groups of the majority population of the respective state. While usually they show a tight linkage with the territory, developed throughout history, rather it is the emerging phenomenon of the newly immigrated minority groups which in many urban areas are giving rise to de facto "multilingual environments", comparable with the Indian urban scenarios.

281 Srivastava, 1977, p.70-71, quoted by N.H. Itagi/Shailendra Kumar Singh (eds.), *Linguistic Landscaping in India*, CIIL and M. Gandhi International Hindi University, Mysore 2002, p. 50

Nevertheless, the cultural imperative in the European "national states" is still that all citizens are required to know and learn the State official language before learning foreign languages. Hence, although linguistic minorities have their own public schools with a mother tongue medium they are obliged to establish such a priority. On the other hand, the necessity of a European link language is a historically new challenge, which emerges more strongly as the economic and social integration of the nation states deepens. European integration is both extending to a larger number of states and deepening with an increasing impact into a wide range of policies and into the daily life of the citizens.[282]

Although the EU has issued recommendations regarding national education policies to ensure that in the future every young European is fluent in at least two other European languages, most States are far from adopting a "TLF" in the Indian style. As English is the absolute favourite foreign language in most European countries, it is learned at the expense of other major languages such as German, French, Spanish, Polish, Italian etc. The national education systems are not bound to transform into systems with three-language-medium-schools, but for the foreseeable future will remain national language medium schools with one or two "foreign languages", although in the foreseeable future the EU will include almost all of Europe. For the speakers of minority languages this strategy in Europe also automatically entails a TLF, as, apart from mother tongue and foreign languages, they are required to learn the national majority language (the "State language") as well. India, operating with two link-languages and the Three-language-formula as a main pillar of the education policy, requires linguistic minorities to learn at least three other languages, apart from their own, which means a "4-language-formula". The Indian youth is, to put it bluntly, under a higher language learning stress as their European counterpart age group.

Practical regulations and instruments are not the only features determining a language policy; psychological and emotional factors are also important in India. Language is a central feature of cultural identity and a political symbol for the integration of major groups, as was the case for the Tamils and other Dravidian linguistic groups of South India. Moreover language conflicts sometimes cover deeper cleavages on a political and social level,

282 These issues are extensively analysed by Peter A. Kraus, *A Union of Diversity – Language, Identity and Polity-Building in Europe*, Cambridge University Press 2008: the best overview on the situation of linguistic rights of minorities is given by Christoph Pan's and Beate S. Pfeil's, *Minderheitenrechte in Europa, Handbuch der Europ. Volksgruppen*, Band 2, Springer, Vienna 2006, screening the situation in all European countries except the microstates (only in German language).

as e.g. the perceived dominance of one group in the political sphere. Decisions of language policy, therefore have manifold effects not limited to the cultural life proper, but affecting the whole architecture of the Indian Union. Fortunately, the language policies in India were discussed and implemented within a federal and pluralist institutional framework, accompanied by a free media and information system. Decisions opposed by strong minorities could be redressed later, and flexible solutions were found instead of forcibly imposing languages on other states. The initial project to develop Hindi as an "indigenous national language" was opposed by several States, which succeeded in maintaining a strong role for English and in reinforcing the single regional State languages. The existence of English as an overarching neutral link language from a historical perspective is a rather fortunate circumstance, which avoided a large-scale "linguistic imperialism" as happened in Latin America and in China.

On the other hand, India has done a great deal to strengthen linguistic pluralism: the strong emphasis on multilingual formal education reinforced by promoting the TLF has contributed to a widely accepted pluralist approach to languages in India's modern society. The efforts to promote multilingualism had to be combined with the Constitutional safeguards for the rights of linguistic minorities. Ensuring primary education in the mother tongue, allowing for media in minority languages, providing safeguards to use minority languages at the local level, whenever a minimum of population speaks them – all such provisions are not to be taken for granted in the difficult social reality of a developing country.

In heterogeneous societies like India's, it is important to promote cohesion or integration at both levels, federal and State. This is also happening through languages and language policy. But it has to be acknowledged that languages are not equal and do not have the same standing. Absolute equality in function, prestige, and status is quite unrealistic, but if linguistic variety is to be preserved – as an overriding political aim - legislation and policy must respond to this goal. Weaker, smaller minority languages must receive major promotion to compensate for their difficulties with regard to dominant languages, provided the goal is to enable their survival. Every language should obtain recognition and the promotion its speakers desire, so to be accepted by all and to avoid the discrimination of linguistic minorities. In India, as in Europe, there is a cleavage between constitutional postulations and material social and political performance.

10.3 The economic dimension of the protection of linguistic rights

For illustrating this point we have to get back to the principal causes of language endangerment as quoted in the introduction. The main symptom of such a process in the dwindling number of speakers, and this is mainly due to the attitude of native speakers of renouncing to pass their language on to their children. Every language is endangered if it is held in low esteem by it speakers and if it is deemed a language with very little or no use in any domain outside the family home. Such languages, instead of being useful for each kind of communication and livelihood, are rather considered a liability. Their speakers prefer and feel compelled to prefer to equip their children with languages of the majority culture, be it the State official or the national one. Bilingual parents, belonging to a linguistic minority, often are not keen to pass on the problems linked to be a "minority language speaker", but to ensure the optimum of professional opportunities for their offspring. Unless learning a minority language, apart from being a cultural heritage, is not important for improving one's social and economic opportunities, such languages will be endangered. Language skills in a modern society turn out to be a resource only if there is a link to utility on the labour market.

Therefore the real issue is how to redress the structural disadvantage of minority languages in States dominated by one linguistic majority, coupled with the general requirement of multilingualism in a multilingual nation. Which kind of legal-political framework must be created for endowing also minority languages with utility and relevance in the modern social, economic and cultural life in their environment? This "redress" of structural dominance can occur only on a territorial basis referring to the traditional "homelands" of such minorities, in India mostly to be identified on district or sub-district level. For the purpose of the protection of minority rights and of rights of tribal peoples in particular, district autonomies have been established under the 5th and 6th schedule of the Constitution. Most of such 6th-schedule-district autonomies were created in the ethnically heterogeneous Northeast, none in the big tribal belt of central India. There are many districts outside the Northeast which have a majority of tribal peoples or, however, groups speaking a different language as their native language than the State official language. District autonomy is not only an issue for so-called tribal peoples, but for linguistic minorities generally. In Europe, out of 36 operating autonomous regions, the major part has obtained this status due to the presence of an ethno-linguistic minority, and several more are striving for this status.

In this regards India's quota regulations for members of STs turn out to be a double-edged sword. On the one hand they are there to ensure equal rights and opportunities to disadvantaged groups of the society and to avoid substantial discrimination; on the other hand due to the ST-quota reservation part of the tribal elite can often get a public job. Then they migrate to major towns and are absorbed in the mainstream. Mostly they don't come back to the communities to work. This "brain-drain" weakens the tribal community and the efforts for modernizing the smaller languages. In the long run the qualified jobs have to be created locally and requiring a certain degree of command of the local or regional languages too, if these languages are to be preserved.

10.4 Language and territory

As has been said, in Europe major linguistic groups (peoples) and linguistic minorities have a tight link with their traditional territory. The local-regional dimension is very relevant in India as well, as it is a society that was much less mobile and migrant in the past, with an economy based on agriculture and less integrated before the industrialisation of the recent decades. But as a political factor, territory does play a much weaker role in India's architecture of state powers. One example is the unusual faculty of the Centre's legislature to carve out new federated States of existing States; a second the relatively scarce powers of the sub-State government level. India's third government level – in the European Union the roughly 250 regions (sometimes identical with federal units), in India the 330 districts – has much less power of self-government than in most European states. In India, commonly there are no legislative powers on the sub-State-level (district, taluq), and territorial autonomy is a rather rare exception, concentrated mostly in the Northeast and West-Bengal, where 11 "Autonomous Hill Councils" have been established under the 6th Schedule of the Constitution[283]. While India is the most populous federal state in the world, most European states, having the size of Indian States, are themselves structured on three levels: the centre or federation, the regions or federal units, and the municipal level.

283 Other two are located in Jammu&Kashmir, the autonomous districts of Kargil and Leh. An analysis and comparison of all world-wide operating regional autonomies has been elaborated by the author. See Sabyasachi Basu Ray Chaudhury, Samir Kumar Das and Ranabir Samaddar (eds.), *Indian Autonomies: Keywords and Key texts*, Kolkata 2005; and Thomas Benedikter, *The World's Working Regional Autonomies*, ANTHEM Press, London/New Delhi 2007

This territorial power sharing structure forms a remarkable difference in the "institutional infrastructure" of a state, which is very relevant for the protection of ethno-linguistic minorities. The more decentralised a State is, the more opportunities regional minorities have for self-government, for shaping cultural and education policies according to linguistic peculiarities, and for implementing such linguistic rights as official bilingualism in public administration. The latter concept is more coherently adopted in cases of full-fledged territorial autonomy, which has been established in 36 areas in 11 European states. India still is much more reluctant in conceding regional autonomy, and it remains to be seen whether the existing forms of autonomy (e.g. Leh & Kargil, Bodoland, Darjeeling, Khasi, Garo and Jaintia Hills, North Cachar, Karbi-Anlong, Chakma. Lakher, Lai etc.) have met the goal of preserving minority languages. At least 50 other Indian districts have a considerable, if not majority indigenous (Adivasi) population. Yet, their languages only exceptionally enjoy official status in those districts. A precise mapping of such areas and an assessment of the requirements of local self-administration has not yet been conducted.

Some provisions of Part XVII of the Constitution on "Official Language" seemingly seek to protect minority languages on a territorial basis. Most, however, have remained ineffective in protecting the rights of linguistic minorities. Article 347 reads: "On a demand being made in that behalf the President may, if he is satisfied that a substantial proportion of the population of a state desire the use of any language spoken by them to be recognised by that state, direct that such language shall also be officially recognised throughout that State or any part thereof for such purpose as he may specify." Instead of making it a duty of the State to determine the size and spread of linguistic minorities for their official recognition at appropriate levels and purposes, Article 347 makes such recognition and use dependent on the subjective satisfaction of the federal President and on the "desire of a substantial proportion of the local population" - quite a vague concept. This is based on the ground that a substantial proportion of the population desires it, and that desire has been expressed in the form of a demand. This amounts to treating numerically inferior groups of citizens as subject people and not as citizens with inherent and inalienable rights, including the right to the use of their mother tongue in important public domains. What proportion should be treated as substantial, 25% or 50%? No precise indication is given, and hence it is not surprising that very few minority languages have been declared co-official on regional or district level. [284]

284 But Ranabir Samaddar, Director of the Mahanirban Calcutta Research Group objects to this statement: „Thus, the idea 'if a majority group could freely adopt ist own language regu-

India's Autonomous District Councils under the 6th schedule are vested with a varying range of powers, but just a few of them covering cultural and linguistic affairs. As the legislative scope and financial fundings are quite restricted, the performance of such autonomies is not prevailingly positive as far as the language policy is concerned. In other terms: this form of autonomy did not provide a sufficient political basis to create a framework for counterbalancing to the dominance of the respective State official language. Whereas the 6th schedule-autonomy was designed around 1950 to take care of the interests of tribal peoples in troublesome Assam, the purpose of a new extended concept of territorial autonomy is much more comprehensive: there is a need of recognition and protection of smaller linguistic communities in many other States, which are in a absolute or relative majority on district level or in their traditional regions. Thus, the real challenge is how to decentralize the existing Indian States in order to cope with the need to provide a local-regional framework for equal linguistic rights and protection of smaller languages.

10.5 Differences in perceiving multilingualism: the hierarchy of linguistic domains

Because of close contacts with other speech communities and possibly because of early alphabetisation in other languages, claims of proficiency or having native-like control over more than one language or dialect is a very common phenomenon in India. Bi- and trilingualism in India is not just a feature of "highbrow-culture" or of the well-educated elite, but is widely spread among all social strata. Due to the TLF-policy, the share of bilinguals is steadily increasing. In such a plurilingual society, one's total linguistic repertoire is influenced by more than one language and/or dialect, and a person's choice of languages is hardly obstructed by linguistic boundaries. The boundary between dialect and language or between two languages (where children have been lingualised, acculturated, and socialised in two languages simultaneously) remains very fluid. Apart from mastery over language at large, Indian people do not show over-consciousness of speech characteristics in operating in various domains, unless a formally high level of accuracy is demanded: "Therefore, in such multilingual societies mere speech characteristics cannot be a strict marker of lingual identification unlike in European countries."[285]

lation in its area, the usage would be quite different' betrays our disregard of the fundamental fact that India has been often plurilingual and linguistic nationalism went hand in hand with Indian nationalism, and the search for such „areas" may at times be fruitless."

285 Shailendra Kumar Singh, *Linguistic Landscaping*, CIIL Mysore, 2002, p. 46

In linguistically heterogeneous countries like India, a child acquires other languages than its mother tongue from everyday life situations as he grows or starts moving from lower-based linguistic environments to successively higher ones, that is, from home to school, from the school to the capital. Therefore, the speech behaviour or course of language choice is guided by various sociolinguistic demands made by close groups, regional societies, supra-regional spaces or functional requirements in different contexts. By learning other languages, a common Indian citizen responds to functional needs at various sociolinguistic layers, without attaching to that a nationality or a ideologically overloaded significance.[286]

Unlike Europe with its "national languages" and first and second "foreign languages", in India there is no strict separation of languages, even if the States try to impose their respective official languages in several domains such as education, public administration and the media. "People's social, cultural and political identity is linked with the language that they speak, that they think in and that they use to communicate. Multilingualism in India is seen as a hindrance in its development by the developed world. Often an anxiety is expressed as to how a government at the centre could function in a hundred different languages! But neither India nor Europe's national or supra-national do operate in a hundred languages. The European Union has 23 official and only two working languages, English and French. India has 22 scheduled languages and also two "working languages", English and Hindi. Hence the need to have a national or supra-national link-language while preserving the State languages in other domains is not linked with the imposition of a dominant culture and language by a centralized leadership. A multicultural and multilingual society can perfectly maintain this fundamental feature, although adopting one or some common languages for political and institutional communication.[287] In the past, at least in some parts of India, Hindi was perceived as a language that was going to be imposed on other states. But today a relaxed approach to multilingualism can be observed based on the hierarchy of languages with their functional differentiation.

10.6 What is an official language? About the politics of recognition

In the past, the multiplicity of languages in India induced some Western,

286 *ibidem*, p. 47

287 See Sadhana Saxena/Kamal Mahendroo, *Politics of Language*, in: Gupta/Abbi/Aggarwal, *Language and the State*, p.151

but also some Indian scholars to issue alarmed warnings of imminent balkanisation (for example O'Barr in 1976). The presence of many languages within a country is often seen as a source of linguistic confusion and local nationalism, which could develop into a counter posture of nation-wide nationalism. But in multilingual countries such as India – as has been said in the previous paragraph - many languages complement one another in different domains or occupy parallel functions when bilingualism in the public sphere is at stake and are not in constant confrontation with one another. Nevertheless, if languages are to be accorded equal footing, there has to be full recognition, based on clear criteria, entrenched in legal provisions. The main premise of an official status is the recognition of a language, made by a legal, possibly constitutional act of the State. Several European states still do not even recognise any linguistic or ethnic minorities (France, Turkey, Greece, Belarus), and several states have not yet ratified the most important legal instruments for the protection of national minorities (FCNM and ECRML[288]). In other European states it can be observed that the official recognition of minority languages has not been followed by an adequate political attempt to implement the provisions linked to recognition.

Whereas recognition in Europe is a matter of the nation-states and the implementation of minority protection is a domestic state affair, the Indian path to language recognition appears quite arbitrary: although India theoretically could apply a Union-wide coherent scheme of official language recognition, including minority languages, there are official languages under the 8th schedule (22 scheduled languages), recognised under unclear criteria and with no clear definition of the rights derived from this position. On the other side there are 92 non-scheduled languages, 33 of which are waiting to be scheduled. These languages are not openly discriminated against, but clearly lack public support and public prestige. There is no numerical criterion for recognition, as there are non-scheduled languages with millions of speakers. Hence, not only does the 8th Schedule have to be revised, but the very institution of such scheduling has to be questioned. If the Constitution assigns federal responsibility for the protection of minorities to the Centre, recognition should be regulated in a transparent and complete manner by federal law. As the concrete minority issues can only be tackled by State policies, a federal legal framework provision should delegate this task to the States, stipulating equal criteria and setting appropriate standards for recognition, for avoiding arbitrary proceedings, and for monitoring its application. In addition, the act of recognition of a language has to be linked to a clearly determined set of group rights in linguistic matters.

---

288 The States which have not yet ratified the ECRML are: Bulgaria, Estonia, France, Italy, Latvia, Lithuania, Macedonia, Poland, Moldova, Romania, and Russia.

The author with Kamala Devi Tomchok, a Manipuri PhD candidate at NEHU Shillong

As for the recognition of smaller languages, it is evident that India has a longstanding tradition of multilingualism as well as of the hegemony of cultural elites and cultural power exerted by dominant languages. This hierarchy of languages, deeply entrenched in history and even in religion, has brought about a systematic depreciation of smaller languages. The former hegemony of an English speaking elite is replaced by a Hindi+English speaking elite. Within the single States, the regional official language policy is bringing about a second level of hegemony: the State official language and its native speakers. This brings Saxena and Mahendroo to affirm: "Today the rise of regional linguistic identities, as a reaction to the metropolitan ruling class, has led to the emergence of the regional ruling classes, whose cultural hegemony over the larger masses is not very different from that of the English speaking elite."[289] It seems time that the 8th Schedule be seriously re-examined. If the State wishes to promote only scheduled languages, the least it can do is not prevent peoples from developing and using their own mother tongues. Official recognition entails to the use of these languages for the official purposes of the State. "Can the state, therefore, preclude other languages from being used by the citizenry in public

289 See Sadhana Saxena/Kamal Mahendroo, *Politics of Language*, in: Gupta/Abbbi/Aggarwal, *Language and the State*, p.150

life? Can the state discriminate and prevent the use of certain languages when equality of status and opportunity is fundamental to our system of constitutional governance? Does it not militate against this basic ideal to permit only a handful of languages to flourish?"[290]

10.7 Minority languages in education

Again, India's education system presents many differences compared with the European "mainstream model". The most striking differences are: almost all European countries (at least the EU member countries) have a school attendance requirement until the age of 18, and the prevailing form of education for the vast majority of students is the public, tuition-free school for everyone from class I to class XII or XIII. In areas or regions with linguistic minorities, this public primary and secondary school operates the languages the local communities desire as medium languages. This system has not only ensured almost complete literacy and much progress for more equal opportunities, but also a much better starting position for linguistic minorities. Under this regime, the State or the responsible sub-State unit has to offer a tuition-free public school system for linguistic minorities, wherever they wish, operating in the mother tongue of the minority students from class I to class XII or XIII. The Indian Constitution lacks both: there is no provision for free education for all students for this duration, nor is there a right for linguistic minorities to have their own public schools on all levels, or at least from class I to class VIII. No wonder linguistic minorities, especially "absolute minorities" (minorities with no kin-state or major cultural references beyond the State borders) can enjoy much less education in their mother tongue. They simply are not in the condition to run private schools and the legal (constitutional) provision for providing mother-tongue classes or schools according to the 10:40 ratio (10 minority children in a class, 40 minority children in a school) is seldom effective and sufficiently funded. However, the minority population has to live in a concentrated form, otherwise separate education institutions will always be difficult to be organised.

Article 350A of the Indian Constitution reads as follows: "It shall be the endeavour of every State and of every local authority within the State to provide adequate facilities for instruction in the mother tongue at the primary stage of education to children belonging to linguistic minority groups; and the President may issue such directions to any State as he considers necessary or proper for securing the provision of such facilities." Being beautifully

290 *ibidem*, p. 173

vague, it has been possible to disregard this article in all the three aspects: "endeavour", "adequate facilities" and "directions to the state" as borne out by the Report of the Official Committee to Examine the Implementation of the Recommendation of the Gujral Committee for Promotion of Urdu.[291] The most blatant case is the denial of the use of Urdu script in primary education in Uttar Pradesh, where the script of Urdu is fast going into disuse. Article 350 (A) was specially provided through the 7th Constitution Amendment Act (1956) to protect the minority languages used at the primary stage of education upon the recommendation of the States Reorganisation Commission. Because of the way it is phrased, however, it has been possible to render it a "mere teasing illusion, and a promise of unreality."[292]

India by its very nature needs to cope with multilingualism, much more than Europe. The TLF of the future will have to provide proficiency in three languages for all, but these languages will be introduced at different stages. By introducing different languages at different levels of schooling, different values or weights are automatically attributed to those languages. This weight is expressed in teaching time per week, the duration of teaching in years, and the subjects taught in the language concerned. For the typical Indian student enrolled in the compulsory school the problem is not to learn three languages, but which methodology is used with which performance. But for minority language speakers also the amount of time devoted to the teaching of languages becomes a problem. Generally schools in different states devote between a quarter and two-thirds of the total teaching hours to teaching languages. The allotment of greater or lesser time to the teaching of particular languages is judged as a prestige status issue for that particular language. Strategies for teaching contact languages in different regions are designed to satisfy the immediate and long-term societal need. This speaks to the necessity of undertaking a critical assessment of the TLF as implemented in most India States vis-à-vis the teaching of minority languages. To put it bluntly, in order to cope with the TLF-system, at present India's youth has to face an overload of language teaching, let alone the requirement to learn the mother tongue if it is an absolute minority language. There is much evidence that in most schools challenged to cope with India's national multilingual requirements, the interests and needs of the speakers of minority languages are systematically disregarded. The feeling that millions of minority language speakers get in the classes is: if small languages don't matter in education, why should we take it up? Thus all players, learn-

291 Iqbal Ansari, *Minorities and the Politics of Constitution Making in India,* in D.L. Sheth/ Gurpreet Mahajao (eds.), *Minority Identities and the Nation State*, Oxford University Press, 1999, p. 113-135

292 *ibidem*, p. 134

ers, language teachers, the society and families have to seek a new balance between mother tongues and dominant languages.

10.8 Minority languages in the public sphere

The Indian Constitution grants some rights to linguistic minorities whenever the number exceeds 60% of the population in a district, tehsil or municipality. with the right of such a majority language to be declared a co-official language does not accrue automatically, but can be accorded by the President on demand. It is not reported in how many cases the Indian President has taken this decision. The very co-official character of a minority language on the State or sub-State-level has to be questioned: what does recognition entail in legal terms? Which rights are the minority members entitled to in their interaction with the public administration? From a European point of view, these provisions appear vague and insufficiently strict. Why can minority language rights be accorded only if there are 60%-majority of speakers on a given territory, if in Finland the public administration has to serve the citizens of both language groups, Swedish speakers and Finnish speakers, wherever 8% of the local population are Swedish speakers? Are there any provisions to ensure that public employees have to be fluent in both languages in order to meet their duties? Does co-official mean only the right of the citizen to address the local administration in his language, and the right to receive written answers in his language, or does it mean comprehensive bilingualism in the whole public sphere starting from the signboards and every kind of official publication and extending to the obligatory bilingualism of public employees?

10.9 Minority protection as a constitutional issue

First of all, it should be recalled that by far not all European states have enshrined the protection of minorities in their constitutions and this constitutional obligation has not been transformed in State acts, legal provisions and political action in all States. Several States' domestic legislation on minority rights is still half-hearted, incoherent and insufficient for this purpose. India, on the contrary, conferred constitutional value on the right of minorities to protect their identity from the very beginning. But can granting primary education in the mother tongue and the right to run private schools in minority medium languages be truly sufficient for ensuring their survival? The Indian constitution is clear in its principles, but far less advanced in the level and substance of the single rights seen as indispensable for cultural survival in the modern world.

If minority rights are entrenched by the Constitution, who is safeguarding these rights and how are these rights enforced? If more than half of the living minority languages are not even taught as a subject in primary schools and several are only taught for 2-3 years before being replaced by regional majority languages, the minority members are deprived of a fundamental cultural and linguistic right. As States are responsible for the implementation of the educational right, how can it be enforced? How can the States be obliged to cater to the educational needs of linguistic minorities? Is it not a bitter experience for millions of tribal community members to have quota regulations in public employment and in universities, but not enough schools with appropriate curricula and funding to ever allow a sufficient number of students to reach the educational level entitling them to apply for such a course or job?

Indeed, under the present legal setting the multilingual fabric of the country is not questioned with regard to the regional official languages. These 14-15 languages, along with the two nation-wide link-languages, all have a secure legal and societal space and power to be stabilized and further developed. On the other hand, linguistic legislation and the language policy of India's States' does not assign enough importance – either on a territorial or on a cultural basis – to absolute linguistic minorities in public administration and in the educational system. In fact, such minority languages are not contemplated as languages for education beyond the primary stage.[293]

This is due to a fundamental "missing link". The minority languages that India's "Founding Fathers" had in mind, were not the small tribal languages, but the major languages which became minority languages after the linguistic re-organisation. The provision for private community action to promote and preserve minority languages only makes sense for those large languages and linguistic communities with powerful elite lobbies and kin-States, not for tribal languages or smaller and poorer, marginalised people. Protection of the absolute minority languages was therefore conceptually limited from the very beginning with clear-cut linguistic rights linked to the presence of minorities on their traditional territories. Fifty years after India's "linguistic re-organisation", could it be time to re-organise the States internally along linguistic lines?

What remedies are available in the event of violations of linguistic rights?

293 See Sadhana Saxena/Kamal Mahendroo, *Politics of Language*, in: Gupta/Abbbi/Aggarwal, *Language and the State*, p.151

After long debates and complicated decisional procedures, India has found a solution for the official languages which could stabilise the whole system and display an integrative effect on the State and federal level. The very existence of many States has been decided on the federal level in response to claims stemming from parts or groups within a pre-existing state at a sub-state level. The federal state in a certain sense has taken on the role of mediator of conflicts between the States and minority groups at the sub-state-level. The implementation of the legal provisions on language in India goes through different steps of control and revision: the political parties, the media, pressure groups of civil societies and also State institutions, such as the Commissioner for Linguistic Minorities. He represents the interests of the linguistic minorities irrespective of relative or absolute kind. Thus, the centre is in charge of defending the interests of linguistic minorities and their individual members, particularly against the powerful policy of the States to affirm and promote their respective official languages. But is the Centre really doing what it is required to do? The annual reports of the NCLM are more than sceptical about this issue.

10.10 Tribal peoples and the modern society

The victims of the inadequacy of many Indian States' language policies towards linguistic minorities are the tribal peoples. Out of more than 80 million (the current number of members of scheduled tribes) only about half have retained their traditional language, while others have shifted to regional languages, but maintain a tribal cultural identity not based on language. There are tribes in India who do not want schools with their mother tongue medium language, and others who live dispersedly can hardly be provided adequate central infrastructure. Many others, counting hundreds of thousands members, despite a clear need and common will do not enjoy the right to education in their mother tongue, the right to a bilingual school, or the right to use their mother tongues in the local public administration.

The tribal languages are those Indian languages that not only face attrition, but in many cases are close to extinction. "Language should not be perceived just as a tool for learning, reading and writing and to master other subjects. It should be a process on which social values and traditions of a society are passed on leading to identity building, critical thinking, creativity and the capacity to learn other languages. Every smaller language has a rich literary or orally tradition. The replacement of such languages by standard regional languages not only denies the right of speakers to preserve their languages, but also brings about a loss in articulation of cultural and social experience and identity."[294] Both are at stake: the cultural values of many ethno-linguistic communities as well as the linguistic human rights of individual citizens.

In India the absence of a written script often serves as a pretext to deny education in a mother tongue. But is this enough to deny not only education, but language acquisition planning? Is it legitimate to deny public structures for language development because they are allegedly too costly? Can the additional costs of print work, the formation and employment of teachers, and the creation of additional school facilities be presented as decisive obstacles? Certainly India does not boast the wealth of some European states, but on the other hand the country is developing nuclear armament and space research programs. The financial cost is one of the major arguments put forward to reject serious programs of linguistic empowerment, as the protection of minority language faces few problems relating to political acceptance. But in a democratic state, education should made accessible to all citizens, according to fundamental rights, which in India as elsewhere include education in the mother tongue.[295]

10.11 Summary

The UNDP-Report 2004 on cultural rights states: "In multilingual societies plural language policies provide recognition to distinct linguistic groups. Plural language policies safeguard the parallel use of two or more languages by saying in essence: 'Let us each retain our own language in certain spheres, such as schools and universities, but let us also have a common language for joint activities, especially in civic life. Language conflicts can be managed by providing some spheres in which minority languages are used freely and by giving incentives to learn other languages specially a national or official language. This can be promoted by an appropriate social reward structure, such as by making facility in a national language a criterion for professional qualification and promotion."[296] The UNDP is substantially wrong, as the market dynamics are providing sufficient social and economic rewards for learning and using dominant languages, while the minority languages need additional rewards and empowerment to compensate for their general lack of cultural and professional importance and social domains. The question at this point is whether India's States, in response to such a challenge formulated by the UNDP, are ready, first to con-

294 See Sadhana Saxena/Kamal Mahendroo, *Politics of Language*, p.150
295 This is the opinion of the NCLM, 42 report, p.10 at: http://nclm.nic.in
296 UNDP, Annual Report 2004, p.60

cede certain spheres of official use to minority languages on their territory of traditional settlement; second, to empower the very status of minority language according means, funds and devices to stop attrition and foster development. The Indian Constitution of 1950 was well ahead of its time not only in recognizing diversity, but also in providing for representation of the diverse collectivities in the formal democratic structures. But 60 years later, some of those provisions proved to be insufficient.[297]

What are language rights generally? The right to learn in one's own mother tongue, the right to learn through a language of choice, the right to learn other languages, and also to use one's mother tongue in the social environment, public and private, in which it is spoken. The resulting picture concerning India's linguistic minorities is rather contradictory, and the very issue of minority languages and threatened languages does not seem to take priority on the federal or State political agendas. On the one hand, language policy is under stress to cope with the challenge of India's complex multilingual societies, on the other hand many linguistic minorities are left without adequate protection, which is ultimately a serious denial of cultural human rights.

There are external factors, relevant for Europe and for India as well, in the form of external pressures from the society in which the linguistic minority is embedded. Such factors are a product of the modern centralised and rapidly industrialising societies that favour the standardisation of national languages, consumer styles and cultural patterns, at the cost of minor languages and cultures. Given a multiplicity of languages, minority languages may be considered a structural obstacle to trade, mobility of labour, transfer of technology and innovation, interregional and international communication and efficient governance. National networks of media, education and administration are encouraged to facilitate uniformity of ideology and culture through the use of standardised national languages. What was once centralised planning on different government levels, today appears to bow to the constraints of big corporations, which cannot invest time and money to adapt their languages to a specific regional minority situation. These processes of acculturation and assimilation pose a grave threat to the survival of minority languages. Their functions first are reduced to religion, traditional customs and the home, while the functional loads of the majority languages are continuously extended through media, education, administration and business life. Then majority languages also penetrate into the private domains and ultimately bring about the surrender of minority languages.

297 See Ashutosh Kumar, p. 94

Tarun Kom, member of the Kom minority of Manipur

As we have seen, Europe and India, with a comparable degree of linguistic complexity and comparable number and size of minorities, share most key problems faced by linguistic minorities. The core demands of hundreds of linguistic minorities are very similar in both geographical areas:

- The recognition of minority languages, according them a minimum standard of linguistic rights, if possible under a supra-national or national constitutional regulation.
- Language acquisition planning tasked with establishing an education policy for minorities to grant each the opportunity to learn and develop its own language and to speak it in several important domains of its own territory.
- Keeping Minority languages in artificial reserves or marginalizing them to mere usage in homes and family will foster their attrition. Languages need publicly funded development (status planning) to enable their speakers to have both a chance to tackle modern life through bi- or multilingual use of a language widely used in a State or the Union, as well as a chance to use one's own language in the home-region.

But several fundamental conditions for the language policy are markedly different: the organisation of the states and internal power sharing in sub-national and supranational entities, the level of social and economic development, the historical and ideological background, the role of multilingualism, the legal instruments on all levels: international – national – sub-national.

The question at this point should be: what can the political actors of both concerned parties (states and minorities) learn from each other in Europe and in India? Which active responsibility do state actors have in both areas as well as worldwide?[298] Today minority languages are not often openly discriminated against. They are just left alone, exposed to the arbitrary forces of social and economic developments. Language movements seldom have sufficient momentum to gain the national or international attention. Militancy in defence of languages is blamed for both cultural backwardness and anti-modernism, as well as ethno-political activism leading to movements of rebellion and secession. In the present situation both Europe and India need improved recognition and implementation of linguistic rights, which should be enshrined on all levels: national constitutions, international covenants, State acts or sub-state regional statutes (in Europe regions, in India districts). If all states, either united in a common federation or a supranational organisation (27 EU member states, 28 States of India) agree on a common minimum standard of protection of minority rights and linguistic rights with the required legal remedies or supranational mechanisms of implementation and monitoring, it would be much easier to achieve linguistic human rights. Whereas in Europe a more compulsory and strict legal framework must be established throughout the whole continent, in India the constitutional provisions have to be reviewed, to spur the States to attach more importance to linguistic minority protection.

298 J. Castellino quotes K.M. Munsha, who in the Constituent Assembly discussing the fundamental rights of minorities, addressed a series of recommendations to the Sub-committee on Minorities; see Joshua Castellino, *Minority Rights in India*, in J. Castellino/Elvira Domínguez Redondo, *Minority Rights in Asia, A Comparative Legal Analysis*, Oxford University Press, 2006, p.66. As this approach is totally defensive (anti-discrimination) no active political commitment om behalf of linguistic minorities is required by the State actors.

Conclusion: towards a comprehensive protection of linguistic rights in India

India's world of languages is as colourful as her peoples, and as rich in cultural heritage and spiritual energies. When addressing the issue of linguistic rights, one must acknowledge that minority situations are different in kind and in size. Generally, linguistic minorities in federal India are defined in relation to their State of residence, and the vast majority of more than 120 million Indian citizens belonging to linguistic minorities are "relative minorities": speaking one of the "scheduled languages", which is an official language in another State of the Union, but not in their own State, as their mother tongue. Only 3% of India's total population, about 30 million people, mostly tribal communities, speak "non-scheduled languages" – India's less protected and often most threatened languages. They can be termed "absolute minorities", as no kin-state or major speech community is taking care of their protection. Most of these languages are not taught in any school, or recognized for any use in public administration. Many of these languages have no script and thus are deprived of any representation in modern culture and media. This fact does not mean that mere inclusion in the 8th Schedule of the Indian Constitution will be sufficient to solve all their problems.

Examining an overview of the general features of linguistic minorities in India and a brief analysis of major issues concerning official language policy aimed to protect their rights, we find that the result is not overwhelmingly positive. India, the most populous democratic country in the world, must cope with a unique linguistic complexity, which raises far more problems than does the multilingual reality in some major neighbouring states like Russia and China, let alone the few multinational European states. In a federal state like the Indian Union, all government levels are responsible for such fundamental aims as the protection of minorities. Since the 1960s, public institutions are committed to using the regional official languages as working languages. When considered from the viewpoint of the official goals of minority protection, the Indian language policy demonstrates major achievements, but there is also evidence of serious shortcomings. As shown above, State implementation of official language policy has made great progress in the last decades, but quite often in this ongoing process of "linguistic homogenisation" the needs and interests of the linguistic minorities are seriously neglected.

A first problematic issue is the arbitrary and incomplete approach taken regarding the recognition of languages and minority languages in particular, under the 8th Schedule of the Constitution. The major victims are the tribal languages, irrespective of the numbers of speakers and their literary traditions. Other "absolute minorities" face many hardships in obtaining both legal recognition and the necessary minimum resources for safeguarding their survival. The "relative minorities", which have a "kin-State" or a major speech community as their cultural reference area beyond their State of residence, are better off and can rely on greater cultural production, better educational facilities, larger numerical size and other advantages deriving from their status as a scheduled language. Apparently the forces of economic, technical, and social change are putting the minority languages under stress, and the governments' commitment is too weak to effectively implement the constitutional safeguards for minority languages in education and administration to counteract their slow erosion.

A second problematic issue is to be found in the field of education, where the prevailing strategy to cope with multilingual complexity is the famous "Three-language-formula". This again acts to the disadvantage of the smaller, non-scheduled linguistic minorities. Major contradictions have emerged in the implementation of this formula. The major conflicts appear to arise between equal implementation in the Northern Hindi-belt vis-à-vis the States with Dravidian official languages in the South. But this ambiguous formula can hardly be combined with linguistic minorities' right to education in their mother tongues, let alone with the rights of tribal peoples who already suffer under weak education structures. Despite many laudable efforts, the number of minority languages used in education is continuously declining. The duration of the use of minority languages in education, the availability of trained teachers and textbooks, the content of the curricula, the social appreciation of minority languages in public education, and the existence of institutions for the development of educational support are, in many cases, insufficient to meet tribal peoples' fundamental right to education in their mother tongues, as enshrined in the Constitution. There is no numerical or juridical criterion for offering mandatory public education for linguistic minorities at higher levels, and even on the primary level the majority of minority languages are no longer taught. Many minority language speakers had to accept "superposed languages", and many tribal groups accepted the regional languages as the language of education, neglecting their own traditional languages. Of course, the use of minority languages as medium of instruction and as a symbol of identity is not only the responsibility of state official boards and institutions; it also depends on the attitude of the minority communities themselves.

The use of minority languages in administration and the media is constrained by economic, administrative and socio-cultural factors. No coherent and comprehensive approach to grant equal rights in public administration to linguistic minorities and to minor groups like scheduled tribes could be found. The situation is better wherever minority languages are declared "official languages" on a territorial level (district, tehsil, municipality) or where former minorities or tribal peoples can obtain their own federated State (Meghalaya, Nagaland, Manipur, Mizoram). The analysis, however, revealed the problem that many minority languages, though constituting a major percentage of the population at the local level (approximately 50 out of 330 districts) are not recognized as official languages. Even if there is no comprehensive regime of bilingualism, some rights for the use of mother tongues in public administration are upheld.

What are the main reasons for this situation? In addition to general factors of social change such as national economic integration, free migration and opening to global markets, there are other constant factors impeding and hampering the maintenance and development of minority languages. These factors are absent in environments in which a language is in a majority or dominant position and is endowed with the necessary functional load and transparency to survive. There are internal shortcomings and external pressures that may jeopardize efforts to preserve minority languages.

First, members of the minority may be divided – as is often observed in India – in their opinion regarding the economic, social, administrative and educational advantages to using their mother tongue. When the elite of a linguistic community, due to economic self-interest, is divided on such a crucial issue, no social and political mobilization will occur to ensure the maintenance of the language and culture. Under such conditions the language risks becoming insignificant, paving the way for acculturation and assimilation.

Second, there are external factors, in the form of external pressures from the society in which the linguistic minority is embedded. Such factors are a product of modern centralized and rapidly industrializing societies, which favour the standardization of national languages, consumer styles and cultural patterns, at the cost of minor languages and cultures. Given a multiplicity of languages, minority languages may be considered a structural obstacle to trade, mobility of labour, transfer of technology and innovation, interregional and international communication and efficient governance. National networks of media, education and administration are encouraged, through the use of standardized national languages, to facilitate uniformity of ideology and culture. What was once centralized planning on different government levels, today appears constrained by the concerns of big corporations, which do not wish to invest time and money to adapt their languages to a specific regional minority situation. These processes of acculturation and assimilation pose a grave threat to the survival of minority languages. Their functions are first reduced to religion, traditional customs and the home, while the functional load of the majority languages is continuously extended through media, education, administration and business life. Then majority languages penetrate into the private domains and ultimately bring about the end of minority language use.

The Indian Constitution contains several provisions of the utmost importance in granting some rights to linguistic minorities. The fundamental right to preserve identity is enshrined, along with the right to education in the mother tongue, and the right to have minority languages declared as 'co-official languages', if some basic conditions are fulfilled. Nevertheless, by recognizing some (22) of India's languages and denying this recognition to many (92) others, without applying transparent criteria for such a selection, the Constitution, creates two classes of languages. Moreover, it does not determine which rights derive from the inclusion of a language in the 8th Schedule. The Constitution, furthermore, does not establish a State duty to provide for compulsory tuition-free school education up to class XII in the medium language desired by the families concerned. Linguistic or religious minorities' mere right to run private education institutes is not enough. The provision stipulating that in areas with more than 60% speakers of a minority language this language can be declared as co-official, is not enough to ensure full parity of rights of all languages, if the implications of such recognition are not clearly set out. If the Constitution in some articles stresses the prohibition of personal discrimination on linguistic grounds, there are few duties enshrined that oblige the Government and the States to take action to prevent structural discrimination and allow comprehensive bilingualism with minority languages. In sum, the constitutional safeguards, after 60 years of an independent India, are neither sufficiently comprehensive or exhaustive to effectively protect linguistic minorities, as:

- There is no duty of the States/Governments to recognise linguistic minorities
- There is no clear-cut right to benefit from mother tongue instruction at the primary level
- Compulsory education in one's mother tongue at the secondary level is not contemplated
- There is no comprehensive right to establish a bilingual public administration in minority areas
- The only institution of control and monitoring on the federal level,

the NCLM, lacks powers to redress shortcomings and violations of constitutional or State provisions

- There are no rights for linguistic minorities to be represented on a political level (mainly at the State and district level)
- There is no public responsibility to support language status planning and language acquisition planning, enshrined on federal level and part of State official language policy.
- There is no right for tribal peoples to claim cultural or local autonomy, including basic linguistic rights, and to be vested with adequate financial funding in order to preserve their languages.
-

In order to evaluate the real situation of linguistic minorities in the single States "on the ground", a further detailed assessment has to be made based on appropriate empirical research. In India there are many very committed public institutions (e.g. the NCLM and the CIIL) that are carrying out serious political programs ensuring the rights of linguistic minorities as enshrined in the Constitution. But how can India cope with this challenge if the Constitution itself is not complete in this regard? How is India to cope with it if public efforts, particularly in terms of funds earmarked for this purpose, are grossly inadequate to meet the great demand? Language policy cannot be improvised, if no general legal framework on federal level is set obliging all States to enhance minimum standards of language protection. India's polities seem much more worried about coping with and effectively implementing the Three-language-formula than trying to invest funds in minority language medium schools, bilingual education programs, full bilingualism in public administration on local and regional level, and minority language media. Of course, it must be kept in mind that a multinational state such as India will always be much more concerned with the major task of national integration, which encompasses not only languages, but also ethnicities, religions, and castes.

In India such integration is pursued by exploring unity in diversity. But one can explore unity only if one recognises diversity. The present problems are the result of the failure to recognize the diversity of some weaker groups and their fundamental rights. What are language rights generally? These include the right to learn one's own mother tongue, the right to learn through a language of choice and the right to speak it in the public sphere. This is not a revolutionary agenda, but language rights have far reaching implications for social and economic rights as well. The resulting picture concerning India's linguistic minorities is rather contradictory, and the very issue of minority languages and threatened languages does not seem to be given priority on the federal or State political agendas. On the one hand, language policy is under stress from coping with the challenge of India's complex multilingual societies, on the other hand many linguistic minorities are left without adequate protection, which in the end is a serious denial of a cultural human right.

If we were to assess the achievements and failures of the Indian language policies over a period of time, first of all we should discover what goals, declared or implicit, these policies set forth. "The philosophical basis and goal of Indian planning is the development of a society with cultural and linguistic pluralism within the framework of national solidarity. Given this goal and the constitutional commitment for equal opportunity of education for all, educational planning must have a programme of education for linguistic minorities which recognizes the identity of those groups and yet provides a strategy for regional and national integration. This visualizes elementary education through the language of early childhood experience and a programmatic transfer to the mainstreams, both regional and national."[299]

299 D.P. Pattanayak, *Multilingualism and Mother-tongue Education*, 1981, p. 83

ANNEXES

Annex 1: Institutions

The Central Institute of Indian Languages (CIIL)

The Central Institute of Indian Languages (CIIL) was established on July 17th, 1969 to assist and co-ordinate the systematic development of Indian languages. The Institute was charged with the responsibility of serving as a nucleus to bring together all the research and literary output from the various linguistic streams to a common head and of narrowing the gap between basic research and developmental research in the field of languages and linguistics in India. The CIIL is headquartered in Mysore (Karnataka) and has seven regional offices employing some 500 collaborators. With its specialised sections and regional centres, the CIIL is committed to meeting the demand for trained teachers and textbooks for all levels in the educational system. The CIIL also provides scientific assistance and practical support for the protection of the languages of linguistic minorities and tribal peoples all over India. It acts as an editor – with a catalogue of currently more than 300 deliverable titles and media products – and runs a multimedia library in Mysore, which rightfully can be described as a "National Information Centre on Linguistics and Indian Languages". More on this institution at: www.ciil.org

The Official Language Commission

The Official Language Commission was appointed by the Government of India to make recommendations to the President as to

a) the progressive use of the Hindi language for the official purposes of the Union;
b) restrictions on the use of the English language for all or any of the official purposes of the Union;
c) the language to be used for all or any of the purposes mentioned in Article 348 of the Constitution;
d) the form of numerals to be used for any one or more specified purposes of the Union;
e) the preparation of a time Schedule according to which Hindi may gradually replace English as the official language of the Union and as a language for communication between the Union and the State Governments and between one State Government and another.

The Report of the Official Language Commission presented an in-depth study of problems relating to language use in administration. According to its terms and conditions the Commission was concerned about the progressive use of Hindi for official purposes, the restriction on the use of English language, etc. The Commission found that "a common linguistic medium for Official Union purposes is administratively necessary (whatever view one may hold about the non-official sector). The need for establishing Hindi as such is of significance correspondingly to the significance of maintaining the country's political unity and integrity". It made specific recommendations relating to the official language of the Union; progress in the use of Hindi in State administration, language of legislation, Union language and Public Service Examination, propagation and development of Hindi and regional language, etc.

The National Commissioner for Linguistic Minorities

Article 350B of the Constitution provides for the appointment by the Indian President of a "Special Officer for Linguistic Minorities" (NCLM). The NCLM has the duty to investigate all matters relating to safeguards provided for the linguistic minorities, and reports to the President at such intervals as may be fixed. These "Annual Reports" of the NCLM, to be presented to the President of India, are the major source of information on minority languages (available at: http://nclm.nic.in). As of 2008, 43 reports can be retrieved on this website. The office of the NCLM has its national headquarters at Allahabad in Uttar Pradesh (where the regional office for the Northern and Central Zone is also attached) and regional offices in South India

(Chennai), West India (Belgaum) and East India (Kolkata). In June 2006 A. Keswani, an ex-member of the Indian Parliament, took over as NCLM. The "Combined scheme of safeguards of linguistic minorities in India" (as presented by the National Commissioner for Minority Languages):

1. the translation and publication of important rules, regulations, notices, etc. into all languages, which are spoken by at least 15% of the total population at district or sub-district level;
2. the declaration of minority languages as second official languages in district where persons/speakers of such languages constitute 60% or more of the population;
3. the receipt of and reply to representations in minority languages;
4. instruction through mother tongues/minority languages at the primary stage of education;
5. instruction through minority languages at the secondary stage of education;
6. advance registration of linguistic preference of linguistic minority pupils, and interschool adjustment;
7. provision of textbooks and teachers in minority languages;
8. the implementation of the Three-Language-Formula;
9. no insistence upon knowledge of State's official language at the time of recruitment. Test of proficiency in the State's official language to be held before completion of probation;
10. the issue of pamphlets in minority languages detailing the safeguards available to linguistic minorities;
11. establishment of proper machinery at the State and district levels for looking after the interests of linguistic minorities.

Apart from these institutions and India's major actors in matters of language policy, namely the Federal Government and the States, there are important national organisations such as the Hindi-Sahitya Sammelan and the Anjuman-e-Taraqi-e-Urdu, which serve as political platforms for linguistic interests.

Language boards or academies for minority languages?

When a new language policy is being explored or implemented, a special public language board or academy should be created, as was done Catalonia, the Basque Country and the Baltic States. The board should include experts to analyse the socio-lingual situation, draft policy proposals and organise language learning programmes. This is especially needed if a new language policy includes language requirements for civil service jobs, licensing or naturalisation. If the state openly acknowledges that facility in a language is required for access to public services, it has a duty to assist and monitor the acquisition of that language, in order to overcome linguistic conflicts and to provide for language status planning and development. A state language board with expert commissions and a permanent staff naturally requires substantial resources, as do language learning programmes. In the present analysis it could not be assessed whether such boards in India already exist at State or District level.

2: Legal provisions

Legal provisions on the language of the Indian Constitution

Part XVII OFFICIAL LANGUAGE – CHAPTER I – LANGUAGE OF THE UNION

Article 343 - The language of the Union
1) The official language of the Union shall be Hindi in Devanagari script. The form of numerals to be used for the official purposes of the Union shall be the international form of Indian numerals.
2) Notwithstanding anything in clause (1), for a period of fifteen years from the commencement of this Constitution, the English language shall continue to be used for all the official purposes of the Union for which it was being used immediately before such commencement:
Provided that the President may, during the said period, by order authorise the use of the Hindi language in addition to the English language and of the Devanagari form of numerals in addition to the international form of Indian numerals for any of the official purposes of the Union.
3) Notwithstanding anything in this article, Parliament may by law provide for the use, after the said period of fifteen years, of -

(a) the English language, or
(b) the Devanagari form of numerals for such purposes as may be specified in the law.

Part XVII – OFFICIAL LANGUAGE - CHAPTER I – LANGUAGE OF THE UNION

Article 344 Commission and Committee of Parliament on official language
(1) the President shall, at the expiration of five years from the commencement of this Constitution and thereafter at the expiration of ten years from such commencement, by order constitute a Commission which shall consist of a Chairman and such other members representing the different languages specified in the Eight Schedule as the President may appoint, and the order shall define the procedure to be followed by the Commission.
(2) It shall be the duty of the Commission to make recommendations to the President as to
a) the progressive use of the Hindi language for the official purposes of the Union;
b) restrictions on the use of the English language for all or any of the official purposes of the union;
c) the language to be used for all or any of the purposes mentioned in Article 348;
d) the form of numerals to be used for any

one or more specified purposes of the Union;
e) any other matter referred to the Commission by the President as regards the official language of the Union and the language for communication between the Union and a State or between one State and another and their use.
4. In making their recommendations under clause, the Commission shall have due regard to the industrial, cultural and scientific advancement of India, and the just claims and the interests of persons belonging to the non-Hindi speaking areas in regard to the public services.

5. There shall be constituted a Committee consisting of thirty members, of whom twenty shall be members of the House of the People and ten shall be members of the Council of States to be elected respectively by the members of the House of the People and the members of the Council of States in accordance with the system of proportional representation by means of the single transferable vote.

6. It shall be the duty of the Committee to examine the recommendations of the Commission constituted under clause and to report to the President their opinion thereon.

7. Notwithstanding anything in article 343, the President may, after consideration of the report referred to in clause, issue directions in accordance with the whole or any part of that report.

PART XVII - CHAPTER II.-REGIONAL LANGUAGES

Article 345. Official language or languages of a State.-
Subject to the provisions of articles 346 and 347, the Legislature of a State may by law adopt any one or more of the languages in use in the State or Hindi as the language or languages to be used for all or any of the official purposes of that State:
Provided that, until the Legislature of the State otherwise provides by law, the English language shall continue to be used for those official purposes within the State for which it was being used immediately before the commencement of this Constitution.

Article 346. Official language for communication between one State and another or between a State and the Union.-
The language for the time being authorised for use in the Union for official purposes shall be the official language for communication between one

State and another State and between a State and the Union:
Provided that if two or more States agree that the Hindi language should be the official language for communication between such States, that language may be used for such communication.

Article 347. Special provision relating to language spoken by a section of the population of a State.
On a demand being made in that behalf the President may, if he is satisfied that a substantial proportion of the population of a State desire the use of any language spoken by them to be recognised by that State, direct that such language shall also be officially recognised throughout that State or any part thereof for such purpose as he may specify.

PART XVII - CHAPTER III.-LANGUAGE OF THE SUPREME COURT, HIGHCOURTS

Article 348. Language to be used in the Supreme Court and in the High Courts and for Acts, Bills, etc.-
1. Notwithstanding anything in the foregoing provisions of this Part, until Parliament by law otherwise provides-
2. a) all proceedings in the Supreme Court and in every High Court,
 b) the authoritative texts-
3. i. of all Bills to be introduced or amendments thereto to be moved in either House of Parliament or in the House or either House of the Legislature of a State,
ii. of all Acts passed by Parliament or the Legislature of a State and of all Ordinances promulgated by the President or the Governor of a State, and
iii. of all orders, rules, regulations and bye-laws issued under this Constitution or under any law made by Parliament or the Legislature of a State, shall be in the English language.
4. Notwithstanding anything in sub-clause (a) of clause (1), the Governor of a State may, with the previous consent of the President, authorise the use of the Hindi language, or any other language used for any official purposes of the State, in proceedings in the High Court having its principal seat in that State:
Provided that nothing in this clause shall apply to any judgement, decree or order passed or made by such High Court.
5. Notwithstanding anything in sub-clause (b) of clause (1), where the Legislature of a State has prescribed any language other than the English language for use in Bills introduced in, or Acts passed by, the Legislature of the State or in Ordinances promulgated by the Governor of the State

or in any order, rule, regulation or bye-law referred to in paragraph (iii) of that sub-clause, a translation of the same in the English language published under the authority of the Governor of the State in the Official Gazette of that State shall be deemed to be the authoritative text thereof in the English language under this article.

Article 349. Special procedure for enactment of certain laws relating to language

During the period of fifteen years from the commencement of this Constitution, no Bill or amendment making provision for the language to be used for any of the purposes mentioned in clause (1) of article 348 shall be introduced or moved in either House of Parliament without the previous sanction of the President, and the President shall not give his sanction to the introduction of any such Bill or the moving of any such amendment except after he has taken into consideration the recommendations of the Commission constituted under clause (1) of article 344 and the report of the Committee constituted under clause (4) of that article.

PART III – FUNDAMENTAL RIGHTS - CULTURAL AND EDUCATIONAL RIGHTS

Article 29. Protection of interests of minorities

Article 29(1) Any section of the citizens residing in the territory of India or any part thereof having a distinct language, script or culture of its own shall have the right to conserve the same.

(2) No citizen shall be denied admission into any educational institution maintained by the State or receiving aid out of State funds on grounds only of religion, race, caste, language or any of them."

Article 30 Right to establish and administer schools

(1) All minorities, whether based on religion or language, shall have the right to establish and administer educational institutions of their choice.

(2) In making any law providing for the compulsory acquisition of any property of any educational institution established and administered by a minority, referred to in clause I, the State shall ensure that the amount fixed by or determined under such law for the acquisition of such property is such as would not restrict or abrogate the right guaranteed under that clause.

(3) The State shall not, in granting aid to educational institutions, discriminate against any educational institution on the ground that it is under the management of a minority, whether based on religion or language.

Article 120 Language to be used in the Legislature.

120 (1) Notwithstanding anything in Part XVII, but subject to the provisions of article 348, business in the Legislature of a State shall be transacted in the official language or languages of the State or in Hindi or in English:

Provided that the Speaker of the Legislature Assembly or Chairman of the Legislative Council, or person acting as such, as the case may be, may permit any member who cannot adequately express himself in any of the languages aforesaid to address the House in his mother tongue.

(2) Unless the Legislature of the State by law otherwise provides, this article shall, after the expiration of a period of fifteen years from the commencement of this Constitution, have effect as if the words "or in English" were omitted there from.

Article 210 Language used in the Legislatures of the States

1. Notwithstanding anything in Part XVII, but subject to the provisions of Article 348, business in the Legislature of a state shall be transacted in the official language or languages of the state or in Hindi or in English: Provided that the Speaker of the Legislative Assembly or Chairman of the Legislative Council, or person acting as such, as the case may be, may permit any member who cannot adequately express himself in any of the languages aforesaid to address the House in his mother tongue.

2. Unless the Legislature of the state by law otherwise provides, this article shall, after the expiration of a period of fifteen years from the commencement of this Constitution, have effect as if the words "or in English" were omitted there from: Provided that in relation to the Legislature of the states of Himachal Pradesh, Manipur, Meghalaya and Tripura this clause shall have effect as if the words "fifteen years" occurring therein, the words "twenty-five years" were substituted.

PART XVII – CHAPTER IV SPECIAL DIRECTIVES

Article 350 Language to be used in representations for redress of grievances

Every person shall be entitled to submit a representation for the redress of any grievance to any officer or authority of the Union or a State in any of the languages used in the Union or in the State, as the case may be.

Article 350A Facilities for instruction in mother tongue at primary stage

It shall be the endeavour of every State and of every local authority within the State to provide adequate facilities for instruction in the mother tongue at the primary stage of education to children belonging to linguistic minority groups; and the President may issue such directions to any State as he considers necessary or proper for securing the provision of such facilities.

Article 350B Special Officer for Linguistic Minorities
(1) There shall be a Special Officer for linguistic minorities to be appointed by the President.
(2) It shall be the duty of the Special Officer to investigate all matters relating to the safeguards provided for linguistic minorities under this Constitution and report to the President upon those matters at such intervals as the President may direct, and the President shall cause all such reports to be laid before each House of Parliament, and sent to the Governments of the States concerned.

Article 351 Directive for development of the Hindi language
It shall be the duty of the Union to promote the spread of the Hindi language, to develop it so that it may serve as a medium of expression for all the elements of the composite culture of India and to secure its enrichment assimilating without interfering with its genius, the forms, style and expressions used in Hindustani and in the other languages of India specified in the Eighth Schedule, and by drawing, wherever necessary or desirable, for its vocabulary, primarily on Sanskrit and secondarily on other languages.

Annex 3

Bibliography

Mahadev L. Apte, Multilingualism in India and its sociopolitical implications: an Overview, in: William and Jean O'Barr (eds.), Language and Politics, Mouton –The Hague/Paris 1976

E. Annamalai, Language Movements in India, at: http://www.languageinindia.com/index.html
- , Language Use in Administration and National Integration, at: http://www.languageinindia.com/index.html
- , Managing Multilingualism in India, Sage Publications, New Delhi 2001

Benedict Anderson, Imagined Communities, Reflections on the origin and spread of Nationalism, London/New York 1983

Iqbal Ansari, Minorities and the Politics of Constitution Making in India, in D. L. Sheth/Gurpreet Mahajao (eds.), Minority Identities and the Nation State, Oxford University Press, 1999, p. 113-135

Sanjib Baruah, Durable Disorder – Understanding the Politics of Northeast India, Oxford University Press 2005

Jennifer Bayer, Language Law and National Integration, at: http://www.languageinindia.com/index.html

Thomas Benedikter, Threatened Languages and Linguistic Rights of Minorities: some Empirical Background, in: S. K. Singh (ed.), Rethinking Multingualism – Issues and Problems, Eastern Publ., Guwahati 2009;
- , (ed.), Europe's Ethnic Mosaic, A Short Guide to Minority Rights in Europe, EURAC, Bozen 2008
- , The World's Working Regional Autonomies, ANTHEM Press 2007, Delhi/London 2007

S.S. Bhattacharya, Languages in India – Their Status and Function, in: Itagi/Singh (eds.), Linguistic Landscape in India, CIIL Mysore, 2002

Di Bona J., Critical Perspectives in Indian Education, Bahari Publications, New Delhi 1989
Michael E. Brown/Sunti Ganguly (eds.), Language Policy and Ethnic Relations in Asia, on: http://www.books.google.co.in

Roland J.L. Breton, Languages and Ethnic Communities in South Asia (updated edition), Sage publication, London/New Delhi 1997

William Campbell, In Defence of Vernaculars, edited by M. S. Thirumalai/B. Mallikarjun, Critical Quest, New Delhi 2006

Chaklaer S., Linguistic Minority as a Cohesive Force in Indian Federal Process, New Delhi, Associate Publishing House, 1981

Joshua Castellino, Minority Rights in India, in J. Castellino/Elvira Domínguez Redondo, Minority Rights in Asia, A Comparative Legal Analysis, Oxford University Press, 2006

David Corson/Ruth Wodak (eds.), Encyclopaedia of Languages of Languages and Education – Language Policy and Political Issues of Education, Kluwer Dordrecht 2008 (2d edition)

Das Gupta, Jyotirindra, Language Conflict and National Developmentnt, Group Politics and National Language Policy in India, Berkeley/Los Angeles/ London 1970

C.J. Daswani (ed.), Language Education in Multilingual India, UNESCO, New Delhi 2001

H.R. Dua, Language Planning and Linguistic Minorities, in: E. Annamalai/B. Jernudd/J. Rubin (eds.), Language Planning: Proceedings of an Institute, CIIL Mysore 1986, p. 43-72

Government of India, Group on Minorities Education, Report of the Group 1991, New Delhi 1991

Cynthia Groff, Status and acquisition planning of Linguistic Minorities in India; on: http://www.sil.org/asia/ldc/parallel_papers/cynthia_groff.pdf

R.S. Gupta/Anvita Abbi/Kailash S. Aggarval (eds.), Language and the State, Creative Books, New Delhi 1995

S. Imtiaz Hasnain, Minority Rights and Education, Question of Survival of Minority Languageş, in Language in India, April 2006

-, Place of Minority Language in Education, Language Education in multilingual India, UNESCO, Delhi 2001, p.59-103

N.H. Itagi/Shailendra Kumar Singh (eds.), Linguistic Landscaping in India,

CIIL and M. Gandhi International Hindi University, Mysore 2002
Jayaran, B.D./Rajyashree K.S., State Official Language Policy Implementation, Central Institute of Indian Languages, Mysore 2000

M.A. Jawaid/K.N. Jehangir/Shankar Bose (eds.), Minorities of India – Problems and Prospects, MANAK publications, New Delhi 2007

Braj B. Kachru/S.N. Sridhar (eds.), The Minority Languages and their Status – Languages in South Asia, Cambridge University Press 2002
Braj B. Kachru/Yamuna Kachru/S.N. Sridhar, Language in South Asia, Cambridge Press, 2008

Lachman Khubchandani, Tribal Identity: a Language and Communication perspective, Indian Institute of Advanced Studies, Shimla 1992
- , Minority Cultures and their Communication Rights, in: Tove Skutnabb-Kangas/Robert Phillipson (eds.), Linguistic Human Rights – Overcoming Linguistic Discrimination, Mouton de Gruyter, Berlin/New York 1994
- , Language Demography and Language in Education, in: Language Policy in India, UNESCO, Delhi 2001
- , Language Policy and Education in the Indian Subcontinent, in: S. May and N.H. Hornberger (eds.), Enyclopaedia of Language and Education (2d edition), Vol. I, Language Policy and Political Issues in Education, p. 369-381, Springer Science, New York 2008
- , Language, Education and Social Justice, Poona 1986

Omkar N. Koul, Language, Education and Communication, Indian Institute of Language Studies, New Delhi 2005
Omkar N. Koul, Use of Tribal Languages in Administration, in: Koul, N.O./J. Imtiaz (eds.), Linguistics: Theoretical and Applied, IILS, Delhi 2004
Omkar N. Koul and L. Devaki, Medium of Instruction across Levels of Education in India, in Daswani C.J., Language Education in Multilingual India, UNESCO, Delhi 2001

Mallikarjun, B. The Eighth Schedule Languages - Critical Appraisal. in Language and The State: Perspectives On The Eighth Schedule, Creative Books, New Delhi 1995, pp. 61-83.
- , Language Use in Administration and National Integration, Mysore CIIL, 1986
- , Bilingualism And Census Of India 2001. Language in India, Vol.1(3), May 2001.
- ,.Language According To Census Of India 2001. Language in India, Vol.1(2), April 2001.

- , Globalization and Indian Languages. In Linguistic Cultural Identity and International Communication, J.Vieberth/G. Drexel (eds.), AQ-Verlag Saarbrücken, June 2003, pp. 148-173.
- , Language rights and education in India, Language in India, February 2004
- , Language and the digital divide, in Language in India, April 2004
– , An Exploration into Linguistic Majority-Minority Relations in India, Language in India, 2004

S.P. Massey, Minority Rights: the Constitutional Vision, in: Language Education in multilingual India, UNESCO, Delhi 2001

National Council of Education, Research and Training, Fifth All India Educational Survey, New Delhi 1989
- , Third All India Educational Survey, New Delhi 1982

Rajendra Pandey, Minorities in India – Protection and Welfare, APH Publishing Corporation, New Delhi, 1997

Rajeshwari Pandharipande, Minority matters: issues in minority languages in India, in: International Journal of Multicultural Societies, Vol. 4, No.2, UNESCO 2002

D.P. Pattanayak, Tribal Languages in Education, in: Language Education in multilingual India, UNESCO, Delhi 2001, p. 48-57
- , Multilingualism and Mother-Tongue Education, Oxford University Press 1981

Peter L. Patrick, Linguistic Human Rights: A Sociolinguistic Introduction, at: http://privatewww.essex.ac.uk/patrickp/lhr/lhrintro.htm

Robert Phillipson – Mart Rannut – Tove Skutnabb-Kangas, Linguistic Human Rights – Overcoming Linguistic Discrimination, Mouton De Gruyter, Berlin-New York 1994;

Sanjay Radhan, Educational Deprivation of scheduled Tribes in India, in: D.C. Sah/Yatindra Singh/Sisodia, Tribal Issues in India, Rawab Publications, Jaipur/New Delhi 2007, p.148-156
J.C. Sharma, Multilingualism in India, in Language in India, December 2001

Horst Friedrich Rolly, Bildungsrecht und Bildungspraxis religiöser und linguistischer Minderheiten in Indien, Peter Lang Verlag, Frankfurt 2002

Suresh Sharma (ed.), Language in Contemporary India, VISTA Internat. Publishing House, 2 Volumes, New Delhi 2006

R.D. Singh (technical Director), Census of India – Language Atlas of India 1991, Registrar General&Census Commissioner, Delhi 2004

Shailendra Kumar Singh (ed.), Rethinking Multingualism – Issues and Problems, Eastern Publ., Guwahati 2009

Smita Sinha, Linguistic Human Rights in Tribal Education in Orissa, in: Language in India, May 2005

Selma K. Sonntag, National Minority Rights in the Himalayas, SAI Working Papers, on http://www.sai.uni-heidelberg.de

R. Srivastava, Linguistic Minorities and National Language, in: Florian Coulmas (ed.), Linguistic Minorities and Literacy: Language Policy Issues in developing Countries, p. 99-114, Mouton De Gruyter, Berlin 1984

A.K. Srivastava, Multilingualism and school education in India: special features, problems and prospects. In D.P. Pattanayak (ed.), Multilingualism in India, Clevendon, Mulitlingual Matterss, 1990, p. 37-53

UNDP, Report on human development 2004, Cultural and linguistic rights, New Delhi 2005

K. Vishwanatham, The Eigth Schedule and the Three Language Formula, in: Language Education in multilingual India, UNESCO, Delhi 2001, p. 298-333

Christian Wagner, Das politische System Indiens, on: http://books.google.de

Bharati Wangkheimayum/Anjani Kumar Sinha, Survival of Minority Languages in a Multilingual Set-up, in: South Asian Language Review, Vol IX, No 1-2, Delhi 2000, pp. 141-158

Virginius Xaxa, The Concept of Indigenous Peoples in India, in Christian Erni (ed.) The Concept of Indigenous Poeples in Asia – A Resource Book, IWGIA Document No. 123, Copenhagen/Chiang Mai, 2008

Useful websites:

The Constitution of India, at: http//www.constitution.org/cons/india/

The National Commissioner of Linguistic Minorities (publishes also an inhouse magazine Basha Sagar) at: http://www.nclm.nic.in

The National Commissioner of Minorities, at: http://www.ncm.nic.in
Central Institute of Indian Languages – Mysore, at: http://www.ciil.org

Asian Centre of Human Rights – Human Rights Report on SAARC countries, at:
http://www.achrweb.org/reports/SAARC-2008.pdf

Maps and statistical figures about India at: http://www.mapsofindia.com or also at:
http://freeindia.org:8088/india_maps/statemaps/images

Education of scheduled tribes and scheduled castes in India at:
http://education.nic.in/scst/SCST-special.asp

UNESCO documents on languages at: http://lesla.univ-lyon2.fr/IMG/pdf/doc-461.pdf

India's Ministry of Tribal Affairs: http://tribal.nic.in/index1.html

Language in India , the online review of the CIIL at: http://www.languageinindia.com/index.html
The Virtual Library of the CIIL at: http://www.ciil-ebooks.net/html/disorder/index.htm

Portal of the Santhals: http://wesanthals.tripod.com/

General overview on Government websites: http://goidirectory.nic.in
General issues of Constitutional issues on: http://supremecourtofindia.nic.in Constitutional judicial activities and verdicts: http://courtsjudgement.com
Parliamentary activities and laws at: http://rajyasabha.gov.in
News on legal activities of the States' assemblies: http://legislativebodiesinindia.gov.in
Union and State Acts and Law: http://www.legalservicesindia.com and http://www.indlaw.com

AITPN, The State of India's Indigenous and Tribal Peoples 2009, New Delhi 2009, at: http://www.aitpn.org/Reports/Tribal_Peoples_2009.pdf

Population figures and other statistical information: http://www.censusindia.net/t_00_005.html

UNESCO, Language atlas and endangered languages of India, available at: http://www.unesco.org:80/culture/ich/index.php?pg=00206

The author: Thomas Benedikter

Economist and social researcher in Bozen (South Tyrol, Italy, 1957), graduated in Economics at the University of Munich (D) and in Political Economy at the University of Trento (I). Besides many years of professional activity in empirical social and economic research in his home region South Tyrol, since 1983 he has been continuously committed to activities in development co-operation projects and human rights NGOs with particular regard to minority and indigenous peoples rights, peace and international conflict, information on North-South-issues. T.B. has been director of the South Tyrolean branch of the international NGO "Society for threatened Peoples" (based in Germany) and some other international solidarity initiatives. He spent about two years with research and project activities in Latin America, the Balkans and South Asia (especially in Nepal, Kashmir, India and Sri Lanka) and is writing for several news-magazines and reviews. Since 2003 he is collaborating with the European Academy of Bozen EURAC (Department for Minority Rights) for the EURASIA-Net-Program on "Europe-South Asia Exchange on Supranational (Regional) Policies and Instruments for the Promotion of Human Rights and the Management of Minority Issues". Apart from other books on ethnic conflicts and minority protection systems, in 2007 he published "The World's Working Regional Autonomies" (ANTHEM Press, London/New Delhi).